Jonty's
Boot Fair
Secrets

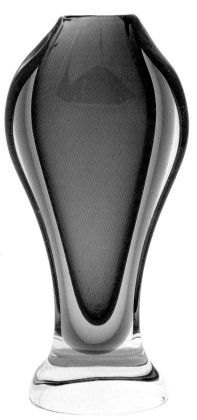

MITCHELL BEAZLEY

Jonty's Boot Fair Secrets by Jonty Hearnden

First published in Great Britain in 2008
by Mitchell Beazley,
an imprint of Octopus Publishing Group Ltd
2–4 Heron Quays, London E14 4JP
Miller's is a registered trademark of Octopus Publishing Group Ltd,
A Hachette Livre Company

ISBN 978 1 84533 4321

A CIP catalogue record for this book
is available from the British Library

Set in Univers and Sabon
Colour origination by United Graphics, Singapore
Printed and bound in China by Toppan

Consultant Editor: Jonty Hearnden

Specialist Consultants: Phil Ellis, Will Farmer, Nick Goodman, Steven Moore

Commissioning Editor: Valerie Lewis
Designer: Philip Hannath
Project Co-ordinator: Deborah Wanstall
Editor: Anna Southgate
Picture Research: Melinda Williams
Indexer: Hilary Bird
Jacket Design: Mark Winwood
Photographers: Paul Harding, Jeremy Martin, Graham Rae,
Robin Saker, Mark Winwood
Production: Lucy Carter

Jonty's
Boot Fair
Secrets

Jonty Hearnden

Contents

CONTENTS

How to use this book

This book covers nine collecting areas which can be navigated by the colour-coded tabs. If you are looking for a particular item, refer to the contents list on pages 4–5 to find the appropriate sections. Having located your area of interest, you will see that each section has its own contents page which will guide you further. If you are looking for a particular maker, factory or object, consult the index which starts on page 301. If you want to find out about how to buy or sell an item, turn to page 288.

The introduction to each chapter will help you to get started with your chosen field. It gives advice on where to search, what to look for and how to check for condition.

On these spreads you will find a general introduction to the featured subject as well as more specific information about styles, makers, designers, types of wares, decoration and marks.

These pages highlight a particular type of product, providing information about selected factories, designers or types of ware.

Foreword

There are countless books that specialize in the A to Z of the antiques business – each one covering anything from the 19th-century Aesthetic Movement to Staffordshire pottery zebras. However, there are very few books that can give you all the information you need in order to make instant decisions when trawling the rows of traders as they unpack their wares at dawn at a car boot fair. That is the time when an instant decision is vital if you are going to get snap up a bargain. If you are selling rather than buying, you need to have a good idea of the value of your items before the experienced dealers and collectors pounce in the hope of finding a winner.

Now that 20th-century antiques and collectables have become the flavour of the month, there are literally thousands of objects that not so long ago would have

been thought fit only for a charity shop or the dustbin. *Jonty's Boot Fair Secrets* has been designed to help you find your way around this amazing new market. This book is an indispensable tool that will enable you to identify and value the vast treasure trove that is out there waiting for you. Be sure to keep it in your bag or in the glove compartment of your car so that it is always to hand when opportunity strikes.

Jonty Hearnden

Introduction

If there is one thing above all others that has changed the landscape of the collectors' world over the last 20 years, it has to be the now familiar sight and sound of the car boot fair. At weekends, fields and car parks are filled with expectant sellers setting out their unwanted possessions in the hope of making some money.

There was a time when antiques were regarded as a better investment than money in the bank. However, tastes have changed and prices with them. For many the heavy lines and decoration of the Victorian and Edwardian eras are no longer fashionable, opening the door to a whole new field of 20th-century collectables.

I first worked in the London salerooms 25 years ago, and can remember seeing tea chests full of unwanted post-war ceramics and glass that were being sold for next to nothing. Without exception, they were regarded as designs of yesteryear, only fit for the nearest junk shop. Today the contents of those tea chests would probably be worth a small fortune. If only I had had a crystal ball...

In recent times a sea change has occurred in the way many people trade and this is directly attributable to the Internet. Online

A spun fibre and teak Rocket floor lamp, 1960s.
£75–85

dealing has taken the world by storm, allowing people around the globe to connect and trade with one another. On a daily basis millions are buying or selling online at any one time. I believe that one of the big winners in this phenomenon has to be 20th-century collectables, for two main reasons. Firstly, this is an area to which many people can relate and secondly, modern day collectables tend to be accessible and affordable.

Modernism has taken a firm grip on interior design since the start of the 21st century. Almost any object with a clean line that complements the minimal approach to design is likely to appeal to the collector. For example, there has been massive growth in areas such as 20th-century glass, including the hand-blown and moulded designs of Geoffrey Baxter from Whitefriars. Recently I found a Whitefriars Drunken Bricklayer vase in an Italian market for £25. On returning home I sold it to a collector for £300. A record price was achieved for a 1970s Mdina glass vase that fetched £1,100.

Another major growth area in recent years has to be that of 20th-century ceramics. Names such as Moorcroft and Clarice Cliff are more than holding their own, with rare and unusual pieces fetching ever higher prices on the open market. Post-1945 ceramics are achieving a rapid rate of growth and it is not unusual to have seen increases of 500 per cent in the last ten years. Here, the designs and shapes of the 1960s and '70s in particular seem to

Mdina glass vase, 1970s.
£1,200–1,800

appeal to interior designers and collectors who are looking for accent pieces to make bold statements. Poole, Rye Studio Pottery and West German ceramics are all growing in popularity.

In recent years, high street fashion has been inspired by the designs of the 1950s, '60s and '70s and, as a consequence, original garments are also being collected. Clothes that your parents once wore and have long been languishing at the back of the wardrobe have become must-haves among the younger generation. This is also true of fashion accessories, where costume jewellery from the likes of Trifari and Miriam Haskell have become highly desirable. In a recent auction sale a Hermès Kelly handbag, made famous by Hollywood actress Grace Kelly, fetched in excess of £30,000.

The doll market has seen a softening in the traditional field of 19th- and early 20th-century bisque-headed dolls; conversely, post-war plastic and vinyl dolls, including familiar names such as Barbie, Sindy and Tammy have all shown signs of a rise in value.

The post-war toy market, especially toys associated with film and television, is growing. Very large sums of money now exchange hands for items that were once purchased for the equivalent of a week's pocket money. Recently a set of *Star Wars* figures in their original packaging sold for £10,000.

The purpose of this book is to help you value your possessions, and to unearth those golden nuggets that are now worth buying. Begin by asking yourself some questions: Does the item look as though someone took time to make it? Does it have any detail? Is it aesthetically pleasing? Does it look as if it was once expensive? Does it have provenance – a maker's name, a history or identifying marks? However, if it was mass-produced, is it in its original packaging? If so, this will definitely add to value. Does it look old or could it be a fake? Is it rare or a cult item? Is it in good condition? When it comes to 20th-century collectables, this is an important factor and can make the difference in value between pence and pounds. Most important of all, however, is the question of how rare and desirable the item is. And remember, collect what you love and love what you collect.

A pair of plastic sunglasses, c1970.
£1–3

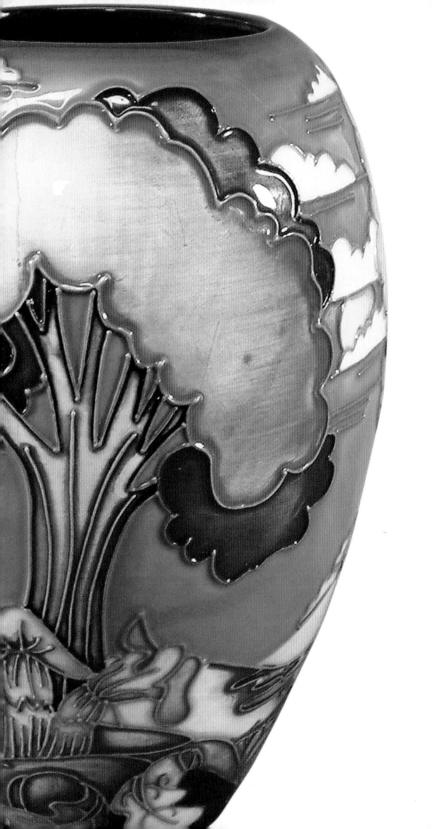

Ceramics

My very first job, in 1979, was in the porcelain department of one of London's top auction houses. It was there that I was first introduced to the intricacy and romance of European design, as well as the mystery and majesty of works from the Orient.

At that time, many 20th-century ceramics were considered to be inferior, with little more value than second-hand goods. Consequently, scant attention was paid to a market that has grown rapidly and can now only be described as booming. Almost on a daily basis collectors are discovering pieces by designers and manufacturers that not so long ago would have been regarded as worthless, and there is now a growing demand for these wares.

CERAMICS

There is something thrilling about hunting down antiques and collectables, whether at a flea market, car boot sale or charity shop. Each visit to one of these events has the potential to discover treasure – but you need to be able to tell the good from the bad.

How do you begin?
Reading books about ceramics is a good way to start. Books will tell you what type of product each manufacturer has produced and, hopefully, enable you to identify the genuine article when you find it. Visiting places where ceramics are sold helps, too. New collectors

Carlton Ware sugar shaker in the form of a cottage, c1930. £100–120

should think of specialist dealers and antiques fairs as temporary museums where all kinds of ceramics can be handled – this is important as it is the only way to get a feel for the real thing. What's even better is that you can buy the goods when you find something you really like. Thorough preparation is vital; do not automatically believe everything you are told, unless you know it to be true. Taking a chance on an item costing a few pounds is fine, but never risk a large amount of hard-earned cash on a purchase you think (or want to believe) is right.

Moorcroft perfume bottle and stopper with Spring Flowers pattern, 1939–49. £650–700

So what do you collect?
This is, of course, a matter of personal choice, but many collectors choose to collect one type or style of ceramics. Collecting a particular designer is a popular route, or the work of just one factory, perhaps one local to where you live. Collecting by period is another popular method – it certainly provides a much wider choice of items. Whichever method of collecting you decide on, always buy something that you like – you will be living with it, after all – and always buy the best you can afford.

How do you know what is hot right now?
Well, what is hot now is not what new collectors should be looking for. You have to find out what's warm and is (or may) get hot soon. If you are wondering how on earth you tell without the benefit of a crystal ball, do what I do and try to spot the look-alikes. For example, Clarice Cliff has been popular – and pricey – for years so it is no surprise that Myott's funky Clarice-inspired wares are rocketing in price. The recently

Carter, Stabler & Adams ring posy vase, 1950s. £20–25

published book *The Mystery of Myott* by Anne Myott and Philip Pollitt has helped too. Often an exhibition or new book will push up prices but one thing remains constant – any ceramic that is well made and not too difficult to come by could, sooner or later, increase in value.

When considering a purchase do remember that quality is always key, as is condition. Try to buy perfect items if you can, and any damage should be reflected in the price.

How do you look for damage and restoration?

Condition is very important where ceramics are concerned. Big cracks should be obvious, but smaller ones can be less so, especially if a piece is not clean. In fact, if something is dirty I am always suspicious, as surely any self-respecting vendor would want to show his or her wares at their best. Look closely at areas that are prone to damage, such as knobs on tureens, tails and fingers on models. Restoration is harder to see, but be aware that there is no foolproof way of restoring ceramics. Restorers simply fill in or paint over damage and then cover it with a soft varnish. The restored area will feel softer and more waxy than the rest of the item.

Collectors' clubs

Joining a collectors' club is a great way to learn more about your subject and meet other collectors who share your passion. Many groups hold regular meeting and produce newsletters or have a website packed with information. Collectors' clubs can keep you informed of the latest research – this is often published online before it is available in reference books. This can be particularly useful if, for example, you want to know how to identify fakes.

Kahler Keramik earthenware vase by Svend Hammershoj, 1930s–40s.
£200–250

Where to collect

You can find bargains anywhere. Although today much is made of buying online, there is nothing better than the thrill of the chase at a car boot sale or flea market. Last but not least, remember to enjoy your collections.

Ruscha wall plate, 1950s.
£45–50

Art Pottery

Art Pottery was out born of the Arts & Crafts Movement which began in Britian in the 1850s. Exponents of the Movement rejected mass production and strove to incorporate the ideals of hand craftmanship of the medieval age into the 19th century. True Art Pottery was largely handmade and items were decorative rather than functional. It was produced either as one-off pieces or in small quantities and is usually signed.

As Art Pottery became fashionable its style was copied with varying degrees of success by makers who used mass-production techniques to make pieces on a semi-industrial scale. These more 'arty' pieces are still more decorative than they are functional but will, in the main, be moulded rather than hand thrown.

Generally speaking, Art Pottery is all about quality of design and the materials used. Shape, glaze, craft techniques such as sgraffito and hand decoration, as well as lustre, are all employed to produce items that purport to be art. Emphasis is placed on individually-made pieces, which are often signed by their creators.

Many early makers, such as Ault, Linthorpe, Bretby, Della Robbia and Brannam, produced great Art Pottery during the 19th century. This tradition was continued into the 20th century by firms such as Ruskin and Pilkington. Art potters often strove for perfection and idealism which meant that, although they often believed in egalitarianism, it was only the rich who could afford their products.

Ruskin Pottery

Established in 1898 by William Howson Taylor and his father, Edward, the then principal of Birmingham School of Art, the Ruskin Pottery is famous for its glazes. Howson Taylor sought inspiration from the Orient and was well aware of the work of other potters, particularly those in Scandinavia and the firm enjoyed close links with Rörstrand in Sweden. Well-known as a perfectionist Howson Taylor destroyed many pieces that did not meet his high standards. Collectors will pay a premium for a signed piece such as that on the left, as they interpret this as proof of Howson Taylor's 'approval'.

Manufacturers

Ault Pottery vase, c1895.
£60–70

Bretby Rocket vase, 1900.
£330–370

C. H. Brannam jug, 1900.
£300–330

Van Briggle Pottery jardinière, 1905. £750–900

What to look for

The Della Robbia pottery in Birkenhead, Merseyside was established by Conrad Dressler and Harold Rathbone in 1894. When Dressler left in 1897 to establish his own pottery near Windsor, in Berkshire, he was replaced by Carlo Manzoni. The business closed in 1906.

This 'running' in the glaze is typical of Art Pottery.

This sgraffito (scratched) decoration is a typical feature of this ware and had to be done while the clay was semi-hard.

The body is made from the local red clay. The base shows the original white glaze, which was applied first, allowing the colour of the clay to show through when incised. This typical incised mark has the initials 'DR' for Della Robbia, 'JS' for the potter and 'EMW' for Miss E. M. Wood, the artist who painted it.

Vase by Miss E. M. Wood, 1900. £750–850

Pilkington's Lancastrian vase, c1920. £400–450

Ruskin Pottery jug, 1932. £230–260

George Ohr vase, c1935. £750–1,000

Trentham Art Ware jug, 1934–41. £20–25

CERAMICS

Art Deco

Dozens of British factories embraced the Art Deco style to create eye-catching table and decorative wares. Many of these were produced in Staffordshire for the mass market, allowing many households to own a piece of the latest fashion. A strong export trade brought in the money to experiment and try out new ideas and innovations. Where major designers lead, smaller factories followed, often adding their own take on a style, making this period a very rich one for the collector. Some smaller potteries did not use factory marks and pieces can only be identified by shape and design. Knowledge, as ever, is priceless.

Charlotte Rhead Born in 1885 into a family of potters, Charlotte Rhead was destined to be a designer. Her father, Frederick Alfred Rhead, was well-known in the business and her brother Frederick Hurten Rhead became a designer in the UK and the US. Charlotte worked at a number of potteries but first found fame at H. J. Wood, where she worked with her father. She then moved to Burgess & Leigh and, in 1931, Crown Ducal, where she produced some of her best work. Charlotte Rhead used a method of decoration known as tube lining. The ceramic equivalent of icing a cake, clay outlines are piped onto the piece and then filled in with colour. The combination of great glazes and colours can produce a stunning effect.

Bursley ware dish, c1930. £140–160

Bursley ware vase, 1922–36. £350–400

Crown Ducal jug, c1930. £550–650

Crown Ducal vase, c1930. £250–300

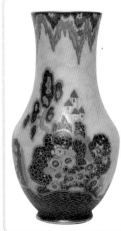

Crown Devon This firm struck gold when it lured designer Enoch Bolton away from arch rivals Carlton Ware. Bolton, who worked at the factory between 1929 and 1950, transformed the firm's image. Among his creations is the 'Mattajade' ground, which works brilliantly on such patterns as Fairy Castle.

Left: Fairy Castle pattern vase, 1920s. £1,000–1,200

Right: Biscuit barrel with hand-painted decoration, 1930. £80–90

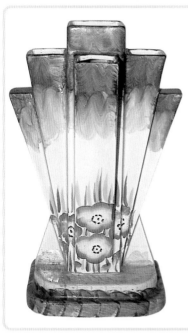

Myott *Long considered a poor relation to Clarice Cliff, in recent years Myott's quirky, very British designs are starting to be recognized and increasing in value. Its funky shapes and bold designs are shooting up in price – just a few years ago they could be picked up for £20–30, but three-figure sums are now normal.*
Left: *Moderne vase, 1930s. £100–125*

Below right: *Persian jug with hand-painted decoration, 1930s. £250–300*

Shelley *Adopted as a trademark in 1910, the Shelley name rose to prominence in the late 1920s under the designer Eric Slater, whose bold geometric shapes and patterns typify the best of British Art Deco and are now very desirable. His classic Vogue or Eve shapes are the most valuable, especially if decorated with an Art Deco pattern. Slater also launched the successful Harmony range in 1934. This colourful 'dripped' pattern is now highly collectable.*
Below: *Jug, c1930. £65–75*

Above: *Mode trio with Blue J pattern, 1930s. £250–300*
Below: *Vase with Harmony pattern, 1930s. £80–90*

Beswick animals

Beswick's realistic animal models are as popular now as they were when first introduced in the 1930s. The firm's reputation was sealed when modeller Arthur Gredington was appointed. His first horse model, the 1938 Derby winner 'Bois Roussel', was followed by champion dogs and cattle. The attention to detail, skilled painting and glazes make Beswick wares stand out. Some models were produced over long periods, others had much shorter runs and are consequently more valuable. Look out for rare colourways or mould variations, which can make a huge difference to value. Gredington retired in 1968 and was followed first by Albert Hallam, and then Graham Tounge in 1972. Beswick's closure in 2002 ensures that the value of their models is likely to increase.

JONTY'S CHOICE

While filming in a pub recently I stumbled across a set of five Beswick huntsmen on horseback, including the rare huntsman on a rearing horse, shape No. 868. The owners were stunned when the set raised over £600 at auction.

Model of a huntsman on a horse, shape No. 868 (second version), 1952–95. £120–145 The earlier first version is worth over £200 more – the horse's head and rider's coat differ.

Compare these models

Model of a Galloway bull, 'Silver Dunn', shape No. 1746C, 1962–69. £900–1,000

Model of a Hereford cow, by Arthur Gredington, shape No. 1369, 1954–97. £100–150

Production run and colour are the two most important factors when valuing Beswick animals. A shorter production run means fewer figures were produced, making those that have survived more valuable. The Galloway Bull on the left was produced for just seven years. Look out for the rarer 'black' or 'belted' versions, which are worth £1,000 more. The Hereford cow on the right was produced over a much longer period, is therefore quite common and, as a result, much lower in value.

Other models

Model of a fish, 'Golden Trout', by Arthur Gredington, shape No. 1246, 1952–70. £200–250

Model of a boy on a pony, 'Palomino', by Arthur Gredington, shape No. 1500, 1957–76. £120–145

The one to look for

Beswick models can come in gloss (seen here) or matt versions, which can be worth more. A matt version of this Jersey bull would be worth twice as much.

Look for damage or restoration at vulnerble points such as the feet, horns or tail.

Model of a Jersey bull, 'Champion Dunsley Coy Boy', by Arthur Gredington, shape No. 1422, 1956–97. £100–125

Model of a pig by Colin Melbourne, shape No. 1473, marked, 1956–62. £450–500 Melbourne was one of the most gifted ceramic designers working in post-war Britain.

Model of a dairy Shorthorn bull, 'Champion Gwersylt Lord Oxford 74th', shape No. 1504, 1957–73. £600–700

Beswick
Beatrix Potter figures

Launched in 1948, Beswick's Beatrix Potter figures proved an immediate success and have been popular with collectors ever since. Originally modelled by Arthur Gredington, there were initially 19 figures including Peter Rabbit and Jemima Puddleduck.

These early figures are generally the ones that collectors seek out, so it is important to know which mark denotes which period (see below). Marks may help with dating, but it is always rarity that collectors are looking for. The rarest Beswick Beatrix Potter figure is 'Duchess with Flowers'. Produced from 1954 to 1967, this little black dog was not popular when first produced and thus was a poor seller. Its rarity has made it very popular with today's collectors, who will pay up to £1,800 to own an example.

Making ceramics is a risky business and the more an item is prone to damage in the kiln the more costly it is to produce. The balance between the wants of the designer can often be set against those of the more commercially-minded management. Collectors are always on the lookout for variation – it can make a massive difference to the price, as shown by the examples on the right.

Backstamps

Date is an important factor with Beatrix Potter figures. On the left is an example of the so-called 'oval gold' mark, in use from 1955 to 1972. A gold mark always adds value to a piece. More valuable is the 'round gold' mark. On the right is an example of the 'line mark' introduced in 1973. Printed in brown, the first version of this mark (1973–74) does have the word 'copyright', but not the date as shown here. It must be understood that the date, 1954 in this instance, is NOT the date of the piece, but the date copyright was issued. This form of mark was in use from 1974 to 1985.

Other figures

Beatrix Potter's 'Pickles', with gold backstamp, 1971–82. £450–500

Beatrix Potter's 'Pig-wig', 1972–82. £350–400

What to look for

Below are two examples of what to look for when buying Beatrix Potter figures. In both cases it is the extra detail in the earlier figures that makes them so much more sought after by collectors.

Here are two versions of 'Mr Benjamin Bunny' – look at the differences between them and how they affect value.

Left: the earlier 'gold marked' example, 1965–74, with the pipe standing out from the body.
£300–350

Right: the later 'line' marked version, 1975–2002, with the pipe modelled into the body.
£50–60

Here are two versions of 'Mrs Rabbit'. Again, look at how prices are affected by the amount of detail.

Left: first version with umbrella sticking out, 1951–74.
£135–150

Right: second version with umbrella moulded to dress, 1975–2002.
£45–50

Beatrix Potter's 'Thomasina Tittlemouse', brown line mark, discontinued in 1989.
£50–55

Beatrix Potter's 'Johnny Town-Mouse', brown backstamp, 1980s.
£200–225

Blue & white transfer-printed wares

During the industrial revolution of the 18th century Britain became a ceramics powerhouse. Traditional methods were replaced by semi-industrial techniques, one of the most revolutionary of which was transfer printing. This process transformed ceramic production, enabling elaborate patterns to be reproduced in their thousands by semi-skilled workers. For a large part of the 18th century British potters had copied Chinese patterns but now newer, Western designs could be developed. The famous Willow pattern is a good example. A wholly Western invention, it was created by Thomas Minton for Thomas Turner of Caughley in 1780.

Spode (later Copeland & Garrett, then Copeland Spode) is one of the most important names in blue and white transfer-printing. They refined the process and made it their own from 1800, introducing iconic Western-themed designs that are highly collectable. Spode's famous Italian design, introduced in 1815, is as popular as ever and still in production today.

Much early blue and white was printed in a fairly pale colour, which gradually darkened as fashions changed in the 1820s and '30s. A much darker shade was very popular with the American market, and a number of English firms made special designs showing American views. Enoch Wood, Ralph Clews and Ridgway are notable examples. Ridgway's Beauties of America series is highly collectable.

Flow blue was another popular style of blue printing and this is now very collectable in the US. It was produced by firing wares in a kiln to which ammonium chlorate had been added, thus blurring the printed image slightly. Flow blue dates from the 1820s and was produced up to the 1930s.

Another famous design, Asiatic Pheasant by Podmore, Walker & Co, also originates from the mid-19th century. Other makers produced their own versions and it is often printed in pale blue, but other colours are available too. Like Spode's Italian, Asiatic Pheasant is still being made today.

TRADE SECRETS

- Early pieces will generally be thinner-potted and of a paler blue.
- Early plates tend to have a flatter profile.
- An impressed mark could be a clue to an early date.
- Real views of real places will always be worth more than a fantasy scene.
- Cracks, staining and chips will affect value but a rare pattern will still be worth buying if the price is right.

Patterns

King's Cottage, Windsor Park, plate by J. R. Riley, 1820s.
£170–180

Arms of Virginia, plate by Thomas Mayer, 19thC.
£6,000–6,500

Furness Abbey, platter by William Mason, c1810.
£600–725

City of Albany, State of New York, plate by Enoch Wood, c1825.
£700–800

CERAMICS

What to look for

The designs or patterns of many transfer-printed wares were based on those of Chinese porcelain. The main reason for this was to satisfy the desire of the emerging middles classes to own items of beauty suitable for everyday use. At that time the cost of imported Chinese porcelain was prohibitive to all but the very wealthy. Generally speaking, earlier tureens will have thinner walls and are of a paler blue than later examples,

This style of knop is fairly typical. Look out for more complex examples such as animal heads as these can add to value.

Check the rims for chips and cracks.

Inspect the handles as they are prone to damage.

This tureen does not have a stand or ladle. If you find one that is complete it will be worth considerably more.

Soup tureen decorated with Willow pattern, 1830–50. **£120–140**

Cistern near Catania, plate by Don Pottery, c1820. **£600–700**

Baltimore & Ohio Railroad, plate by Enoch Wood, c1835. **£550–650**

Ladies' Cabin, platter, c1840. **£450–500**

Footbath, early 19thC. **£1,400–1,650**

Carlton Ware

Carlton Ware was produced by the firm Wiltshaw & Robinson at the Carlton works, Stoke-on-Trent from 1890 to 1989. The Carlton Ware trademark was added in 1894.

In the early 20th century crested wares similar to those by Goss were produced. Carlton Ware's models are often more quirky and adventurous. After WWI the lustre wares that were to make its name famous were developed. At first lustre versions of existing patterns were made, but gradually designs appeared that were created specially for the lustre ranges – collectors now consider these to be the pick of the bunch. The Egyptian-inspired Tutankhamun from the early 1920s, New Mikado and Chinaland are especially prized.

Always moving with the times and fashions, Carlton Ware was the first range to introduce oven-to-table wares.

Art Deco-inspired lustres appeared in the 1930s. Among the most collectable designs are Red Devil,

Devil's Copse, Zig Zag and Sunflower Geometric. The embossed designs of the 1930s were cheaper to produce than the costly lustre ranges. These novel but very useable wares were a huge success and exported around the globe. Many designs were in production until the 1960s, so look for patterns that were exclusive to the 1930s – they are rarer and more valuable.

Post-war Carlton Ware continued with innovation. Peter Foster's Orbit design speaks loudly of the period and is currently undervalued, as is Linen, another 1950s range. Royale, a new line of traditional lustre was introduced, available in Rouge, Vert, Bleu and Noir; it must not be confused with earlier versions. Thankfully this is easy as the designs are simpler and usually bear the 'Royale' backstamp in gothic script. It is worth a fraction of the pre-war range. The most novel, and probably the most collected post-war range is Walking Ware. It kept Carlton Ware in business during a difficult trading period.

Australian backstamps

This mark is often found on the base of pieces from the mid-1930s to the early '60s and it is a popular misconception that these pieces were made for Australia – they were not. During the 1930s Japanese manufacturers unscrupulously copied British pottery, including Carlton Ware. At this time there was no copyright protection but Cuthbert Wiltshaw found a way around the problem. A clause in the South East Asian Treaty stated that if a design was registered in Australia it could not be copied by the Japanese. Thus many Carlton Ware designs were registered in Australia.

Other shapes

Tea caddy with Red Devil pattern, 1920s.
£3,000–3,500

Gondola vase with Devil's Copse pattern, 1920s.
£1,000–1,200

Preserve pot in the form of a cottage, c1930.
£60–70

Chocolate mug and cover with Clematis pattern, 1930–40.
£250–300

The one to look for

A Carlton Ware hand-painted stamp licker, modelled as Humpty Dumpty, c1930, 5in (12.5cm) high.
£200–250

Look closely at the hat, it is separate from the body – twist it and his tongue comes out. The tongue is made from an absorbent material which could be dampened and then used to moisten your stamps. The brick effect has been painted on. Firstly the base was banded in a solid 'brick' colour. Then a dry brush was used to define individual 'bricks' Finally a fine brush was used to draw on defining lines.

This piece (like a handful of Carlton Ware pieces) is not fully marked, but bears a registration number that can be traced back to Carlton Ware.

Backstamps

1906–27	1925–57	1952–62	1970s

Preserve pot in the form of a blackberry, 1940s.
£90–100

Butter or jam dish with Buttercup pattern, 1960s.
£20–25

Walking Ware egg cup, c1973.
£20–30

Bean Bag cruet set, 1980.
£35–40

Chinese ceramics

The first Chinese ceramics were produced around 9000 BC, with the earliest porcelains arriving in about 1000 BC. The East held a virtual monopoly on porcelain production until the early 18th century and exported this precious product to the West in massive quantities. Called 'export porcelain', these wares were designed specifically to meet Western tastes. With China's new booming economy there has been a revived interest in antique Chinese porcelain. Massive prices are being seen at auction for the very best pieces and prices of 19th- and 20th-century examples are also on the rise. However, it is a collecting area that is full of potential pitfalls for the untrained eye. Styles continued to be made for centuries and without seeing the real thing it is very difficult to tell old from new.

Imari *Essentially a Japanese style originating from the 17th century, it was copied by the Chinese for the lucrative export trade and also made in the West. Imari was produced at Arita and exported via the port of Imari, hence its name. An often gaudy look that has never gone out of fashion, it is a combination of underglaze cobalt-blue decoration with overglaze iron-red enamel, finished off by gilding. Early pieces will be finely painted on well formed thin bodies. Generally speaking, the later the piece, the cruder the decoration and thicker the ware.*
Chinese Imari tea caddy, early 18thC.
£125–150

Nanking *This name is associated with the blue and white hand-painted porcelains that were exported to the West during the 18th century from the port of Nanking (now called Nanjing). It was often referred to by Western dealers as 'best Nanking china' and the name stuck. The name is often associated with the so-called Nanking Cargo, porcelains recovered from the Geldermalsen, a Dutch ship that sank in 1751. This important sale, held in Amsterdam in 1986, continued a trend for 'shipwreck ceramics' ie those that have been recovered from ancient shipwrecks. Such pieces are always sold at a premium and come fully authenticated.*
Teabowl and saucer from the Nanking
Cargo, c1750. £250–300

Canton enamel *Wares were produced at the main kilns at Jingdezhen then some were sent to the port of Canton for decoration. Most pieces date from the mid-19th to the mid-20th century and typically have panels of figures or landscapes on a green background of flowers and precious objects. Earlier pieces tend to favour a predominantly pale blue ground followed by the green palette associated with this style.*
Canton enamel bowl, c1870. £450–550

Armorial ware During the 18th century, there was an extensive trade in Chinese porcelain made especially for the Western market. Customers sent out details of family crests and patterns to be copied by Chinese artists. Even shapes were copied. This practice continued into the 19th century but was at its height c1800. Luckily for the collector, these pieces are distinctive as they were painted in a Chinese style. The gilding and body also are good pointers, as is the hardness of the glaze. *Chinese export platter, c1790. £850–950*

Famille verte This was the standard form of decoration until the introduction famille rose in around 1720. It was developed during the reign of the Emperor Kangxi (1662–1722) and was very successful. The predominant green colour on famille verte pieces tends to be a slightly see-through but deep coppery-green. Combined with the typical blue, red and yellow, it can make a stunning design. Like famille rose, this style continued into the 19th and 20th centuries. *Famille verte dish, Kangxi period, 1662–1722. £150–200*

Famille rose Meaning 'pink family', this is a term given to a group of Chinese wares with a distinctive pink enamel colour. Called 'foreign colours' by the Chinese, they were inspired by the western palette.This shade came to prominence during the 1730s and was a fashion must-have. Previously only basic enamel colours had been available: blue, yellow, iron-red and copper-green. The new pink colour enabled naturalistic decoration that was more in tune with a western take on Chinese style. Famille-rose type decoration continued well into the 20th century but the colour itself is not a clue to dating. *Famille rose plate,c1740. £225–275*

Yixing stoneware Pronounced 'Ee shing', this stoneware has been produced in the city of Yixing since the Song Dynasty. It was made in various shades from brown to purple and red. Being stoneware, the body is vitrified and does not require glaze to be watertight, making it particularly suitable for teapots and in fact most early teapot forms were based on existing Yixing shapes for wine pourers. Yixing stoneware is still made today and it is very difficult to distinguish old from new, but as the body is not glazed a patina of dirt will have built up on old pieces. *Yixing teapot, 19thC. £130–150*

Chintz ware

Chintz ware, inspired by chintz fabric designs, is a popular range of British ceramics decorated with an all-over floral lithographic transfer. First seen in the 1920s, it was in production until as recently as the 1980s. It became massively popular during the 1990s collectables explosion, when several firms began to make chintz wares again.

Two factories stand out in chintz production: Royal Winton and Crown Ducal. Royal Winton was the trading name of the Grimwade brothers, a firm founded in 1885 and still trading today. They adopted the name Royal Winton in the late 1920s and their first chintz design was launched in 1928. The Marguerite pattern was an immediate success with the public and was in production until the 1960s. It is less popular with today's collectors, however, largely due to its brownish background and the fact that it is still quite widely available. Crown Ducal was produced by A. G. Richardson and after Royal Winton it is the most collectable factory. Look out for patterns such as Festival, Blue Chintz and Florida.

All chintz designs are 'sheet patterns', that is to say the design covers the whole lithographic printing sheet. Great skill was needed to carefully cut the sheets to fit the complex shapes of various wares. If you look closely at chintz ware you will be able to see where a design has been cut or snipped to fit. Tricky areas such as teapot spouts, handles and knops caused manufacturing problems. The best chintz producers budgeted for the extra time it took to cover these difficult areas, but cheaper, more cost-driven makers skimped or simply left them blank. Lord Nelson ware is one such maker. Their chintz is on a noticeably cruder body and usually has undecorated areas. Lord Nelson chintz is worth less than Royal Winton or Crown Ducal, but look out for their Black Beauty and Green Tulip patterns which are highly sought after, particularly in the US.

Another maker to look out for is James Kent, who also traded as Old Foley. Their most successful pattern was Du Barry (see below), which was reintroduced in 1998.

James Kent cheese dish and cover with Du Barry pattern, 1930s. £165–185

Chintz ware patterns

Crown Ducal centre-piece with Ivory Chintz pattern, 1920s. £200–250

Crown Ducal sweet dish with Peony pattern, late 1920s. £100–130

Royal Winton toast rack with Sweet Pea pattern, c1930. £70–75

Royal Winton bonbon dish with Marguerite pattern, c1930. £65–75

What to look for

Individual pieces such as teapots or cheese dishes are not as commonly found as, for instance, teacups and plates and consequently are highly collectable. This teapot has a classic Art Deco shape which makes it even more desirable.

Look how the teapot handle has been decorated. This is always a good sign of a quality maker – an undecorated handle would be worth less.

Royal Winton Norman teapot decorated with Wellbeck pattern, 1930s.
£200–250
This pattern also came in a black-ground version called Hazel (see below for an example of this colourway).

The all over, tightly packed floral design is just what collectors look for.

Backstamps

Collectors need to know their marks to date pieces properly. Above left is the classic pre-war mark in use from 1934 up to 1951. Due to government restrictions at that time, most pieces seen in the UK bearing this mark will be pre-war as decorated pottery was not sold between 1941 and 1951. The mark on the right was introduced in 1951 when restrictions on the sale of decorative pottery were lifted. Some chintz patterns were in production before and after the war. A pre-war piece is generally worth more, so check those marks!

Royal Winton teapot stand with Cotswold pattern, c1930.
£20–25

Royal Winton teapot with Hazel pattern, 1934.
£450–500

Royal Winton dish with Summertime pattern, 1930–40.
£25–30

Old Foley dish with Rosalynde pattern, 1950s.
£5–10

Clarice Cliff

Clarice Cliff, who was born in 1899, transformed British ceramics. Eighty years after the launch of her first range, her designs are still keenly sought out and can achieve massive prices. As with many collectables, prices have fallen back slightly, but good examples and rarities are still increasing in value. Interestingly, as prices at the top end increase, designs which were once cheap, such as Crocus and Celtic Harvest, are rising in value dramatically.

The Bizarre range was launched in 1927 and was an immediate success, although nothing like it had been seen before. Original Bizarre is typified by broad brushstrokes, mainly in strong geometric designs. The early 1930s is Cliff's most notable design period. The powerful combination of classic shapes and patterns has long been attracting high prices. By the middle of the decade, however, fashions began to change and graphic designs gave way to simpler patterns and embossed shapes. These later designs are generally less valuable.

Post-war designs tend to be traditional and, with the exception of the ever popular Crocus pattern which was introduced 1928, do not appeal to most collectors.

Celtic Harvest

Introduced in 1937, Celtic Harvest was popular with buyers, but until recently not that popular with collectors. With rising prices for painted wares, the once neglected moulded designs are now increasing in value. Produced up to 1963, pre-war examples will have a black printed mark, whereas post-war ones will be marked in green.

Celtic Harvest jug, 1937–41, £100–125

Other shapes & patterns

Bizarre Tankard coffee pot and cover, c1928.
£600–700

Bizarre Lotus jug with Sliced Circle pattern, 1929.
£4,000–4,500

Soup bowl and stand with Spring Crocus pattern, c1930.
£100–120

Bizarre Stanford teapot with tennis pattern, 1931.
£2,000–2,200

The crocus that was almost a lupin

Lynton sugar sifter with Blue Crocus pattern, 1935. £450–550

Lynton sugar sifter with Autumn Crocus pattern, 1928–41. £340–380

Crocus pattern was added to the Bizarre range in 1928. Clarice Cliff had originally intended her new design to be a lupin, but it proved too complex to paint. The crocus flowers were easier to reproduce; the earth is symbolized by a brown band below them while the sun is represented by a yellow band above. The pattern was a massive success when launched and remained popular until 1963. Blue, and the rarer purple, crocus were introduced in 1935. Spring crocus, with pink, yellow and blue flowers, was produced from 1933 to 1963 but did not sell as well as the other colourways with the result that it is as easy to find today.

Bizarre Conical sugar sifter with Windbells pattern, c1930. £500–600

Jam pot with Berries pattern, c1930. £450–500

Plate with House and Bridge pattern, c1930. £900–1,000

Bon Jour biscuit barrel with Coral Firs pattern, 1930s. £800–900

Commemoratives

The area of commemoratives is vast, but it is also one where the savvy collector can find bargains if they know what to look for and know a bit of history too.

Initially, mainly Royal events were commemorated, but by the 18th century politics were included. This was partly due to the fashion for political cartoons, upon which many early political commemoratives were based. Early pieces, that is pre-1840, are desirable and rare although there are interesting later pieces worth searching for. The early pieces tend to be well made but even the cruder items are worth considering.

Queen Victoria's coronation in 1837 was an event for which large quantities of wares were made. Such was her fame that her image can appear without a title,

although it's worth knowing what she looks like because a Queen Victoria coronation mug could be worth in excess of £500. Massive quantities of wares were produced for her Golden and Diamond Jubilees (1887 and 1897); although worth less than earlier items, the more complex and high quality pieces are still prized. Items made to commemorate her death in 1901 are more rare and thus highly collectable.

Politics is another popular subject. Churchill, Thatcher, Kennedy and Roosevelt are names to look out for, as well as Jimmy Carter and Harold Wilson. Look out too for notable events such as the moon landing of 1969 or Olympic memorabilia, especially notable ones such as Berlin, Moscow and Los Angeles.

Churchill plates compared

Paragon bone china plate commemorating the centenary of Sir Winston Churchill's birth, 1974. £70–80

Nelson ware plate depicting Sir Winston Churchill, 1940s. £50–55

Churchill is a massive figure on the commemoratives scene. Anything featuring him is good but, as with all things, rarity and quality bring higher values. The Paragon plate is well made and of high quality, whereas the Nelson plate was mass-produced, and these factors are reflected in the different values. Generally speaking Paragon pieces are usually worth more as they are always well made and well designed.

Political collectables

Plate commemorating W. E. Gladstone, late 19thC. £40–45

Paragon bowl commemorating Neville Chamberlain, 1938. £75–85

Mug commemorating Harold Wilson's devaluation of the pound, 1968. £40–45

Loving cup commemorating Margaret Thatcher's third election, 1987. £150–170

The one to look for

Although Edward VIII pieces are plentiful, better quality pieces like this Paragon plate were not made in massive quantities, so if you want a piece of Edward VIII memorabilia this is a great one to go for.

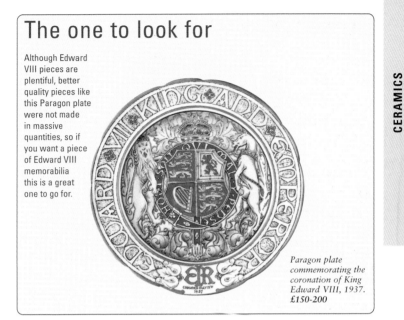

Paragon plate commemorating the coronation of King Edward VIII, 1937. £150-200

Golden Jubilee of Queen Elizabeth II

Caverswall urn and cover, with gilt scrolling, 2002. £70–80

Rye Pottery tankard, hand-decorated, 2002. £30–40

Moorcroft vase with stylized flowers, 2002. £250–300

Caught off guard by supposed public opinion that the 2002 Golden Jubilee would not be popular, few commemorative items were produced. As it turned out the celebrations were a massive success with record crowds flooding the streets of London for the many events. Thus commemoratives are rare and already increasing in value. Just look at this Moorcroft vase, which cleverly commemorates the event by using the UK's national symbols – the rose, thistle, daffodil and shamrock – rather than the usual monograms and Royal personage.

Royal collectables

Mug commemorating Queen Victoria's Diamond Jubilee, 1897. £65–75

Arthur Bowker mug commemorating Queen Elizabeth II's coronation, 1953. £35–40

Coalport mug commemorating the marriage of Prince Charles and Lady Diana Spencer, 1981. £15–20

Queen's China mug, commemorating the 90th birthday of HM Queen Elizabeth the Queen Mother, 1990. £5–10

Other Continental factories

Many continental European factories produced high quality ceramics, but until recently many were relatively unknown outside their countries of origin. The internet, cheap European flights and political changes in eastern Europe have made these pieces more available to collectors. Firms such as Boch Frères in Belgium (later Villeroy & Boch), Longwy in France and Lenci in Italy produced wares that are instantly recognizable. Many of these are of high quality and highly priced. Although reproductions exist they are not common, but it is always worth making sure that you check the authenticity of any piece you consider buying.

Boch Frères *Founded at La Louvière, Belgium in 1844, their stunning Art Deco ceramics are highly collectable, with good examples bringing thousands, especially in the US. Many were designed by Charles Catteau (active 1922–45), who signed his pieces. Wares with the Keramis mark, introduced in 1927, are often associated with the very best Art Deco period pieces.*
Vase, c1910. £160–175

Antelope vase designed by Charles Catteau, c1925. £800–1,000

Centrepiece, late19thC. £500–550

Dresden *The name refers to wares in the style of the Meissen made in numerous factories in Dresden. The wares, frequently painted by independent decorators, were often marked with versions of Meissen's crossed swords. In 1882 the first Dresden mark was registered, a blue crown over the word 'Dresden'. Look for ladies in crinolines with plenty of lace, but be aware that they are prone to damage.*
Figure of a young man, late 19thC. £500–550

Goldscheider *Established in 1885 in Vienna, Goldscheider are mainly known for their stunning models from the 1920s and '30s. The principal modellers to look out for are Josef Lorenzl and Stefan Dakon. Look out, too, for the stylish face masks made in red clay and decorated in strong colours.*
Figure of a young woman, c1930. £1,250–1,500

CERAMICS

Hutschenreuther *Founded in 1814 in Hohenberg, Germany, Hutschenreuther began as a porcelain decorating business. It started producing its own wares form 1822. It expanded rapidly, taking over numerous businesses and is now part of the Rosenthal group. Their output included utility wares and figures, the production of which began in 1917 at the Selb factory. Their natural representations of animals, birds and figures have a sense of movement and realism and, by 1926, were highly sought after. During the 1960s and '70s they produced 'op art' white porcelains.*

Nude figure with borzoi, by Carl Tutter, c1938.
£700–800

Lladro *Established in 1954, Lladro pieces are now making their way onto the collectors' market. Only perfect examples are sought as Lladro is prone to damage. Look out for the cheaper 'Nao' range introduced in 1968. Originally called Rosal, early pieces are keenly sought.*
Right: Figure of boy, 1980s. £160–175
Far right: Figure, 'Angel Praying', 2006.
£60–65.

Rosenthal *This innovative German firm began making porcelain at the end of the 19th century. It employed top designers from the world design community, including Raymond Loewy, Bjørn Wiinblad and Lucienne Day. Their studio line, launched in 1961 used only the best designs from over 100 artists and designers, selected for production by an international panel. Many of the post-war pieces made for export to Britain and the US were marked 'R – Continental China'. This mark is not often recognized so it is worth looking out for.*

Figure of a woman entitled 'Drinking Maiden', by Ernst Wenck, c1930.
£450–500

Rosenthal mark, c1914   *Rosenthal mark, c1937*   *Cup and saucer with Flash pattern, 1982. £15–30*

Susie Cooper

Susie Cooper (1902–95) studied at Burslem School of Art and then joined Gray's Pottery as a paintress in 1922, rising quickly to designer. Some Gray's Pottery items are marked 'designed by Susie Cooper'. A determined and highly skilled designer, she became frustrated with the restrictions of working and set up her own factory.

In 1929 she established the Susie Cooper Pottery. Initially she bought in wares to be decorated, but from 1931 designed her own shapes which were made at Woods Pottery, next door. Her first mark is the rarely seen triangle used from 1929 to 1931 with the words 'A Susie Cooper Production'. Many items bear her painted signature, although this usually denotes that she designed, rather than decorated, the piece. From 1950 she designed new shapes for production in bone china and in 1969 her firm was taken over by Wedgwood.

Buy or Sell?

This is a great example of the Art Deco-inspired designs that Susie Cooper produced during her last few years at Gray's and dates to about 1927 or 1928. Known to collectors as the Cubist pattern, it was the precursor of the more muted version she designed for her own pottery in 1929. Popular with collectors who like the bold geometric design, this is likely to increase in value. I say it's a keeper!

Cubist pattern teapot, c1930.
£700–800

Patterns old & new

Patricia Rose tea plate, 1930s. £50–55

Introduced as Patricia in 1938 and later renamed, this popular design was produced until 1966 – look out for major pieces in classic shapes, like Kestrel coffee pots.

Diablo coffee cup and saucer, 1960s. £20–25

Dating from 1967 Diablo is typical of later designs when the pottery was part of the Wedgwood group. These later pieces are now cheaper than pre-war or even 1950s examples.

Marks

Gray's Pottery mark, 1922–29.

Susie Cooper's first mark, 1930–32.

Leaping Stag mark, 1932–64.

Alternative mark, 1932–64.

CERAMICS

What to look for

Principally known for her tableware designs, Susie Cooper produced a small range of figures, intended as table centre-pieces. This range consisted of flower troughs, a leaping stag (much prized by Cooper collectors), a hound and this fox.

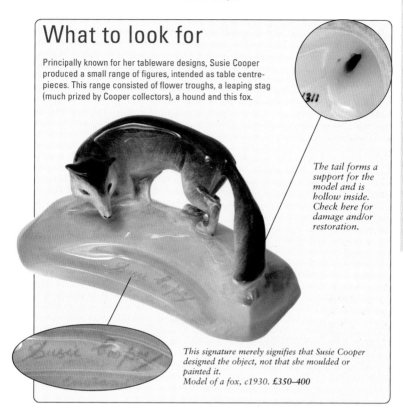

The tail forms a support for the model and is hollow inside. Check here for damage and/or restoration.

This signature merely signifies that Susie Cooper designed the object, not that she moulded or painted it.
Model of a fox, c1930. £350–400

A look at coffee pot shapes

Rex shape with sgraffito decoration, 1930s. £85–95

Kestrel shape with Gardenia pattern, 1932. £100–130

Kestrel Shape with feather design, 1939. £90–100

Introduced in 1932 and still going strong in the 1960s, the Kestrel shape is a Susie Cooper classic. Collectors will always pay more for a Kestrel coffee pot than any other shape.

Facsimile signature, 1932–56.

Simpler signature 1932–64.

Post-WWII period, 1950–66.

Wedgwood mark, post–1969.

Cornish Ware

Established in 1862, T. G. Green's pottery at Church Gresley, Derbyshire, became famous for its Cornish Ware. Introduced in the 1920s, this blue and white banded ware is said to have been named after the blue Cornish sea and white clouds and is still as popular today as it was then. Many other makers produced similarly striped wares, but they simply painted on blue (or other coloured) bands.

Cornish Ware is very distinctive in that it is turned on a lathe. After casting the item in a mould in the usual way, it is dipped into the blue-coloured slip and then turned on a lathe, thus cutting bands through the blue to reveal the white underneath.

As well as the famous blue and white, other colours were available. Green and white made an appearance in the 1920s but is very rare. These early pieces will bear the 'early church' mark. Yellow and white was very popular; first appearing in the 1950s and '60s, it made a comeback in the 1990s. Look out too for the rare red and white and orange and white banded wares.

The Church Gresley works closed in July 2007 and at present it seems to be the end of the line for Cornish Ware. Whether this will push up the value of older pieces remains to be seen.

Many Cornish Ware pieces are inscribed and jars with rare names can fetch three-figure sums – so watch out for fakes. Fakes are actually genuine but undecorated Cornish Ware pieces that have been 'doctored' with a false name that has been added using Letraset and cold glaze. These fake names can be scraped off using a knife. Genuine jars have their names printed under the glaze and these will never come off. The name is critical to value – the rarer the name, the more valuable and sought after it will be. Below is a guide to the names that you might see on Cornish Ware.

Common names include: Coffee, Cream of Tartar, Currants, Flour, Pepper, Raisins, Rice, Salt, Spice, Sugar, Sultanas, Tea and Bi.Carb.Soda

Less common names include: Carbonate of Soda, Tapioca, Thyme, Cloves, Ginger, Mint, Mustard, Nutmeg, Sage, Sago,

Rare names include: All-Spice, Almonds, Custard Powder, Bread Crumbs, Brown Sugar, Cherries, Cocoa, Cocoanut, Cornflour, Icing Sugar, Mace, Parsley, Peel, Prunes, Soda and Suet.

Very rare names include: Apricots, Borax, Cinnamon, Curry, Dripping, Herbs, Lard, Marjoram, Pimento Seeds, Table Salt and Washing Soda.

Shapes

Storage jar, 'Coffee', 1920s–30s.
£350–400

Storage jar, 'Custard Powder', 1930s.
£140–160

Melior Cafétière, c1950.
£250–300

Vinegar bottle, 1950s–60s.
£450–500

The one to look for

T. G. Green made a huge range of items in Cornish Ware. Storage jars are the most common, with the exception of the small spice jar size. Other pieces, like this sugar shaker, are sought after. Red is a very rare colour; look out, too, for green, black and yellow.

The name is important – rare names have a higher value. Check, too, that the name is under the glaze; fakes names will have been added after the item was glazed.

Look at the bands. Genuine Cornish Ware is turned on a lathe. The bands are deeply cut and square in profile

Sugar shaker, 1950.
£900–1,000

Backstamps

Black shield mark, 1930s–50s.

Green shield mark, 1930s–mid-1960s.

Collectors' Club mark, 1997–2002.

Judith Onions mark, 1968–75.

Pepper and Salt pots, c1970.
£350–400

Double egg cup, c1980.
£60–70

Country Road utensils jar, c1990.
£20–25

Limited edition measure, c1998.
£70–80

Cottage wares

There is something about a cottage – wooden beams, a roaring fire and maybe just a whiff of baking bread – that is universally appealing. Not surprisingly, it was not long before potters hit on the idea that pieces shaped like cottages would sell.

Cottage wares first appeared during the early 19th century in the form of pastille burners. These small models usually have a porcellaneous body and are quite distinguishable as they have an aperture at the back and either a hole in the roof or a working chimney. Pastille burners were the air fresheners of their day and were used to burn a 'pastille' of fragrance, which would puff smoke out through the chimney or open windows. These items were popular up to the 1870s and were reintroduced by Coalport during the 1970s. The Coalport models are now sought by collectors, so they are worth looking our for.

The cottage also formed a perfect piggy bank and these were produced throughout the 19th century in various sizes. Bigger is better! More macabre was the fashion for Staffordshire potters to make models of cottages (and other buildings) where murders took place. These are rare and highly collectable.

However, it was during the 1930s that cottage wares really took off. There was quite an obsession with them during this period – so much so that trade papers often referred to traditional floral patterns as being 'of the cottage type'. From simple models of cottages we move into open season – tea sets, storage jars, biscuit barrels – you name it and a potter somewhere has turned it into a cottage.

Prominent among the main makers of this type of ware are Price Brothers in Stoke-on-Trent. Their classic 'thatched' cottage wares were made until the 1950s and came in a myriad of shapes. Price Brothers also produced a rarer windmill 'cottage' as well as a 'log cabin' made for the Canadian market.

Carlton Ware also produced a number of cottage models. Other makers include W. H. Goss, Willow Art and, more recently, David Winter, Hazle Ceramics and Lilliput Lane.

Cottage ware shapes

W. H. Goss model of the Goss oven, 1905–29.
£250–300

Royal Winton preserve pot, 1930s.
£140–160

Lilliput Lane model of 'Spring Bank Cottage', 1986.
£15–20

Cottages compared

A W. H. Goss model of William Wordsworth's birthplace, c1920. £130–145

Age is not always everything in the world of ceramics; rarity and, in this example, a celebrity connection also affect desirability and value. Despite being made in 1920, the Goss model of William Wordsworth's birthplace, shown above, is worth half the amount of the Hazle ceramics piece on the right, which was made just six years ago. The two main reasons for the difference in values are as follows. Firstly, the Hazle piece is a limited edition – just 500 of these dress shop models were made and each is numbered and signed by the artist. The Goss cottage, although older, was made in much greater quantities. Secondly, the Hazle dress shop is associated with Diana, Princess of Wales. The model was commissioned by the Pink Ribbons Crusade, a US breast cancer charity that was established to continue Diana's work. Look closely at the shop windows – they have been painted with pictures of several of Diana's iconic dresses.

A Hazle Ceramics model of a dress shop, 2001. £200–230

Lilliput Lane model of Greenstead church, 1989. £25–30

Hazle Ceramics model of Lily's florist shop, 1990–95. £135–150

David Winter model of The Rectory, by John Vine, 1993. £25–30

Crested china

Established in 1858, the firm of W. H. Goss began by making fine quality Parian wares. In the 1880s, however, they launched a range of novelties that would become synonymous with their name. Adolphus Goss, son of the firm's founder, had a great interest in heraldry and archaeology. He hit upon the idea of combining the two to produce small china ornaments aimed at the booming holiday trade. As the railway network expanded around Britain, day-trippers flocked out of cities to nearby beaches or picturesque villages and they all wanted an inexpensive souvenir to take home.

More expensive pieces were in the form of models of local landmarks or even historic crosses or fonts. All of these items are rare. Such was the phenomenon of Goss that even as early as 1900 a Collectors' Club was formed.

Other makers quickly launched similar wares and by around 1900 many firms were producing crested china, notably Carlton, Arcadian and Shelley.

Goss pieces are generally more valuable than those made by its rivals, but rare models by any maker are sought after. Look for animal figures by any maker or the rare WWI pieces made in the form of tanks, battleships or soldiers.

Arcadian models compared

Arcadian model of a sailor winding a capstan, with New Milton crest, 1914–18. £125–140

Arcadian model of a jug, with Lewes crest, early 20thC. £5–10

Although generally speaking Arcadian wares are worth less than Goss examples, they produced a number of good figure models which always carry a premium, hence the higher value of the item on the left. Look out for military figures and those associated with WWI, Battleships, tanks and even ambulances all command higher prices.

Manufacturers

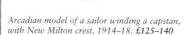

Albion China model of a kettle, with Derby crest, early 20thC. £5–10

Arcadian model of a cockerel, with Eynsham Abbey crest, early 20thC. £35–40

Arcadian model of Shakespeare's house, with City of London crest, c1920. £15–20

Carlton model of a jockey on a horse, with Newmarket crest, c1925. £85–95

The one to look for

This Goss model is based on an object from antiquity. The moulding gives the piece an authentic look.

Look inside for evidence of fine cracks. Goss porcelain is very fine and prone to cracking.

This gilding provides the finishing touch.

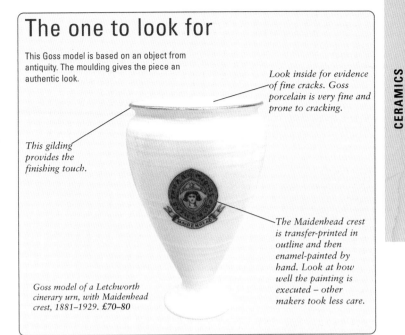

The Maidenhead crest is transfer-printed in outline and then enamel-painted by hand. Look at how well the painting is executed – other makers took less care.

Goss model of a Letchworth cinerary urn, with Maidenhead crest, 1881–1929. £70–80

Backstamps

Arcadian china was produced between 1904 and 1924 by Arkinstall & Sons. They produced many good quality pieces and are particularly known for their animal models.

A typical mark from a piece of crested china made in Czechoslovakia between 1900 and 1920. Generally speaking, these Continental items are worth less than English examples.

Goss model of Eddystone lighthouse, with Corfe Castle crest, 1920s. £35–45

Goss model of whiskey and soda on a tray, with Land's End crest, 1920s–30s. £40–45

Norfolk Crest China model of a Red Cross van, with Canterbury crest, c1919. £60–70

Rita China model of Pontypool Folly, with Pontypool crest, early 20thC. £100–125

Hummel

Love them or hate them, 'Hummels' have been popular the world over ever since they were introduced in the 1930s. Instantly recognizable, they are based on drawings produced by a German nun, sister Hummel. Known to the world as 'M. I. Hummel', sister Maria Innocenta was born Bertha Hummel in 1909. A skilled artist from childhood, she trained professionally and then after meeting nuns from a local teaching order took vows and entered the convent in 1931.

Teaching young people inspired her and she continued to draw. Some of these drawings were turned into postcards and it was one of these that was noticed by Franz Goebels, owner of the German ceramics firm of the same name. Goebels realized that if these charming drawings could be turned into figures they would be sure sellers. In 1935 he approached Sister Hummel and, after some persuasion, she agreed to grant the firm an exclusive licence to produce her work, with strict guidelines. Each figure had to be as close to her drawings as possible, would bear her signature

and must 'bring joy'.

After her death in 1946 an artistic board was established at the convent to maintain her strict standards and even today each new Hummel figure must be approved by the sisters.

Buy or Sell?

Advertising pieces like this are rare and form the centrepiece of any collection. Originally produced for retailers, in recent times there has been a trend for collectors' clubs to reissue copies of these items. Although one can understand this practice it has affected the value of original examples. Saying that, collectors will always want the genuine item. This is a genuine Hummel showroom plaque, so if you are lucky enough to own one, I would say hang on to it!

Goebel Hummel advertising plaque, 'Merry Wanderer', 1970s.
£170–185

Some of sister Hummel's Figures

Pair of Goebel figures 'Umbrella Boy' and 'Umbrella Girl', 1950s.
£100–130

Goebel figure of 'Apple Tree Girl', c1960.
£110–120

Goebel figure of 'Little Gardener', c1970. £65–70

Goebel figure of 'Wayside Harmony', c1970. £50–55

The one to look for

Launched as 'Timid Hunter' in 1940, this figure is one of the original collection and still in production. A new 'collector's' version of the original model was launched in 2005, using original moulds.

The biggest difference between the various editions of this figure is the shape of the suspenders used with the lederhosen. The 'H' shape shown here, which is associated with all the Crown Mark figures, will add about 30 per cent more to the value than those with the 'X' variation.

The rabbit usually appeared in orange until 1981, after which it was changed to brown.

Goebel figure of 'Sensitive Hunter', 1940–59.
£100–120

Backstamps

The so called 'big bee' mark in use from 1950 to 1955. Early marks add to value.

This mark was also in use from 1950 to 1955.

This mark was in use between 1972 and 1979.

Goebel figure of 'Star Gazer', c1970. £60–65

Goebel figure of 'Happy Traveller', c1970. £75–85

Goebel figure of 'Spring Cheer', retired 1984. £120–140

Goebel figure of 'Be Patient,' 1972–79, £60–70

Japanese ceramics

Japan's porcelain industry is a relatively recent one, beginning in the early 1600s, and by the middle of the 17th century Arita was the main centre of production. At the time, Chinese ceramics were unavailable due to the internal conflict within the country so Japanese makers stepped in to fill the void and enjoyed massive export trade. This subsided as the Chinese trade returned in the 18th century, but by the late 19th century all things Japanese were again popular. The tradition continued into the 20th century with Satsuma wares as well as the many inexpensive eggshell tea sets. Makers such as Noritake produced good quality wares mirroring Western styles. In the US in particular, post-WWII pieces marked 'Made in Occupied Japan' are very collectable.

Satsuma *More a style of pottery than a type, it has an earthenware body with a yellowish tinge and finely crackled glaze. Originating in the Satsuma area in the mid-19th century, it became popular in Europe and America after being shown at the Paris Exhibition of 1867 and is still made today. At its best it shows incredible detail, especially in the gilding; at its worst it can be crude, lumpen and ungainly. Names to look for are Meizan and Kinkozan. Much Satsuma is marked with the 'satsuma mon' of a cross within a circle.*
Satsuma chopstick rest, 19thC. £60–70

Arita *Arita is the main centre of porcelain production in Japan. Most early Japanese porcelain was made at factories founded near Arita at the beginning of the 17th century. By the middle of the century items decorated with underglaze blue were being exported and Arita is often associated with these pieces, but other types of ware were made here too, including Kakiemon and Imari. Much of the best Japanese porcelain was being made at Arita by the 18th century.*
Arita noodle cup, 19thC. £100–120

Noritake *Founded in 1904 and still going strong, the Noritake Co was established in the village of Noritake by the Morimura brothers, who had begun as retailers in New York City in 1876. Fine quality dinnerwares were produced for the export market, principaly America. Until the 1920s wares were hand decorated, often with liberal amounts of gold, but later more mechanized methods were introduced. Noritake produced large quantities of decorative pieces, which are very collectable, particularly in the US.*
Trinket set, 1930. £65–80

Imari *Like Satsuma, Imari is a style of porcelain. Initialy made in the Arita area from the mid-17th century, it shows a typical palette of under-glaze blue decoration, with over-glaze iron red and is often gilded. During the late 19th and 20th centuries much Imari was exported. Although very decorative, these later wares are often thickly potted and when compared to 17th- and 18th-century versions are often crudely decorated.*
One of a pair of chargers, 19thC. £400–500

Hirado *Known in Japan as Mikawachi, this finely potted ware was produced from the mid-18th to the mid-19th century at Mikawachi, close to the main centre of Arita. It was initially produced for the Hirado family but was later also made for export. It is often associated with plain white wares, but blue and other colours were also used.*
Pair of models of tigers, 19thC. £1,400–1,600

Kutani *These wares date back to the mid-17th century and were made in the Kutani (which means 'nine valleys') region. The name is mainly associated with the highly decorative pieces produced from the mid-19th century onwards. Kutani is similar to Satsuma but has a porcelain body; thousands of eggshell porcelain tea sets were made and exported in massive amounts. Mid-19th century Kutani decoration is often of a high, if lavish, quality but later pieces can be much poorer.*

Vase, on a metal stand, c1900.
£160–190

Moorcroft

William Moorcroft began to design for James Macintyre & Co of Burslem, Staffordshire in 1897 and by 1898 was head designer. These early wares are known by collectors as Macintyre Moorcroft and are highly collectable. The first range, Florian, is characteristic of the Art Nouveau period – sinuous flowers and leaves cover the pots or are placed in more formal reserves. Peacock feathers, poppies and cornflowers are typical motifs as are large flowing leaves, often in paler shades or tones of blue. Various marks were used; many have the initials 'J' and 'M' for James Macintyre, often with 'Florian Ware', but always with the hand-painted signature 'W. Moorcroft' and sometimes 'Des' meaning designed by.

Moorcroft left to set up his own pottery in 1913 with funding from Liberty, the well-known London store. Post-1913 designs are marked 'Moorcroft Burslem' and 'W. Moorcroft', or initialed 'WM'. Many pieces from this period are marked 'Made for Liberty & Co' or have Liberty's Tudric pewter mounts. Several designs were made solely for Liberty, including Flamminian, introduced in 1905, which has a simple small foliate roundel and often seen in a green or red glaze. Pieces from this period tend to have a softer look with less busy designs. Two great patterns are Hazeldene, showing

trees in a landscape on a green/blue ground. The same design on a dark blue ground is called Moonlit Blue. Claremont shows toadstools in naturalistic settings and comes in various colours. Different shape toadstools were used to fit the shape of each piece.

From the 1920s onwards wares tend to have the classic dark blue ground. Motifs include anemonies and pomegranates. Pomegranate pattern was introduced in 1910 and sold until 1938. It is still one of the most common designs and good examples are highly prized.

Items marked 'Potter to HM The Queen' suggest a date after 1927 but before 1953. Those marked 'Potter to the late Queen Mary' date from 1953 to 1978.

When William died in 1945 his son Walter took over. The post-war designs tend to be simpler, with more space around the design. Waterlily, introduced in 1950, is often seen on a green ground with a pink flower .

The pottery was owned by Liberty until 1962, when the Moorcroft family bought Liberty out. In 1984 the family sold the factory and it looked set to close, but in 1987 it was rescued by Richard Dennis, whose wife Sally Tuffin became principal designer. Rachel Bishop joined in 1993 when Sally left to concentrate on her own business. Rachel is still head designer and her wares are highly collectable.

Marks

Florian ware mark, 1898–c1905.

J. Macintyre mark, 1904–13.

Made for Liberty & Co mark, c1903–1913.

Impressed mark, c1918–26.

The one to look for

Poppy pattern was one of William Moorcroft's early successes and is as popular with collectors today as it was with the buying public when it was introduced in 1902. William Moorcroft designed both shapes and patterns, ensuring each was in harmony with the other. It is this care, and the high standard of decoration, that make this piece so collectable.

Notice how the inside of the vase is painted – this gives it balance.

Applying the poppies by hand ensured that the design fitted the shape of the item.

Florian ware vase with Poppy pattern, 1902–04. £2,500–3,000

Principal designers

William Moorcroft 1897–1945

Walter Moorcroft 1935–88

Sally Tuffin 1987–93

Rachel Bishop, 1993–present

Impressed mark and paper label, c1925.

Impressed mark and paper label, 1928–35.

Painted marks for QEII jubilee, 2001.

Painted marks, 2005.

Nursery ware

Items of pottery and porcelain made for children date back centuries, but much of what is available on the market was made in the 20th century. Whereas earlier pieces were often based on nursery rhymes or simply bore a child's name, much of that produced in the 20th century was based on characters, often developed by artists working outside the field of ceramics.

Wares with character-lead designs are the most sought after. Anything from Disney is popular, especially Mickey Mouse and Donald Duck, where values for pre-war pieces are always higher. Wade produced a large number of Disney pieces, with characters such as Snow White, Three Little Pigs, Mickey Mouse and Donald Duck. All of these pieces are keenly sought by collectors.

The prolific illustrator Mabel Lucie Attwell (1879–1964) designed a popular range of wares for Shelley. From 1926 Shelley produced tea wares with Attwell's designs. The following year she also designed shapes. Many of these feature the green-suited imps which are called 'Boo Boos'. These were followed by figural groups inspired by her drawings. All of these are very collectable.

Slightly later than Shelley's

Attwell range is the Bunnykins series from Royal Doulton. Although it began as a pattern on tea wares, by 1939 a set of 12 figures had been designed by Charles Noke. These are now rare and highly desirable. When Doulton took over Beswick in 1969, Albert Hallam began a new set of figures.

By its very nature – being made for children – nursery wares are very often the victims of damage, with the result that perfect examples are rare and therefore much more valuable. Small items such as eggcups are very collectable, but more common items such as beakers and cups are less popular. Do look out for rarer pieces such as teapots, especially character-inspired ones.

A Shelley cup and saucer, designer by Mabel Lucie Attwell, 1926. £180–200

Other shapes

Empire Porcelain Co bowl with Peter Pan pattern, c1920. £60–70

Midwinter Georgie Porgie egg cup by Peggy Gibbons, c1930. £55–65

Grimwades plate with The Imps pattern, c1930. £40–50

Grimwades Pixie jug, c1930. £270–300

What to look for

This figure was the first in the 'Time' series and Figure of the Year in 2000. This association with the millennium may increase its value in future years.

SUNDIAL BUNNYKINS
DB 213
BUNNYKINS OF THE YEAR 2000
FIRST IN THE 'TIME' SERIES
© 1999 ROYAL DOULTON

Doulton's pieces usually have all the information a collector needs on the base. Here we have the name of the figure as well as its all-important number, DB213. The date of introduction is also shown.

Sundial Bunnykins, No. DB213, 2000. £25–30

Bunnykins

Royal Doulton Bunnykins money box, 1984. £5–10

BUNNYKINS ®
© ROYAL DOULTON
TABLEWARE LTD 1936

Bunnkykins were conceived by Barbara Vernon Bailey, a nun and daughter of the decorating manager at Royal Doulton. The first pieces were launched in 1934. Both printed patterns and figures are available and the range is still made today, so collectors seek out items that are no longer in production.

Shelley night light by Mabel Lucie Attwell, 'Sleepy Head', c1930. £2,400–2,600

Shelley plate by Mabel Lucie Attwell, c1930. £90–100

Washington Pottery bowl, 1960s. £20–25

Royal Doulton Mystic Bunnykins, No. DB197, 1999. £20–25

Poole Pottery

Poole Pottery began in 1873 as tile makers Carter & Co, and rose to become one of Britain's most influential art potteries from the 1920s to the post-war period. A separate firm, Carter, Stabler & Adams, was established in 1921 to produce art wares.

New partners Harold Stabler, his wife Phoebe and John Adams brought a huge amount of influence to the firm's products, introducing faïence ranges and figures. One of the most important introductions of this era was the so-called traditional range which emerged during the early 1920s. A red-bodied earthenware with an opaque white glaze was decorated with, at first, simple hand-painted designs, which by the 1930s had become elaborate and highly stylized. Many of these were the work of John Adams' wife Truda.

Post-war Poole lost none of its momentum with its important Freeform, Delphis and Aegean ranges. Freeform was designed by Alfred Read and Guy Sydenham during the late 1950s. Combining contemporary shapes with hand-painted patterns, these new wares were leading fashion. Just as Freeform captured the 1950s, Delphis was Poole's take on the 1960s with its bright colours and abstract designs. Still popular in the 1970s, it was followed by the more subtle Aegean range.

Aegean dish, 1970s. £60–65

Pattern codes

Poole Pottery has a slightly confusing pattern system that new collectors find frustrating. Instead of being marked with the usual pattern number, most pieces have a two- or three-letter code. These codes are often mistaken for artists' initials but the form in which they are painted is the main clue. Conversely, most artists' marks are monograms or symbols.

CE pattern, 1930s.   *EP pattern, 1930s.*

Backstamps

1930s   *c1952*   *1950s*   *1975*

The one to look for

This typical 1930s example is a great find. These stylized Art Deco designs are often prized above the more traditional florals. This piece is painted in colours and has printed and painted marks.

This 'dash' border is typical of Poole.

Look at these flowers – they are typical Truda Carter's work.

The shape is pure Art Deco.

Vase with TZ pattern, 1930s.
£200–220

KK pattern, 1930s.

LT pattern, c1935.

TJ pattern, 1930s.

TV pattern, 1930s.

1970s

1959–67

c1979

1980s

Post-war English ceramics

The post-war period provides the best opportunities for a budding collector. Ceramics from this time are still readily available and in many cases undervalued or unrecognized. The period is one of innovation, with new styles and influences dominating.

British ceramics are heavily influenced by American designers such as Raymond Loewy and Eva Zeisel. Condition is particularly important. Always buy perfect examples, if you can, as these will hold their value better.

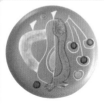

Above: Cloisonné coaster, 1956. £15–20
Below: Pair of Burlington vases, 1959. £40–50.

Denby *An important and interesting factory during this period, the main designers were father and son team Albert and Glyn Colledge, who were responsible for most of the best ranges. Typically the shapes were by Albert with decoration by Glyn. Cloisonné, an important range introduced in 1957, was similar to the previous Cheviot; it used a combination of sgraffito (scratched through) decoration and enamelling. Burlington dates to the late 1950s – its simple lines and pastel shades were well in tune with the period. Denby made large amounts of tableware and Minstrel is characteristic of the 1970s. It is a colour variant of the successful Gypsy pattern designed by Glyn Colledge. As with most post-war ceramics, Denby pieces are always fully marked.*

Mark, 1950–75   *Mark, 1975–85*

Left: Tricorn sugar bowl, 1958. £50–60
Below: Fish pepper pot, 1977. £10–15

Hornsea *This small pottery produced many innovative and still undervalued pieces. Tricorn (above) is typical of the pieces designed by John Clappison, the driving force behind Hornsea's designs. Introduced in 1958, it was not made in large quantities and is already difficult to find. Simpler and more available is the Summit range produced 1960–65, as are the plentiful screen-printed designs Clappison introduced in the 1970s such as this Fish pepper pot form 1977.*

Midwinter More than any other firm, Midwinter lead the way in post-war design. Roy Midwinter ran the factory and designed shapes, Jessie Tait designed many of the best patterns and in the 1970s and '80s Eve Midwinter designed groundbreaking ranges such as Creation. Savanna is typical of Tait's clever designs of 1956. By combining transfer printing and hand painting, Midwinter's wares looked good but were cheap to produce. Sir Terence Conran's designs are popular with collectors, as are Hugh Casson's Riviera from 1954 and Cannes from 1960.

Above: Savanna vase, c1950.

SAVANNA
BY
JESSIE TAIT
PERMANENT UNDERGLAZE COLOUR
ACID RESISTANT HAND ENGRAVING
Midwinter Modern
STAFFORDSHIRE   ENGLAND

Left: Plant Life vegetable dish by Terence Conran, 1950s. £120–135

Portmeirion Named after the Portmeirion village in Wales which was built by her father, designer Susan Williams-Ellis began the pottery in 1960 when she took over the existing factory of A. E. Gray. Known principally for their moulded and lithographed wares, Magic Garden is typical of their output. Introduced in 1970, it is already being collected. Botanic Garden was launched in 1972 and is still in production today but is a bit too traditional for collectors – they prefer the more 'arty' designs.

Above: Magic Garden cream jug, c1970. £40–50
Left: A Botanic Garden plate, 1972. £30–40

Rookwood

Many people consider Rookwood to be America's finest art pottery. It was founded by in 1880 by Maria Longworth Nichols Storer in Cincinnati, Ohio. Storer was a lady of means who had taken up the then fashionable hobby of decorating china blanks. Finding the local kiln not to her liking she set up on her own and then, in 1880, established Rookwood.

Under Storer's direction artists and chemists were brought in to develop new glazes and designs. Quality control was paramount and even the slightest imperfection on a piece would deem it a second which would be clearly marked with an incised 'X' on the base.

The many glazes used at the firm were refined and categorized. The so-called Standard Glaze was a deep gold, red and orange over a dark brown, which fired to a high gloss. This was particularly seen with floral motifs or especially the Native American portraits series.

Other important glazes were developed including the Matt glaze, Vellum (another matt glaze) and Sea Green. The slightly later Iris glaze is a white glossy colour. Rarer still is Tiger Eye, a glaze that has 'gold' streaks from tiny pieces of goldstone in the glaze.

The Matt glaze was developed by Artus Van Briggle. A skilled artist, Van Briggle joined Rookwood

from Cincinnati's Avon pottery and was taken up by Maria Storer, who encouraged him to experiment and even sent him to study art in Paris. Europe was a huge inspiration to Van Briggle and particularly influenced his glazes. Back at Rookwood he tried to recreate the Chinese glazes that he had seen in the Musée Guimet in Paris. Van Briggle suffered from tuberculosis and left Rookwood in 1899 for the drier air of Colorado Springs where he established the Van Briggle Pottery.

From 1905, a production line of less costly pieces was set up. These items were glazed but not decorated by Rookwood's artists. This line helped the factory through leaner times. Rookwood established an architectural section during the peak of the Arts & Crafts movement that produced faïence tiles and fireplaces. These were made to order and occasionally hollow ware artists would make individual tiles and add their signatures to the backs.

Rookwood was badly hit by the Great Depression of the 1930s and the two World Wars and filed for bankruptcy in 1941. The factory was bought by Walter Schot, who attempted to restart the pottery. Somehow Rookwood struggled on until 1967. The pottery was re-established in 2007.

Shapes

Vase decorated with irises by A. R. Valentine, 1885.
£350–400

Jug painted by Mathew A. Daly, 1885.
£150–180

Vase painted with a nasturtium by F. Rothenbusch, c1907.
£650–750

Bowl, No. 956, 1908.
£150–180

What to look for

Vase decorated with carnations and Standard Glaze, c1900. £550–650

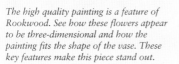

The high quality painting is a feature of Rookwood. See how these flowers appear to be three-dimensional and how the painting fits the shape of the vase. These key features make this piece stand out.

The other side of this piece shows the typical characteristics of Rookwood's Standard Glaze. See how the colour graduates from a mustard yellow through red to darker brown.

Vase painted by Sara Sax with peacock feathers, c1915. £750–1,000

Vase painted by W. Hentschel with birds of paradise, 1916. £500–600

Vase painted with a floral wreath by Louise Abel, c1923. £850–1,000

Vase painted with birds and flowers by E. Lincoln, 1925. £3,000–3,500

Roseville

Founded in Roseville, Ohio in 1890, the pottery began by making utilitarian stoneware and painted flowerpots. Production of slip-painted art pottery began after the business relocated to Zanesville, Ohio in 1898.

Roseville's first range of art wares was the Rozane range, launched in 1900. The name was a combination of Roseville and Zanesville. It is similar to, and no doubt inspired by, Rookwood's pieces. Rozane featured a mainly brown background with hand-painted landscapes, floral designs and animal subjects. Another line, Rozane light, is similar but has a greyish ground. Both ranges were discontinued in 1914.

English born designer Frederick Rhead joined Roseville in 1904 and when he left in 1908 his brother Harry took his place. Many of the best patterns and ranges of this early period are by the Rheads, including the highly prized Della Robbia line.

Frank Ferrel took charge of the pottery in 1917 and was responsible for many of the most collectable of their designs. Roseville switched from more expensive art wares to cheaper relief-moulded pieces around 1920. It is this type of ware that is most often encountered today.

Ferrel was responsible for designing Roseville's most popular pattern, Pine Cone, which was launched in 1935 and sold until the firm closed in 1954. The pottery's management had initially rejected the design but a salesman, Charles Snider, urged the firm to go ahead with production. Pine Cone was an instant hit with the American public and over 75 shapes were produced in brown, blue or green colourways. In a similar style are Ferrel's Sunflower, Iris and Wisteria patterns.

Post-war designs include the ever popular Freesia, Zephyr Lily and Snowberry. Although these proved popular when first produced, Roseville did not keep up with the fashions of the day and the factory closed in 1954.

Roseville fakes abound, but are easily identified by experienced collectors. Not being made from original moulds, shapes differ from genuine pieces. Most fakes are marked 'Roseville' without the usual 'USA', but the real clue is the shape of the mark. On genuine items the mark curves up slightly, following the line of the 'R' of Roseville. On fakes 'Roseville' is straight. Other clues are that the glaze on most fakes is dull and lacks depth, handles tend to be thicker and details not as refined.

Shapes & patterns

Vase with embossed advertisement, shape No. 5, 1914.
£250–300

Vase with White Rose pattern, 1940.
£45–55

Vase with Foxglove pattern, 1942.
£25–30

Creamer with Magnolia pattern, 1943–44.
£20–25

What to look for

Vase decorated with Clematis pattern, c1940.
£30–35

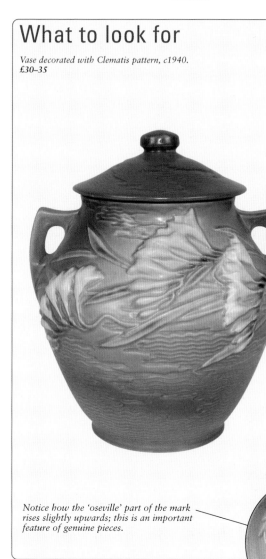

Look at the quality of the painting – it is neatly applied. Fakes tend to be not so well decorated.

This green ground and the muted colour of the flowers is typical of Roseville's output.

Notice how the 'oseville' part of the mark rises slightly upwards; this is an important feature of genuine pieces.

Pair of candlesticks with Clematis pattern, 1944. £75–100

Vase with Freesia pattern, 1945. £45–55

Console bowl with Zephyr Lily pattern, 1946. £100–120

Centrepiece bowl with Gardenia pattern, 1940s. £45–55

Royal Doulton

Founded in 1815 in Fulham, south London, Doulton made sanitary wares and stoneware items for everyday use. Henry Doulton later established an art department at Doulton's Lambeth works and employed one of the pupils from the nearby Lambeth School of Art – George Tinworth. Joining the firm in 1867, Tinworth was allowed to experiment, making and decorating vases and figures, which were exhibited to great acclaim in 1871.

Tinworth was joined in the art department by the Barlow sisters, Florence and Hannah. They specialized in a type of decoration known as 'sgrafitto', where fine lines are drawn into the wet clay to form a picture. Hannah's speciality was studies of animals, while Florence concentrated on birds and flowers.

During the 1880s Doulton expanded, taking over a firm in Burslem, Staffordshire. This pottery was run by John Slater, who was to have a huge influence of the style of Doulton's wares. Slater introduced many new techniques and appointed Charles Noke as modeller. Noke designed many of the new shapes and figures for which Doulton would become world famous.

Noke was also responsible for the introduction of Series ware in 1899. It was intended as a giftware line but also included practical items. Series ware was simply a range of similarly themed designs used on a variety of goods. Popular lines included Dickens, the Gibson Girls and Golfing Themes.

The firm was granted a Royal Warrant in 1901, when it became known as Royal Doulton.

Lambeth Stoneware - Principal designers

One of a pair of vases decorated with donkeys by Hannah Barlow, c1900. **£1,900–2,200**

One of a pair of vases decorated with birds by Florence Barlow, the base with marks of junior artists, c1905. **£1,600–1,750**

Character jugs

Auld Mac, c1938. **£120–140**

Viking, 1959–75. **£60–70**

John F. Kennedy, 2006. **£115–130**

 Royal Doulton are well-known for their character jugs. Based on the Toby jug, the character jug was introduced in 1932. Collectors, as ever, look for rarities. Short production runs and rare colours add value.

Plates compared

Series ware fruit bowl by CharlesCrombie, with a golfing scene, 1930. **£180–200**

Plate by Charles Crombie, with a golfing scene, c1911. **£350–450**

Golfing 'motto' Series ware by Charles Crombie, which was in production between 1911 and 1932, is highly collectable. However, plates sell far better than soup plates or breakfast bowls, which is why the item on the right is twice the price of the item on the left. Plates tend to display the design to better advantage whereas bowls constrict the design. Also, plates are much easier to display, which increases their popularity.

Vase by Eliza Simmance and Jane Hurst, c1910.
£1,350–1,500

Vase by George Tinworth, c1902.
£200–300

Ewer by George Tinworth, c1878.
£450–500

Marks

Doulton's first mark was a simple impressed 'Doulton Lambeth' which appeared in various forms until 1901, when they became Royal Doulton. From this time the marks appears with a crowned lion.

c1920s

1939–41

1973–81

Royal Doulton figures

The name of Royal Doulton is synonymous with figures. The firm had, however, been in business for nearly 100 years before it began to make its most famous line.

The figures were conceived in 1909 by Charles Noke and were launched with Royal approval in 1913 after King George V and Queen Mary visited Doulton's Burslem pottery. Queen Mary admired a figure then known as 'Bedtime', declaring 'isn't he a darling'. In honour of the visit 'Bedtime' was renamed 'Darling'; it is as popular now as it was then.

All figures are given HN numbers and these are all-important to collectors. The initials refer to Harry Nixon, who was in charge of decorating the original figures. The HN number will tell you when a figure was introduced and, when you look this up in a book, for how long it was produced.

The value of all figures depends on rarity. Those produced for only a short period or in a rare colour-way will be worth more.

Generally speaking, earlier figures are more valuable than later ones. Pre-war examples tend to be better modelled and painted, with closer attention to detail, although this is not always the case. For example, figures of characters from J. R. R. Tolkein's trilogy *Lord of the Rings* were produced in the early 1980s and withdrawn in 1984. They shot up in value when the films were released. Likewise, the *Snowman* figures created in the 1990s were a huge success. The 'Skiing Snowman' figure was produced for a short period between 1990 and 1991 – it was withdrawn due to technical problems. Sold for just £12 when new, 'Skiing Snowman' can fetch up to £800 today.

Dickens figures

Royal Doulton produced a large range of figures inspired by the works of Victorian author Charles Dickens and these were hugely popular up to the 1950s. The first range of figures was launched in 1922 and were smaller than other figures produced by Doulton. Dickens figures were originally given the usual HN prefix, but in 1932 were renumbered with an M prefix. All Dickens figures are now prefixed with an M. The Dickens range was added to in 1939 and 1949 and stands at 24 figures, some of which are available as napkin rings.

Right: 'Mr Micawber', 1932–83. £80–90

Centre right: 'Fagin', 1932–83. £60–70

Far right: 'Buz Fuz', 1949–83. £60–70

Figures

'Hinged Parasol', HN1579, 1933–49. **£1,000–1,100**

'The Potter', HN1493, 1932–92. **£220–240**

'Cardinal', HN2554, 1941–46. **£1,000–1,100**

'Summer', HN2086, 1952–59. **£300–350**

The one to look for

Modelled by R. Asplin in 1947 and withdrawn in 1979, 'Belle o' the Ball' is a popular figure. Seated on a *canapé*, she appears to be waiting for the next dance…or is she just dreaming of a handsome beau?

Collectors appreciate the attention to detail. Look at the finely painted face and the flowers on her hat.

The cushion is just the sort of detail that we have come to expect from Doulton.

'Belle o' the Ball', HN1997, 1947–79. £250–300

Belle O'The Ball
COPR 1946.
DOULTON & CO.LIMITED
R^dN° 846738.
R^dN° 23902.
R^dN° 128/46

'Gentleman from Williamsburg', HN2227, 1960–83. £160–170

'The Premier', HN2343, c1970. £125–140

'Fragrance', HN3220, 1988–92. £100–120

'Applause', HN4328, 2002. £135–150

Royal Worcester

The Royal Worcester Porcelain Company is the successor to the original Worcester factory founded in 1751 by Dr Wall. Run by various partnerships during its long history, the business was gradually modernized during the 1840s and '50s, culminating in the formation of the Royal Worcester Porcelain Co in 1862.

Royal Worcester is principally known for its high quality hand-painted wares made between the 1880s and the 1930s. During the 1880s when Japanese-style wares were all the rage many high-quality pieces were produced, often unglazed and with a matt appearance. Many of these, which resemble ivory with gold or bronze decoration, were modelled by James Hadley. Items include dishes, figural candelabra and vases and are usually marked with his facsimile signature. Hadley was also responsible for many charming figures of children after the illustrations of Kate Greenway.

From 1867 items were marked with a date code letter, beginning with A but missing out J, O and Q. The letter O was used in 1889 and A in 1890, before a new dating system came into force.

After 1900 the factory allowed their artists to sign work for the first time. Their signatures are usually found at the end of the painted area and not on the base.

Royal Worcester employed a large number of very skilled artists who painted freehand, as well as other artists who filled in transfer-printed outlines. Many floral designs are a combination of freehand painting and transfer-printed outline. The outlines are often very finely printed in puce, so do examine pieces closely as those that are painted entirely freehand tend to be more valuable. Items may be signed regardless of the method of decoration.

Many Royal Worcester items have a matt ground which may have been restored. This is because those that are matt-glazed are much easier to restore, so it is very important to look carefully at any item you are considering for purchase.

During the 1930s, Royal Worcester diversified into making a range of figures that became a significant and popular part of their output. Freda Doughty's models of children were an early success, followed in 1933 by a commission of American birds which were modelled by Dorothy Doughty. Dorothy also produced a set of British birds in the late 1950s but these were not put into production until 1962. Figure making continued after WWII and Doris Lindner's figures of champion bulls and horses are particularly sought after.

Shapes & models

Set of six porcelain cabinet plates, 1876.
£350–450

Porcelain jug, 1876.
£320–380

Pot pourri jar and cover, 1908.
£2,700–3,000

Vase painted by Harry Stinton, 1912.
£900–1,100

The one to look for

Fruit painting is a speciality of Royal Worcester. This type of decoration has always been highly prized and is still produced today.

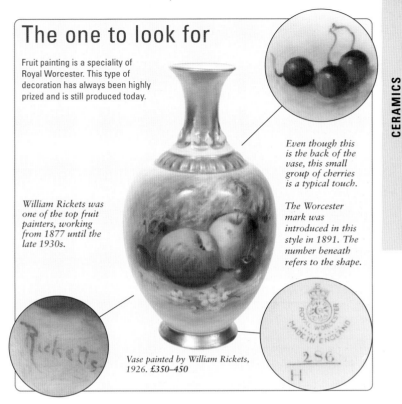

Even though this is the back of the vase, this small group of cherries is a typical touch.

William Rickets was one of the top fruit painters, working from 1877 until the late 1930s.

The Worcester mark was introduced in this style in 1891. The number beneath refers to the shape.

Vase painted by William Rickets, 1926. £350–450

Backstamps

This is the typical Royal Worcester mark that most collectors will encounter. Introduced in 1891, a dot was progressively added above the word 'Royal' until 1915, when 24 dots are seen either side of the mark. In 1916 a star was added beneath, replacing the dots. Dots were added each year up to 1927. A small square was added in 1928 and in 1929 a diamond. The 1930s mark was a ÷, followed by two small interlocking circles in 1931, three for 1932. From 1933 a dot was added to the circles up to 1941. From 1941 to 1948 the mark remained the same, but was replaced by a 'V' in 1949 and a 'W' in 1950. Dots were added each year in progression.

Model of a chaffinch, 1949. £100–125

Figure of a girl, c1959. £200–225

Model of a Hereford bull, by Doris Lindner, 1959. £850–950

Figure of Princess Margaret, 2002. £165–185

Scandinavian ceramics

The Scandinavian countries of Denmark, Norway, Sweden and Finland each has its own distinctive ceramics industry. Scandinavian ceramics are not so commonly seen in the UK, but are growing in popularity with collectors and interior designers. As a consequence of this they often remain unrecognized when they appear on the market, so with some knowledge you could make a lot of money. Scandinavian pottery is also popular in America, where it tends to fetch higher prices.

Gustavsberg *Ceramics were first made in 1825, mainly in the English style. Swedish-style pieces were introduced during the late 19th century and the appointment of Wilhelm Kåge in 1917 brought the company to a world stage. The Argenta range was introduced by Kåge in 1930 as a prestige line and was produced until the 1950s. Stig Lindberg joined Gustavsberg in 1937 and studied under Kåge. He became art director in 1949 and worked for the firm up to 1980. His Pungo vases were designed in 1950. Berndt Friberg began as Kåge's thrower in 1934, and became a designer in his own right in 1944.*

Argenta jar by Wilhelm Kåge, 1947.
£1,750–2,000

Rörstrand *Established in 1726, Rörstrand are known for their crystalline glazes. They began making faïence, then English-style cream wares. Under Alf Wallander fine quality pieces were produced in the Art Nouveau style from 1895 and between 1939 and 1959 Gunnar Nylund introduced many graceful forms. Carl-Harry Stålhane worked for Rörstrand from 1939 to 1973 and specialized in tin-glazed earthenwares. He trained in both painting and sculpture and his work often shows French and Egyptian influences as well as that of abstract art.*
Stoneware vase by Gunnar Nylund, 1940s–50s. £320–360

Palshus *Established in 1948 by Per and Annelise Linneman-Schmitt, Palshus produced simple craft-inspired pieces until the early 1970s. Early examples such as the one shown on the right tend to have matt glazes, but later techniques included incising and rough glazes.*
Stoneware vase, 1950s–60s.
£230–260

Royal Copenhagen Established in 1755 under Royal patronage, this factory came to prominence during the late 19th century under the direction of Arnold Krog who developed the famous underglaze painting in blue, greys and pink. Japanese and French influences were important at this time. Nils Thorsson worked at Royal Copenhagen from 1912 to 1975; their most enduring designer, he is principally known for his highly popular Baca and Tenera series. Designer Ellen Malmer produced several Baca pieces. Tenera, another collaborative project coordinated by Nils Thorsson, involved artists such as Marianne Johnson, Inge-Lise Koefoed and Kari Christensen.

Above: Tenera series vase by Nils Thorsson, c1960. £70–80
Left: Vase by Kari Christensen, c1967. £100–120
Below: Royal Copenhagen mark showing monogram of designer Ellen Malmer, design and pattern number and artist's mark.

Saxbo Established in 1930 by Nathalie Krebs, Saxbo became the most important and influential independent pottery in Denmark. Many of Denmark's top potters worked at the company before moving on to other factories. Saxbo are known for their oriental-inspired glazes, of which this piece is typical.

Stoneware figural group depicting lovers, by Jens Jakob Bregno, 1930s. £420–460

Staffordshire figures

'Staffordshire Figures' is a generic term for figure groups made in many British potteries from the early 18th century up to the early part of the 20th century. The vast majority of these were produced in Staffordshire, hence the name.

The figures fall into two distinct groups – those made before and those made after c1835. Early pieces tend to be well modelled 'in the round', ie designed to be seen from all angles, and are more naturalistic. They were usually made from moulded sections, which allowed for complex designs. Staffordshire figures of the 18th century tend to copy more expensive porcelain models, but by c1800 they had their own style and are seen with a floral 'bocage' behind them. This style, often associated with rustic themes, was fashionable in porcelain in the 1760s.

As the 19th century progressed, figures became simpler and more two-dimensional. Those dating from 1840 onwards are often known as 'flat backs', where the back is flat and often unpainted. In the main these were inexpensive pieces destined to sit on the mantle shelf of workers' homes and depicted popular figures of the day. Up to 1860, figures tend to be

well painted with plenty of orange, blue and green, whereas later ones are almost all white with a minimum of decoration.

As well as figures, many models of dogs were made. Pairs of King Charles spaniels were popular and made by many factories up to the 1950s. The early examples are usually well modelled with separated legs and are often on bases. They can also be found with baskets of flowers in their mouths and are naturalistically coloured, or painted with red or black detailing. Later examples have legs moulded into the body and less colouring – sometimes just a few gold sprigs or a gold chain at the neck. From around 1900, spray-painted rusty-orange coloured dogs with glass eyes were made.

Figures of popular and infamous characters abound. Any named figure will be worth more than a similar, unnamed example. Worth collecting are Royalty, military figures, especially those on horseback, and theatrical characters, which were often made in smaller quantities. Look for models of houses or places where famous murders took place, such as the infamous 'Red Barn'. Models of animals are always prized – the more exotic the better.

Figures & models

Figure with bocage, c1820.
£700–800

Group of children bird-nesting, c1850.
£300–350

Pair of models of dogs with children, c1860. £600–650

Pair of Disraeli dogs, c1850.
£1,700–1,900

The one to look for

Figure of General Sir George Brown, c1860.
£350–400

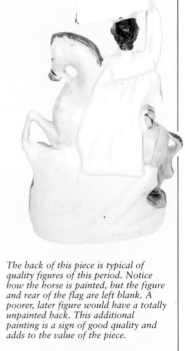

The back of this piece is typical of quality figures of this period. Notice how the horse is painted, but the figure and rear of the flag are left blank. A poorer, later figure would have a totally unpainted back. This additional painting is a sign of good quality and adds to the value of the piece.

The mossy green and brown base and strong orange are signs of a good quality figure. Notice the detailed areas such as the horse's bridle and the rider's face, and how his left arm is modelled.

Pair of spill vases with sheep, c1870,
£400–450

Spill vase with an elephant, c1855.
£650–750

Pair of models of zebras, c1860.
£700–800

Tureen, hen on a nest, c1875.
£400–450

Studio Pottery – post-war

Studio Pottery is a potential minefield for the budding collector. However, it is also one where those armed with some knowledge can bag a bargain. The period after WWII is a fascinating one – designers and artists sought new ideas and direction. Potters such as Lucie Rie and Hans Coper produced beautifully made pieces that were expensive in their day and now command three- and four-figure sums. Lower down the scale potters such as Marianne de Trey and many examples of Rye Pottery are still affordable and possibly undervalued.

Briglin Pottery *Established in 1948 by Brigitte Appleby and Eileen Lewenstein, the Briglin Pottery set out to produce handmade, well designed pieces for the home that would be sold at affordable prices. Although Eileen Lewenstein left the pottery in 1959 to establish her own studio, Briglin continued until 1990. Most Briglin pieces bear the impressed mark 'Briglin'.*

Vase, 1960s–70s. £70–80

Michael Cardew *After studying with Bernard Leach in St Ives, Michael Cardew set up the Winchcombe Pottery in Gloucestershire in 1926 with Elijah Comfort and Sydney Tustin, who was then only 14 years old. Cardew's purpose was to produce pottery in the 17th-century English slipware tradition, suitable for everyday use and at an affordable price. As the range developed he was joined by Charlie Tustin and Ray Finch. Cardew left in 1939 to set up the Wenford Bridge Pottery.*

Winchcombe Pottery jug, c1930. £450–500

Iden Pottery *Dennis Townsend worked with David Sharp at Rye Pottery. In 1959 he opened his own pottery in his garden shed in the neighbouring village of Iden. Although he moved to larger premises in Rye in 1962, the Iden name was retained. Townsend successfully produced wares until he retired in 2002.*
Mug, 1960s. £5–10

Bernard Leach *Born in Hong Kong in 1887 to a colonial family, Leach studied potting techniques in Japan. Returning to Britain in 1920 he established the Leach Pottery in St Ives, Cornwall with the young Japanese potter Shoji Hamada. They focused on traditional Eastern-style wares combined with English techniques such as slip decoration and salt glazing and prized practicality over fine art, calling their wares 'ethical pots'. The Leach pottery was an important training ground for many of the best British potters, and several members of Leach's own family entered the business.*
Stoneware vase, 1932–74. £400–500

Katherine Pleydell-Bouverie *From an aristocratic family, Pleydell-Bouverie studied under Bernard Leach before establishing her own pottery in the grounds of her family home, Coleshill in Berkshire, in 1925. She produced simple well-made pots which were fired in a wood-burning kiln. Katherine worked until her death in 1985.*
Bowl, early 20thC. £60–70

Rye Potteries *Wally and Jack Cole opened Rye Pottery after WWII and trained many of the town's potters, including David Sharp and George Grey. Sharp left to set up Rye Art Pottery with Grey, but was forced to change the name to Cinque Ports Pottery in 1956. The company was renamed Cinque Port Pottery when it became a limited company in the early 1960s. Grey and Sharp parted in 1964, Sharp setting up the David Sharp Pottery, which is still run by his family. Grey continued with the Cinque Port name.*
Jardinière, 1950s. £50–60

Sydney Tustin *As an apprentice at Michael Cardew's Winchcombe Pottery in 1927, Tustin started his career by turning the potters' wheels by hand. When powered wheels were introduced Tustin began to throw his own pots and worked up to his retirement in 1978. Sydney Tustin produced high quality wares that were influenced by Michael Cardew.*
Jug, c1940. £35–40

SylvaC

SylvaC is the trademark of the Sylvan Pottery (1894–1982), founded by William Shaw and William Copestake. They traded as Shaw & Copestake until 1936 when the name SylvaC, taken from the firm's Sylvan factory with the addition of a 'C' for Copestake, was introduced for their decorative products. The name was not used as an impressed mark until 1937.

Many SylvaC pieces are marked with a paper or foil label – this is prized by collectors as it indicates that the item is genuine. Some may just be marked with impressed numbers and 'Made in England'. The numbers are quite distinctive and easy to spot once you are familiar with the style.

Perhaps the most famous items produced by SylvaC are the rabbit models. The 'snub nosed' rabbit was introduced in 1930 and continued in production until 1975. Other rabbits include 'lop-eared' versions as well as models with a match-holder at the rear. They are most commonly found in matt green, but fawn, blue and other colours can also be found. Pink is a very desirable shade for SylvaC items and adds a premium.

Recently, prices of SylvaC have fallen considerably. This is partly due to the number of fakes on the market that have knocked the confidence of collectors. Most of these fakes are produced from existing examples, which means they are slightly smaller than genuine pieces. They are often marked overglaze with a very black version of the 'SylvaC Made in England Ware' mark, whereas a genuine SylvaC example will be marked underglaze with a more smoky-looking mark.

More worryingly, however, are new pieces made in genuine SylvaC moulds. These are very hard to distinguish from authentic examples. If you are in any doubt about the authenticity of an item do seek expert advice.

Buy or Sell?

Prices for SylvaC pieces have fallen back in recent years and this horse is no exception, so it is all a question of when it was bought. If you have just found a horse like this at a flea market for a few pounds, then well done! If you bought it a few years ago it is likely to be worth less than you paid for it, so it would be far better to hang on to it until the market improves.

Model of a horse, 1930s–50s. £50–60

Shapes & colours

Model of a dog, 1930s–50s. £30–35

Model of a rabbit, 1930s–50s. £70–80

Model of Harry the Hare, introduced 1936. £60–70

Model of Sammy the Dog, introduced 1936. £70–80

The one to look for

Prices have remained stable for SylvaC green and blue rabbits, which are easy to find and very popular with collectors. This rare pink bunny is highly sought after and, therefore, able to command a higher price.

Turn this rabbit over and look for authentic marks such as the mould number and SylvaC stamps to the base.

Model of a rabbit, No. 1026, 1930s–40s.
£135–150

Backstamps

Foil label, 1930s.

Impressed mark and pattern number, 1930s.

Be sure to look at the marks on SylvaC pieces as they will almost always have an impressed pattern number on the base. This number refers to the pattern name and date of introduction. Not all SylvaC will be marked with the name, perhaps just a number and 'Made in England'. A foil label indicates authenticity and is therefore always prized by collectors.

Model of a rabbit,
1930s–60s.
£60–70

Beetroot face pot,
1950s.
£15–20

Pixie posy vase,
1930s.
£20–25

Evening Fantasy
vase, 1970s.
£100–120

Troika

The Troika pottery was founded in 1963 by Benny Sirota, Lesley Illsley and Jan Thompson, each partner paying £1,000 to buy the former Powell & Wells pottery in St Ives, Cornwall. The name, taken from the Russian sleigh drawn by three horses, denotes the three partners in the business. In fact, Troika was run by Illsley and Sirota while Jan Thompson took a back seat. He was bought out by Sirota and Illsley in 1965.

Initially tiles and door handles were made but new shapes were soon added. Sirota would form a shape from which Illsley would produce a mould – Illsley's background in sculpture was an important influence on Troika's overall look. The decoration was the responsibility of Benny Sirota.

Although principally known for their rough textured wares, during the 1960s Troika also produced smooth, sculptural items, often in white. These avant-garde pieces were sold in top London stores such as Liberty and Heal's, the latter providing a constant stream of orders until 1978. In 1970 the pottery was forced to move to nearby Newlyn where it remained until 1983, when the loss of the Heal's business and falling sales forced its closure.

Like all collectors, Troika aficionados look for rarity. Larger pieces are always in demand as are the wall plaques, which were produced in small quantities. Items made for the special exhibition at Heal's in 1968 (which bear Heal's mark) are also avidly sought.

Iconic shapes

Wheel vase by Colin Carbis, 1976–77.
£200–220
Available in various sizes from 4½in–12½in (11.5–32cm) diameter these are a popular shape. Bigger is definitely better.

Cube vase by Alison Bridgden, 1977–83.
£200–200
The size of the cube varies and they also come with square 'legs' or a plinth. They are available in textured or smooth ranges.

Marks of prominent decorators

Benny Sirota,
1963–80.

Marilyn Pascoe,
active late 1960s to
1973.

Linda Taylor, active
late 1960s to
early 1970s.

Honor Curtis,
1966–74.

The one to look for

The Anvil vase is a typical Troika shape. Produced during the Newlyn period, it was decorated by Avril Bennett (active 1973–79) who was head decorator.

Anvil vase by Avril Bennett, 1973–79.
£500–550

Mask by Simone Kilburn, 1975.
£800–1,200

Objects of great desire to many collectors, few were produced as the large size, 10in (25.5cm), and complex shape lead to many kiln failures.

Ashtray by Alison Brigden, c1980.
£125–250

Very much an entry-level piece, this is a late example by top-notch decorator Alison Brigden.

Avril Bennett,
1973–79.

Louise Jinks,
1976–81.

Jane Fitzgerald,
1977–83.

Alison Brigden,
1976–83.

West German ceramics

The post-war period was difficult for West Germany. However, such times often bring invention and West German potters developed new styles that are now being recognized by savvy collectors. Wares produced during the 1950s fit into a more generalized European style, similar to Italian pieces. Many have matt, sometimes off-white, grounds, with bold abstract designs. Much more distinctive are

wares from the 1960s to the 1980s. They are gloss-glazed with bold, often clashing colours or more matt 'volcanic' glazes with lava-like trails in loops or spirals. Shape is also an important factor – vases with one or two handles, large jugs, bottle shapes and more abstract forms, as well as the so-called floor vases which were ideal for holding the 1960s fashion must-have, pampas grass.

Scheurich *Founded as a wholesaler, Scheurich began making pottery in the 1950s and were the biggest producer and exporter of this style of ware. Their pieces are marked with a paper label and a three- or four-digit number representing the shape, together with the size in centimetres, around the base.*

Floor vase, 1960s. £220–250

Ruscha *Founded as Klein & Schardt in 1905, the firm was renamed Ruscha in 1948 after Rudolf Schardt took over. The art department was headed by Cilli Wörsdörfer, who produced many hand-painted abstract designs including the popular Milano pattern. Made from both red and white clays, Ruscha's pieces are usually marked on the base with a three-digit shape number, sometimes followed by a slash and a single number representing the size. Wall plate with Torero pattern, 1950s. £45–50*

Bay *In existence between 1933 and 1996, this firm produced great ceramics. They are particularly known for their late 1950s and 1960s pieces designed by Bodo Mans, who had worked with Picasso in France. Abstract designs, often combining curving lines filled in by bold blocks of colour, are highly collectable but seldom seen in the UK. Later pieces are similar to those made by Scheurich, with which they are easily confused. Many Bay items are marked 'Bay', followed by numbers.*
Far left: Vase, c1970. £10–15
Left: Vase with Rimini pattern, 1950s. £25–30

Carstens In operation between 1948 and 1984, this factory's wares are made from a brown clay. Carstens' pieces are well marked, making them readily recognizable to collectors – a bonus, as identifying West German ceramics can be quite frustrating. Almost all examples are marked either with a 'C' followed by numbers in the usual manner of shape, number, size or the same notation beneath two stylized pitched-roof houses and a 'CT' monogram.

Vase designed by Gerda Heukeroth, 1962–54. £85–95

Dumler & Breiden This company began in 1883 as a maker of more traditional ceramics. During the the post-war boom years Dumler & Breiden successfully produced good quality pieces, often with a slightly metallic-looking glaze that contained metallic powder, thus giving a slight sheen. Items are almost always marked with a 'D & B' forming a cross and the usual number, followed by 'Germany'.

Floor vase with copper glaze, 1970s. £180–220

Jasba Formed in 1926, this pottery shared a designer with Ruscha in the form of Cilli Wörsdörfer. Jasba's 1950s pieces are similar to Ruscha's, although markings differ. Wares are often numbered with a prefixed 'N'. In the 1960s and '70s items were marked 'Jasba' in an oval. Production of art pottery ceased in 1975 when the firm switched to making tiles, for which it is still known today.

Jasba dish with metallic glaze, 1970s. £45–55.

Glass

A new generation of glass collectors is developing an interest in the products of 20th-century designers and manufacturers. Particularly desirable are works from the past 40 years. Indeed, with its clean lines, form and colour, 20th-century glass now sits very comfortably in the 21st-century home.

Although some glassware can fetch large sums of money, there are still plenty of very affordable pieces available. This is a trend that has continued for some time and shows no signs of diminishing, making glassware an excellent target for the collector.

GLASS

You could say that the love of collecting is almost inbred in some people. There are those who spend much of their free time in antiques shops, auction rooms or at antiques fairs, carefully looking through boxes of mixed lots and inspecting the wares in the hope that there is treasure to be found. Such diligence can be very rewarding, but even if not, it is great fun and can be a very absorbing way of spending one's time.

What to look for

Looking for glass can be extremely rewarding although many people often find glass

Ariel bowl designed by Sven Palmqvist for Orrefors, c1948. £200–250

difficult. Compared with pottery it can be a little challenging as, more often than not, pieces are unmarked. When there is a mark it may only be a faint acid stamp or illegible hand-engraved mark. Do not let this put you off, however, as over time and with experience the shapes, colours and designs become their own signatures and all too soon you will be able to spot an Orrefors bowl or Holmegaard vase from 20 paces.

Over recent years new markets have emerged, especially for 20th-century makers. Trends in interior design have meant that

Two Pulcino birds designed by Alessandro Pianon for Vistosi, c1960.
Blue: £1,200–1,500
Orange: £1,000–1,200

pieces from the post-war period are fashionable again and fit into modern homes with ease. Makers such as Whitefriars, Wedgwood, Dartington, Blenko, Viking and Mdina have been given the star treatment with a number of wonderfully illustrated books and associated exhibitions. These help to catapult designers back into the public domain with a fresh and new collecting field while at the same time throwing more traditional styles out of fashion.

What's worth buying

Collectors are always looking for the next big thing. Only time will provide the answers to this. However, in my opinion, there are still a number of areas where gains could be made. Post-war mass-produced Czechoslovakian glassware is still in fair abundance. Many factories produced cheaper press-moulded pieces inspired by the high-end studio pieces from top designers. These are often heavy, simple and abstract and look typically post-war and funky. It is possible to find these in charity shops, antiques centres and fairs for as

Bottle or club vase designed by Michael Harris for Isle of Wight Glass, c1973. £500–600

GLASS

little as £3 to £5. If you manage to get a good group of them together they look fantastic, and the sheer quality of their design should reward a savvy buyer.

Doing your research
It is worthwhile taking time to learn the different technical processes in glass making as they affect value. For example, a mouth-blown piece will generally be worth more than a piece made in a mould, although as with everything there is always an exception to the rule. Learn the difference between engraving and cutting, and blown and moulded glass. Consider the weight of the piece, its quality and whether it looks well finished or feels cheap and mass-produced. Try to handle or view as many different pieces as you can, either in auction houses or at antiques fairs, as it will help you get a feel for what people are buying and, better still, what they are prepared to pay for it. In time pieces and their prices will start to become familiar.

Condition
There are a few things to consider here. Firstly, if a piece

is cracked it will remain so as, unlike porcelain, there is no magic wand that can restore it. Chips and scratches can be polished out, but cracks are there forever. Secondly try to avoid 'sick' glass; this is when

Leerdam Unica vase designed by Floris Meydam, c1950.
£250–300

years of water damage, detergents and over use have turned the glass milky in colour. Sometimes this can be treated by means of an acid dip but the results will depend on the quality of the glass. High lead crystal will respond to treatment but lesser types of glass will not. My view, however, is that it is often better to own a damaged and rare piece than never to own one at all.

Availability
Glass is all around you, piled high in salerooms, antiques centres and charity shops. Take the time to look through the shelves and boxes and apply the lessons you have learned as they will help you to spot the treasures. Glass can gve you immense pleasure; collect it, live with it and, best of all, use it.

Art Deco Stuart decanter and two glasses, c1935.
£400–500

GLASS

Carnival glass

The inspiration for iridescent glass came from the lustrous glow of excavated Roman glassware. Across Europe and America major firms such as Loetz, Steuben and Tiffany created magical colour effects for glass by using a cocktail of chemicals, but their wares were expensive and only affordable by wealthy patrons.

In 1907, America's Fenton glassworks introduced a cheaper alternative with its Venetian art glass. This was the birth of what we know today as 'Carnival glass'. The term 'Carnival' is generally thought to stem from the 1950s, when the wares fell out of favour and were given away as carnival prizes at fairgrounds and amusement parks.

Over the years many other manufacturers produced similar wares, with companies such as Northwood, Dugan, Millersburg and Imperial all producing their own ranges. Items were made using the press-moulded method, with some being finished by hand to create a waved rim or lip. The bodies were relief-moulded with a varied range of approximately 200 patterns, the majority of which were mostly a transparent orange. Other colours introduced include tones of purple, green, blue and the rarest of all, red.

America is recognized as the greatest producer of Carnival glass but wares were made in other countries including Czechoslovakia, Australia and England. In recent years some of the original makers and other companies have remade pieces using existing moulds. When hunting for Carnival glass today look for a combination of unusual patterns and ground colour – marigold is common but ice green could fetch a high price.

JONTY'S CHOICE

Fenton's Kittens pattern is always a popular choice with Carnival collectors as it is rare; this pattern was developed with children in mind and shows a number of kittens at play. It was produced in a range of colours including marigold, blue and amethyst. Animals are among some of the rarer subjects to be found.

Fenton Kittens marigold saucer, early 20thC.
£35–50

Shapes & colours

Fenton Horses' Heads marigold bowl, early 20thC.
£30–50

Imperial Ripple pattern amethyst vase, early 20thC.
£30–50

Fenton pink candlestick, early 20thC.
£35–50

Sowerby Thistle and Thorn marigold creamer, early 20thC.
£10–15

The one to look for

This piece draws a great deal of inspiration from Moorish Middle Eastern influences with its repeat roundel motifs. The pattern, which was first introduced by Fenton in 1911, remained in their catalogue until the early 1920s and was used on a great range of items from plates to hair tidies.

The ruffle-edged bowl is one of the most commonly found shapes in this pattern. The bowl would have been press-moulded then heat-treated and hand-finished to create the simple wave effect. The iridescent effect, a combination of liquid metallic salts, is then sprayed onto the bowl while it is still hot, thus creating the lustrous finish.

Fenton Persian Medallion pattern bowl, early 20thC. £100–140

This pattern was re-introduced by Fenton in the 1970s on a number of items following renewed interest in Carnival glass. The later pieces will bear the Fenton mark. This is a more unusual pattern and as such slightly more valuable. While the Carnival glass market has seen a drop of around 30 per cent over the last ten years, rare pieces still command a premium.

Northwood Three Fruits marigold bon-bon dish, early 20thC. £30–45

Northwood Singing Birds blue mug, early 20thC. £100–125

Fenton Pine Cone green candy dish, early 20thC. £100–150

Northwood Good Luck marigold bowl, early 20thC. £80–120

Depression glass

Today this simple product is considered to be an important part of the period in history with which it shares its name, the Great Depression. The Wall Street Crash of 1929 turned America on its head and caused economic fallout that was felt across the globe. Workers who had not lost their jobs were forced to take severe pay cuts and day-to-day life was reduced to managing with, and being grateful for, what they already had. Throughout these difficult times, however, simple, cheap, cheerful and mass-produced glassware remained popular.

For a great many factories business had been strong during the 1920s, enabling them to invest huge sums in automated production. Now, they were able to produce bulk quantities of household domestic and decorative glasswares. The process removed the hand-crafted element and created a product that could be quickly brought to market, reflecting the trends, tastes and styles of the modern home. Surface decoration ranged from simulated cut-glass styles through to lighter and more decorative wares with an etched surface.

This glass was everywhere, available from 'five-and-dime'

bargain stores for the price of a loaf of bread, or slipped into boxes of oatmeal or detergents as an incentive to buy the product. Shoppers would be rewarded with a free gift when their spending had reached a particular level. Gas filling stations were known to offer punch sets with an oil change. Movie theatres were more generous and would give customers a piece of glass just for buying a ticket.

Most of the key glass manufacturers of the day created Depression glass and, as such, it is in abundance. However, as with all collecting fields there are unusual and more valuable items out there waiting to be found. Identification is difficult as Depression glass was rarely marked, so collectors categorize pieces into 'known' and 'generic' classes. The array of wares is mind boggling, with jugs, bowls, vases, plates and much more to choose from. For a collector the only decision is where to start. Many collect by factory while others concentrate on a particular pattern or colour. Either way, this simple product has a place in history, with a status that is a far cry from the function for which it was originally made.

Shapes & colours

Hazel Atlas Glass Moderntone cobalt blue sherbet glass, 1934–42. £1–5

Imperial Glass Cape Cod Crystal water goblet, 1932–84. £1–5

Green serving plate with applied handle, c1930s. £30–35

Jeannette Glass Adam pattern pink cup and saucer, 1932–34. £15–20

The one to look for

This popular hobnail design was introduced as the 'American' pattern by Fostoria in the 1920s and produced for many years in various colourways. The American pattern is often confused with a similar range from the Jeannette works known as Cube or Cubist pattern. However, while similar, each has a different finish. Jeannette also produced different colours, including pink, green and the rarer blue and canary yellow.

This piece was produced by the Indiana Glass Co who had purchased the Fostoria works in the mid-1980s, merging a number of the old Fostoria patterns into the production range.

Indiana Glass Co American Whitehall pattern amber jug, late 1980s. £20–25

Green measuring cup, c1930s. £10–15

Pink jug with hinged tin cover, 1930s. £30–40

Pink lemon squeezer, c1930s. £30–35

Green measuring cup with beater, 1920s–30s. £30–35

European makers

The glass houses of Europe have for centuries been inextricably linked with the finest glasswares, from the complicated yet delicate pieces made on the island of Murano to the ornate and experimental wares from the glass makers of Stourbridge. Each has brought to the trade their own individual stamp that has then influenced the next generation, creating a maelstrom of colour, form and design for modest everyday objects and elaborate cabinet pieces. The few examples shown here represent any number of factories whose output could be found lurking in the bottom of that car boot box, cast aside as nothing more than an ornament, but to the trained eye a small gem.

Caithness *The firm was established in 1961 at Wick, in Scotland by Robin Sinclair, who employed a number of international glass workers, headed by Paul Ysart, formerly of Monart. Early works were similar in style to Scandinavian wares of the day. In 1969 the paperweight range, which was to become the core business, was launched under the artistic directorship of Colin Terris. The firm continues today as a manufacturer of paperweights and some art glassware.*
Vase, 1970s. £35–40

Dartington *Glass making began in 1967 using the skills of of designer Frank Thrower and his team of Scandinavian glass makers. Over the following years their skills were passed on to British workers, who established Dartington as a leading manufacturer. Thrower's work was influenced by Scandinavian designs and 18th-century English glass, and amounts to some 500 designs across a range of techniques.*

Decanter designed by Frank Thrower, No. FT4, c1960. £200–300

Bagley *This was once one of the most successful glass manufacturers in the United Kingdom. Originally a bottle-making enterprise, Bagley began making crystal and pressed glass for domestic use in 1912. In 1924, Queen Mary purchased several items of glassware from a range that was later marketed as the 'Queen's Choice'. In the 1930s the firm introduced a highly successful range of decorative glass in typically period colours in both frosted and transparent glass with the trademark name of 'Crystaltynt'.*

'Sunburst' amber pressed glass jug, 1930s. £30–50

GLASS

Mdina *Michael Harris established the Mdina glassworks in Malta in 1968. Helped by two Italian glass blowers from the Whitefriars works, Vicente and Ettore Boffo, Harris trained local apprentices. His work includes a number of dramatic pieces such as the Fish Head vases in the now classic colour combinations of green and blue and ochre and gold. Harris left Mdina in 1972 to establish Isle of Wight studio glass. Today the firm is owned by Joseph Said, the first apprentice to be hired by Harris.*

Bottle with trailed decoration, late 1970s.
£35–40

Monart *Made at Moncrieff glassworks in Scotland between 1922 and 1961, Monart glass was designed by Salvador Ysart and later by his sons Paul, Augustine, Vincent and Antoine. They made distinctive wares with mottled grounds, swirls and bubbles in many different colour combinations and forms. Three of the brothers began producing Vasart glass after WWII.*
Glass bowl, 1930. £70–80

Ravenhead *Glassware has been made on Merseyside at Ravenhead since the middle of the 19th century. However, it was the arrival of Alexander Hardie Williamson in 1947 that changed the firm's fortunes. He created over 1700 designs, including the dimpled beer tankard and widely used Paris goblet. Annette Meech and John Clappison also designed successful ranges of tableware and stemware.*
Conical glass by Alexander Hardie Williamson, with Festival Pattern, early 1950s. £15–20

Wedgwood *The designer Ronald Stennett-Willson founded King's Lynn Glass in 1967, employing Scandinavian craftsmen. The firm was acquired by the Wedgwood group in 1969 and continued with Stennett-Willson at the helm. Over the years a number of important design pieces were created, many of which were given industry awards for excellence. Ranges cover small novelty paperweights, cased vases and candlesticks. The Sheringham is one of the most sought-after and valuable of these.*

Sheringham candle holder, 1967–69. £30–50

Whitefriars

Over recent years there has been a greater understanding and awareness of Whitefriars' work, largely due to numerous television shows and reference books. However, the lack of signatures across the Whitefriars range means that some pieces will slip through the net.

The firm adopted many different manufacturing techniques including blow moulding, free blowing, texturing, applied and cut decoration. Often influenced by historical references or other active design movements, they always seemed to be in step with trends, especially during the 20th century.

Today, most people recognize the textured range of vases designed by Geoffrey Baxter from the early 1960s, with their quintessentially '60s feel and colour palette. In recent months prices for these pieces have fallen back somewhat, maybe because the big collectors have managed to locate all the shapes and patterns they require. It is worth remembering that these items were mass-produced and are not particularly rare. With the exception of the very large pieces, they fit well with modern ideas in interior design.

As well as Baxter's retro-looking pieces, keep an eye out for the simple 'optical' and 'trailed' wares

of the 1920s and '30s. These have simple loop and line patterns, usually in one colour, but two colours are more desirable.

However, rarest and most valuable are the early 20th-century pieces by Harry Powell. Harry was interested in historical glassware and spent hours at museums drawing ancient vessels. Powell's early pieces such as the Hugo van de Goes vase shown below can fetch four-figure sums at auction.

JONTY'S HOT TIP

Fake Drunken Bricklayer vases

- Counterfeit Drunken Bricklayer vases at 8in (20.5cm) high have recently been spotted in the market place.

- Some fakes are easier than others to identify as they have been made from colours that were not originally used, including amber, acid-yellow and dark blue.

- Check that the base of the vase has a polished circular pontil (the point where the glass blower held the vase). Recent fakes do not have this.

Selected shapes & colours

Hugo van de Goes vase by Harry Powell, 1901.
£1,000–1,200

Minoan vase by Barnaby Powell, c1903.
£350–400

Wave-ribbed tumbler vase by Marriott Powell, 1930s.
£135–150

Cased cut-crystal vase by Geoffrey Baxter, 1959.
£150–200

The one to look for

One of the most iconic vases from both Geoffrey Baxter and Whitefriars, the Drunken Bricklayer was produced from 1967 in a range of colours. The colour is the most important factor determining the price.

Classic examples have the middle brick to the left with a textured front and smooth back. Look out for the very rare reversed example – this is not just the vase turned round!

Drunken Bricklayer tangerine glass vase, by Geoffrey Baxter, 1967. £270–300

The Whitefriars story

Records show that glass was being made on the original site just off Fleet Street, central London in 1720. In 1834 the premises was acquired by entrepreneur James Powell for his three sons and during the 19th century the firm became renowned for design and innovation in glass manufacture. In 1923 the company relocated to a new purpose-built factory in Wealdstone, Middlesex and held a strong position as market leaders until the outbreak of WWII. Output during the post-war years was heavily influenced by the Scandinavian style and the strong influence of senior designer Geoffrey Baxter. Whitefriars finally closed its doors in 1980.

Swingout cased glass vase by Geoffrey Baxter, c1960. £250–300

Textured range Bark vase by Geoffrey Baxter, c1967. £30–50

Onion vase by Geoffrey Baxter, c1964. £1,300–1,500

Banjo vase by Geoffrey Baxter, 1966. £650–800

Murano

On a small island in the lagoon of Venice lives a community of artists, designers and craftsmen who are responsible for some of the most beautiful, technically proficient and important pieces of glass the world has seen. Year after year travellers visiting Venice make the short journey to the island of Murano, where they can witness the centuries-old craft of glassmaking that has become synonymous with the Italians and envied the world over. Many of these visitors will go home with a small souvenir, but such souvenirs do not not necessarily represent the best of the island's ouput in terms of skill and artistry.

The Venetians have a history in glass manufacture that goes back hundreds of years, and it is a craft that was cloaked in secrecy. The masters were made to swear an oath upon pain of death that the skills they learned would not be taken from the city or divulged to any individual outside their circle. From the 15th to the 17th centuries the glass of the Venetians was revered as the finest in the world, placing them firmly at the centre of the industry.

However, the appeal of Venetian glass did eventually wane as, by the 19th century, other countries had developed alternative types of glassware. By then the fashion for lead crystal was sweeping through Europe, suddenly making Murano glass appear dated and out of touch. The taste changed from the typical colourful hot-worked wares of the Italians to the more simplified forms cool-worked with cut and engraved decoration. In a short period of time the highly decorative techniques of the Venetian masters were consigned to history and the manufacture of glass from Murano was confined to historical replicas.

The 1920s and 1930s saw a change in fortunes for the Muranese makers as new blood began to pump into the heart of the island. Young and dynamic artists and designers were employed to rejuvenate tired factories such as Barovier & Toso or Fratelli Toso, or create new companies such as A.V.E.M. and Seguso Vetri d'Arte. The talented but traditional glass blowers and workers quickly and easily interpreted the new bold and experimental designs created by sculptors, artists and architects. The combination of strong personalities and natural Italian flair with centuries-old techniques led to the creation of pieces that would once again take the world's breath away.

Other shapes

Vase by Archimede Seguso, 1980s. £65–75

Bowl in the form a bird, by Dino Martens, 1950s. £120–135

Bucella Cristalli vase, 1970s. £125–135

The one to look for

Fulvio Bianconi began working for Venini around 1946. He originally trained as a graphic designer and is credited today as being one of the most innovative and talented glass designers of the post-war era. Bianconi was constantly experimenting with traditional techniques and sought to push glass to its extreme boundaries.

Tessere is a very ancient and traditional technique. The process begins with panels of sheet glass arranged in the desired pattern. They are then uniformly heated to fuse them together then worked into the desired form.

This vase shows how glassmakers took traditional techniques and used them to make bold, modern pieces in simple, clean shapes.

Vase by Fulvio Bianconi, 1953. £4,300–4,800

Geode bowl, 1950s. £50–55

Venini handkerchief vase, c1950. £450–500

Venini Messico jar by Toni Zuccheri, 1966. £700–800

Murano

Venini is today one of the most respected Italian glass studios of the 20th century. They remain at the forefront of development, constantly striving to push the boundaries of the material. Over the 20th century they worked with such great names as Carlo Scarpa, Gio Ponti and Fulvio Bianconi to create many new and exciting techniques in surface pattern, including a simple cut pattern called battuto that gave glass the appearance of hammered metal.

The new look was characterized by the abstraction of traditional techniques applied to new organic forms. For example, murrine canes were blown up in scale and fused with many others in bright and bold colourways to form a kaleidoscope of colour; the glass was decorated with splatters of other colours, or wrapped around metal foil to give a glittering finish.

By the post-war years this expansion seemed unstoppable and more firms were established including Cenedese and Vistosi. More and more talented artists aspired to be associated with the glassmakers of Murano and ever more increasingly inventive vessels were created. The colour scheme of the post-war years also suited the palette of the Italians with its unashamedly strong colours almost colliding across the body of the wares.

Later, many smaller factories sprung up to produce items that echoed the new creative styles of the top masters. These firms helped to spread the 'Murano' look across the globe and today their wares make collecting Murano affordable. The pieces from large manufacturers such as Venini, A.V.E.M. and Barovier will probably continue to perform well, regardless of market forces, as the complexity of their manufacture deserves the price ticket they command. There is however a huge quantity of affordable wares available on the market from more general factories such as Carlo Moretti and Campanella that provide the Murano style.

Over the last century and into the present there have been many re-assessments of the major glass centres of the world. When looking back at the cool elegance of Scandinavia, the refined quality of Stourbridge or the innovative production of North America, it is impossible to say who has left the greatest legacy. One thing is for sure, however, and that is the Murano legacy is as bold, colourful and confident as the vessels it produced.

Other shapes

Vase attributed to Seguso, c1950. £1,350–1,500

Two birds, 1950s, £50–55

Sommerso bowl, 1950s. £35–40

Sommerso vase, 1950s. £100–120

GLASS

The one to look for

In 1934 Carlo Scarpa developed the sommerso technique while at Venini. Two to four layers of coloured glass are fused together to create a multicoloured sculptural effect. The technique requires great skill.

Bottles such as these were also produced with stoppers, which were often very tall and slender. Few survived so if complete the value of the bottle will be increased.

Note the combination of bright colours which echo the fashion and trends of interior design of the period. These pieces were created to add that extra lift to a home.

The different layers of glass are clearly visible around the base. Working with this thickness of molten glass requires great skill.

Sommerso bottle, mid-20thC.
£100–120

Sommerso fish, 1950s.
£25–30

Figure of a clown, 1950s–60s.
£30–50

Jug, possibly by Ercole Barovier or Giorgio Ferro, 1950s. £75–85

Sommerso vase, 20thC.
£70–100

Scandinavian glass

The glassmakers of Scandinavia represent a group of artists, designers and manufacturers who arguably produced some of the finest glassware of the 20th century. Among their ranks are giants such as Orrefors and Kosta who today still influence trends and continue to develop techniques in glass manufacturing. Other names to look out for include Nuutajärvi Notsjö, Iittala, Flygsfors, Rhiihimäki and Holmegaard.

The Scandinavians have always been associated with fine design and quality craftsmanship – they see art and design as an all encompassing discipline. A skilled designer can just as easily design a vase as a table, create a necklace or paint a picture and it is this all round ability that has created a legacy of design that is envied the world over.

The skill of the manufacturers is in their ability to combine the talents of exceptional craftsmen with dynamic designers who, through combined experimentation, learned to manipulate this most magical of materials. Scandinavian glass was shaped into a number of key styles which together conveyed the statement on style that this group of countries wanted to make.

Designers drew their inspiration from the dramatic landscape outside their studios. They replicated in glass in abstract and fluid forms the texture and appearance of ice, rocks, trees and other plant life. The post-war years also saw a huge recognition of the ever-changing world around them and many firms began producing post-modern Pop Art-inspired vessels and sculptures in bold shapes and dramatic colour palettes.

Each of the many glass-making companies manufactured items across all levels. Output ranged from the more domestic and accessible everyday examples to the immensely complicated exhibition pieces, from the most expensive to the most affordable. However, all were created with the same simple principle that everything should be just as good as they possibly could be.

Today there is a huge interest in all things Scandinavian. The look that was created all those years ago appears just as fresh and appealing to a whole new audience and it is that interest that has created such a strong secondary market. These are living memory pieces that may be thrown out by one generation, only to be snapped up by the next to enjoy all over again.

Makers & designers

Alsterfors cased glass vase by P. O. Ström, c1960s.
£125–140

Holmegaard cased glass Carnaby vase, c1960.
£200–240

Iittala I-glass bottle vase by Timo Sarpeneva, 1960s.
£180–200

Kosta sommerso vase by Vicke Lindstrand, 1950s.
£80–90

The one to look for

Holmegaard's success was largely due to its ability to address the trends and fashions of the day. It carved a strong place in the market with the production of simple forms inspired by Pop art.

Holmegaard Napoli vase by Michael Bang, 1969–71. £100–130

Vases were often cased (layering one colour over another) using bold vivid colours over a white ground, giving a dramatic futuristic appearance.

The distinctive Holmegaard label shows the company's appointment to the Danish Royal family. These are small paper discs and can add value if still present.

Palet series

Michael Bang developed the successful cased glass Palet tableware range for Holmegaard in 1968. Many copies of this line were made but they tend to be of lower quality.

Palet tea and coffee jars, 1970s. £50–55

Nuutajärvi Notsjö vase by Gunnel Nyman, 1947. £250–300

Riihimaki Taalari bowl by Tamara Aladin, 1970. £45–50

Riihimaki Fenomena vase by Nanny Still, 1968–72. £125–150

Strombergshyttan vase by Gunnar Nylund, 1950s. £125–150

US makers

Glass manufacture in America has a heritage dating back to the start of the 17th century and can be classed as one of the country's first industries. However, pieces from this period are not just rare but almost impossible to come by, except from specialist dealers.

The great majority of items on the market today were made during the late 19th and early 20th centuries. The huge array of wares produced over this period have many influences, from the elaborate and decorative styles created in central Europe and the British Isles, to the simple and elegant lines preferred by the Scandinavian designers. The range of items is substantial and provides the keen collector with boundless opportunities.

Blenko *The company was founded in 1893 in West Virginia by William J. Blenko, who was originally from London. They began with the manufacture of glass for stained glass windows, but when William's son joined the firm he brought a dynamism and drive that was to place Blenko on its future path. William Jnr employed Scandinavian craftsmen, and together they developed ranges of free-blown stem wares and vessels. Blenko's wares are distinct with their simple colour palette and European style and form.*
Shouldered ovoid jug with crackle finish, 1950–60. £50–55

Cambridge *Formed in 1873 in Cambridge, Ohio the firm became one of the most successful American glass manufacturers of the early 20th century. Under the artistic management of English-born Arthur J. Bennett it developed many successful ranges of press-moulded decorative wares created to simulate expensive European cut crystal. The company weathered the 1930s Depression but then suffered the affects of cheap European imports after WWII. Unusual decorative items are keenly sought but keep an eye out for coloured pieces rather than the less valuable clear examples.*
Tazza on a chrome-plated stand, 1930s–40s. £10–15

Fenton *The largest manufacturer of handmade coloured glassware in the US, this firm was founded in 1905 by the Fenton brothers. They were heavily influenced by Steuben and Tiffany. The introduction of iridescent glass known today as Carnival glass was a huge success and helped the company emerge from the depression years. Collectors also look for the Victorian-inspired glass of the 1950s and '60s.*

Cranberry glass 'Coin DA' vase, shape No. 1458, 1950s. £75–100

Morgantown *Founded in the late 19th century, the company rose to become a leading maker of high-quality hand-blown tablewares and pressed glass. Over the years it rebranded and reinvented its products, producing drinking glasses for commercial and domestic use. Morgantown's popularity rose again after the introduction of many new and exciting colours in the 1940s and '60s. Today, availability is mainly limited to drinking glasses, but these can be difficult to find as, being everyday objects, they naturally got broken or replaced.*
Crinkle iced tea glass, 1940s. £5–10

Mount Washington *This company stands as one of the great Art glass manufacturers of the 19th century. Its wares reflected the styles and trends being executed in Europe and especially at Stourbridge, England. It produced a great number of high art wares such as epergnes, vases and bowls, using complicated manufacturing methods, hand-enamelling, gilding and applied decoration. Its exquisite pieces, which are housed in private and public collections all over the world, are in very high demand.*
Amberina pitcher, 19thC. £150–200

Phoenix Glass Co *Although founded in 1880, the production of Art glass began in 1932 when the firm acquired some 50 moulds from the Consolidated Glass Co. These early pieces were called the Reuben line and are distinctive with a strong and simple colour palette. Today collectors seek the sculptured art wares made from their own moulds to designs by Kenneth Haley from the 1930s until the mid-1950s. In 1970 Phoenix became part of Anchor Hocking, and was sold to the Newell Group in 1987.*
Mould-blown sculpted Art Glass vase, 1930s–50s. £150–175

Viking Glass Co *After several incarnations the Viking Glass Co was established in Connecticut in 1944. The post-war era saw the company flourish with the development of brightly coloured wares developed by Billy Reinbeau with dramatic yet simple organic forms. The firm continued to make decorative household ornaments and some tablewares until it closed its doors in 1984.*

Crackle glass patio light, 1970s. £25–30

Paperweights

Paperweights as we know them were created in the 1840s but their origins go back to the ancient Egyptians and Romans. Many techniques have been developed in the manufacture of paperweights but the most common today is millefiori, which means a 'thousand flowers'. The technique involves bundles of small glass canes grouped in a range of patterns and designs and cased within a solid glass dome, which magnifies the design within.

In 1845, the Muranese glass artist Pietro Bigaglia exhibited weights using scrambled millefiori canes. The French recognized the commercial possibilities and by 1846 France had become the centre of paperweight production with factories such as St Louis, Baccarat and Clichy. It is believed that between 50,000 and 100,000 weights were produced over the the next 15 years. By the 1850s, English and North American firms such as George Bacchus, New England, Mount Washington and Sandwich were all producing fashionable weights.

The paperweight's success was due to a combination of factors; they could be relatively inexpensive and, being both useful and decorative, were a popular gift item. They were sold in stationery stores and fine glass shops in Europe, Great Britain and America.

By the 1870s, however, paper-weights had begun to fall out of favour. There was a resurgence of interest in the early 20th century when firms such as Whitefriars in London, and several years later the Ysart family in Scotland, began making them again. The 20th century has seen dramatic developments in production, with centres of excellence in the British Isles and North America making examples in both traditional and very modern styles.

When purchasing paperweights there are a number of points to consider. The size is important as classic weights tend to measure between 2in (5cm) and 4½in (10cm) across, whereas both larger examples, known as magnums, and smaller miniatures are more popular. Also, hold the weight in your hand and, if you can, compare it to an identified example as older weights are generally heavier.

As far as condition goes, surface scratching and marking can be a problem. These can be removed by a professional polisher but serious reductions in height will devalue the item. Bruises, however, are far more difficult to remove. With regard to pattern there are so many variants to look out for, from patterned millefiori to blown and lampworked florals. Keep a look out for animals and birds as these can be very valuable.

Paperweight makers

Baccarat bouquet paperweight, 1986.
£400–450

Caithness Glass ribbons paperweight, 1980s.
£20–25

Ken Rosenfeld paperweight, 2005.
£200–220

St Louis millefiori paperweight, 1987.
£400–450

The one to look for

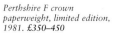

Stuart Drysdale, a former manager for Strathearn glass, formed Perthshire Paperweights in 1968. They produced fine paperweights in the French style and their exquisite artistry, combined with affordable prices, ensured the rapid growth of the company. Most Perthshire weights remain affordable at below £100 but unusual or complex patterns such as this are far rarer and more desirable.

With the exception of limited editions early weights were generally unmarked. All weights after 1974 carry a small signature cane with a letter 'P'.

Perthshire F crown paperweight, limited edition, 1981. £350–450

Victor Trabucco

Bee and flowers paperweight, 2004. £500–550

Flowers paperweight, 2004. £500–550

Victor Trabucco is recognized as one of the most talented glass artists working today. He further developed the traditional lampwork technique, first employed by glasshouses such as Pantin, to create his astonishingly life-like masterpieces. Today his works are housed in some of the greatest collections and change hands for three- and four-figure sums.

Paul Stankard bouquet paperweight, 1981. £2,250–2,500

Strathearn moulded star paperweight, 1964–80. £35–40

Whitefriars paperweight by William Wilson, 1953. £45–50

Paul Ysart butterfly paperweight, 1930s. £800–850

Around the House

The 20th-century witnessed a rapid development in technology, and gadgets for use around the home saw many innovations. Comfort was the buzzword, and manufacturers vied with each other to produce ever more effective versions of labour-saving devices designed to raise living standards and take the drudgery out of domestic chores. Thus a state-of-the-art and cutting-edge possession became obsolete in no time – reinventing itself later as the latest sought-after collectable. The ever-increasing list of products in this field includes Tupperware and Pyrex, post-war stainless steel and even mobile telephones.

Works of art are sought for their beauty and craftsmanship, but many collectors like to focus on everyday items that can be found in the average home. Every room in the house yields something that is of interest to the modern collector, from kitchen utensils to telephones. These are objects that were made to be used and, for many people, are practical antiques that put us in touch with the past. In some cases it is still possible to use them today, which is perhaps the best part of owning these domestic relics of yesteryear.

Vico Magistretti plastic table lamp with swivel globe, 1966. £220–250

How to collect

Parker metal and faux tortoiseshell musical lighter, 1970s. £15–20

Objects from around the house constitute a huge field, and you will almost certainly want to specialize. There are plenty of opportunities to build a collection that is very personal to your own life. For example, if you are working, or have worked, in the IT industry, what could be better than to have a collection of vintage computers and calculators from the dawn of the microchip revolution? If you are a cook, or simply love fine food, why not choose kitchenware? If you are a carpenter, or just have a keen interest in DIY, then build a collection of fine old tools that reflect your interest.

Finding out more

A good way to get started is to visit your local museum. There are many good collections reflecting social history and most local museums have displays of domestic objects from the past, or even room settings. Museums sometimes publish books or pamphlets on their collections, and these can be the start of a reference library. Some areas of collecting are quite specialist and there are few books available.

If there are no dedicated collectors' clubs in your area, try searching the Internet as many clubs have some kind of online presence. Another way of familiarizing yourself with objects from domestic settings of 60 or 70 years ago is by watching films of the period, although as a form of research, this is rarely taken seriously.

Condition

Condition is important, but sometimes a certain degree of wear can be quite acceptable. Collectors of kitchenware and tools know that these items were designed for regular use, and are not put off as long as the wear is not too severe.

In some cases, condition of the inner workings of an item may be more significant than its outer appearance. Clocks are a good example of this, where a high quality or unusual movement can be of great interest to horologists, who will often buy a clock purely for its movement. On the other hand, those who are interested in design will look for an attractive, well-made case, rather than a good movement.

When buying old electrical appliances always remember that they can be extremely dangerous. If you are buying for display only this is obviously not a problem. However, if you intend to use any old electrical items it is essential to get them checked by a qualified electrician first.

Where to buy

Auctions can be good places to buy from as some include domestic antiques in mixed lots, making it possible to pick up bargains. Dealers and fairs are also good sources. Specialist dealers may not be the best choice if you are looking for a bargain, as they are well aware of the value of their stock.

However, a big advantage is that you should get what you pay for and you can learn a lot by talking to someone with a genuine experience.

With fairs the large, showground-type events can be a bargain hunter's paradise. Specialist fairs exist in fields such as vintage communications and these are worth visiting if you have a specific interest and, again, they are good places to learn and to meet

Kockums enamel coffee pot, 1930.
£30–35

fellow enthusiasts. Many domestic antiques are still quite affordable. Not everyone appreciates their value so it is possible to make genuine finds at places such as car boot sales. This varies depending on the type of collectable, and its age. For example, most people are now aware that old radios of the 1930s can be valuable, but fewer realize that transistor radios from the 1960s are collectable. Similarly, not many people would overlook a pair of Victorian cast-iron kitchen scales, but plastic storage jars of the 1950s and '60s are less likely to be noticed – so it is possible to pick up some bargains.

Bush pocket transistor radio, 1960s.
£5–10

Silver

Man has been fascinated by this most versatile of materials for many thousands of years. Ancient civilizations stumbled upon silver deposits, which were plentiful on or near the earth's surface and began working them into jewellery, vessels and religious articles. Silver was used for trade and was held as a symbol of wealth and status, second only to gold.

The area of the world we now know as modern-day Turkey is considered to be the first source of mined silver ore c4000 years BC. The following millennia, leading up to 1st century AD saw central Europe and its civilizations make great strides in the mining of this material and the processes required to extract the ore. Ancient Greece was particularly active in the production of silver and grew at a phenomenal pace. With huge mines around Athens, it became the largest centre of silver production, developing alongside the trade of the silver across Asia Minor and North Africa.

By the 1st century AD other important ore discoveries were made in Spain, making the country a major source of silver for nearly 1,000 years. This supply of raw silver was hugely important, as it provided a huge proportion of the needs for the Roman Empire and was a vital economic source for the spice trade in the Far East. During the following centuries more and more important silver discoveries were made across Europe, and combined with important developments in mining and processing technology.

The silverware that we see on the market today has it origins in relatively recent centuries. Prior to the 16th and 17th centuries, bullion was the preserve of the extremely wealthy, the monarchy or the church. Developments in trade saw the rise of a new and powerful merchant class, however, who indulged in the trappings their success afforded them.

By the 18th century, the acquisition of silver became an important display of one's standing in society and the silversmith was considered an important figure. Up until this time many silversmiths were under the patronage of the aristocracy and church in the production of religious silverware. Now, however, the influence of society and emerging etiquette created a requirement for specific pieces of domestic metalware.

The Georgian period made popular items such as tea and coffee wares, cutlery, table ornaments, baskets and all manner of other decorative wares, and to this day Georgian silver remains some of the most highly prized.

Other silver shapes

Silver teapot by John Walton, Newcastle 1823. £500–600

Silver castle-top card case by Taylor & Perry, Birmingham, c1835. £1,300–1,500

Pair of silver candlesticks, London 1896. £280–320

Silver hand mirror, c1880. £575–650

The one to look for

The Art Nouveau movement is synonymous with a fluid and organic style, which was predominantly mastered by the European makers of the late 19th century.

Silver buckle by Kate Harris, made by William Hutton & Sons, London 1901. £2,250–2,500

A buckle like this would have been worn by a very fashionable lady of the time. Note the very typical whiplash lines and floral motifs around the central figure, influenced by the Asian styles that became fashionable at the end of the 19th century.

Hallmarks

Maker's mark.

Lion passant, the mark of all silver.

Leopard's head, city mark for London.

A letter denotes year of manufacture.

Hallmarking can be classed as the first method of consumer protection and dates back as far as the 4th century AD. English hallmarking dates back to 1300 and the reign of King Edward I, whose act stated that all silver must comply to a standard of 925 (parts of silver per 1,000) commonly referred to as 'sterling'. In 1327, King Edward III granted a charter to the Worshipful Company of Goldsmiths based in London at Goldsmiths Hall, from where the English term hallmark is derived. There are a number of marks, including city marks, small date codes and maker's marks, which may be all manner of initials and monograms.

Silver-gilt vinaigrette by John Reily, London 1815. £200–250

Liberty silver cake forks with fitted case, by Archibald Knox, Birmingham 1913. £1,000–1,100

Silver frame by H. M. H. Matthews, Birmingham, c1903. £300–350

Silver chamberstick by Silvester Lenny-Smith, Sheffield 1903. £720–800

Silver boxes & novelties

By the end of the 19th century and into the modern era, the production of silverware became heavily industrialized, with small and affordable pieces quickly and efficiently manufactured. Centres of excellence, such as Birmingham, provided employment for 50,000 people at the peak. As a result, there is a tremendous choice when it comes to collecting silver pieces from this period.

A good place to start is in deciding what you want from your silver. Is it to use, is it a gift or do you want to place it on display? The next step, and an important one, is to learn how to identify the different silver marks (see page 105). Investing in a small pocket guide will provide you with a list of all the different date codes and associated marks that guarantee the authenticity of a piece of British silver. Be wary of marks on silver plate, however, as this was often stamped with pseudo marks that were applied to give the impression that a piece was correctly hallmarked solid silver.

Collectors will find many different avenues to follow, either by concentrating on periods such as Georgian, Victorian or contemporary; styles such as Neoclassical or Art Nouveau; or certain designers or manufacturers. Focusing on specific objects, however, may be the simplest way of entering into this market. At the affordable end there is a multitude of items such as vesta cases (made to hold matches), pincushions, table salts, wine labels, spoons or buttons – the choices are endless. However, there are some very important, yet simple, rules to learn before starting out.

Check for wear and damage; light scratches can be polished and small dents can be worked out by a professional silversmith, but splits can be a problem. Occuring where a piece has been joined together during manufacture, these often happen when the silver is worn thin, or years of polishing has weakened the joints.

Also, be wary of alterations, which sometimes occur as a natural progression of the history of a piece. For example, the Victorians had a passion for taking plain and simple Georgian silver and transforming it with the more fashionable styles of the day. In the current market the trend is for pieces that are as original as possible. A Georgian tankard later embellished by the Victorians will be worth at least half the value of an untouched example. Also, pieces may have been decorated with a dedication or monogram; these are, of course, personal to the original owner and can add to value. In some cases they can be removed, but the gauge (thickness) of the silver has to be sufficient to survive the polisher's wheel.

Other boxes and novelties

Silver elephant pincushion, Birmingham, 1905. £240–260

Silver pincushion, in the form of a pig, Birmingham 1905. £90–110

Silver snuff box by Joseph Anthony, late 18thC. £170–200

Silver snuff box by Karl Verlin, c1880. £650–750

The one to look for

Cigarette cases can be very affordable objects to collect. The prices are often quite low, as they no longer meet the requirements for modern cigarettes. This example is unusual, however, as it features a golfer, making it an ideal cabinet gift for a keen fan of the sport.

Silver cigarette case embossed with golfer, Birmingham, 1900. £360–400

The rear of the case is quite clearly and beautifully engraved with the previous owner's monogram. Although these can be removed, they form part of a piece's history.

Once made, the manufacturer would send a piece to an assay office, where a very small sample of the silver would be tested to confirm its standard. The piece would then be stamped with this series of small marks before going on to be sold.

Silver vesta case by W. Neale, Chester 1889. £500–600

Silver vesta case, enamelled with head of a terrier, London 1896. £200–240

Silver vinaigrette, Yapp & Woodward, Birmingham 1844. £130–160

Silver vinaigrette, in form of an articulated fish, c1850s. £300–350

Stainless steel

As with so many products we take for granted in today's modern home, stainless steel grew out of need. Silver requires laborious cleaning, as do brass, copper and iron which are also heavy. Over the years there have been some lively debates regarding the exact origins of stainless steel, with a number of sources claiming credit for the discovery of this corrosion-free material.

Although there were various experiments and developments towards stainless steel during the course of the 19th century – particularly in France and Germany – it is an Englishman, Harry Brearley, who is most widely recognized and credited with the eureka moment. Born in Sheffield, in 1871, he was appointed lead researcher at Firth Brown Laboratories. In 1912 Brearley was given the task of prolonging the life of gun barrels, which were eroding away too quickly. Through experimentation he noticed that steel with a high chrome content was resistant to attack and, on August 13th 1913, Brearley created a steel with 12.8 per cent chromium and 0.24 per cent carbon, argued to be the first ever stainless steel.

Brearley subjected his new compound to household acids, such as lemon juice and vinegar, and found that it withstood them. He immediately recognized the potential of this new material in the manufacture of cutlery and, lacking the support of his employers, he took his findings to local cutlers R.F. Moseley. Brearley was marketing his material as 'rustless steel', and it was only after sample tests in vinegar that the manager, Earnest Stuart, dubbed the compound 'stainless steel', after which the name stuck.

The use of stainless steel soon became wider reaching than simple cutlery and, during the course of the 20th century, it was used in many disciplines including industry, architecture and aeronautics. By the latter part of the 20th century it had also become and integral substance in the space race.

Today, stainless steel can be found everywhere, from charity shops to car-boot sales. The nature of the material means that it is usually in very good condition. Having been designed as a household material, it is not unusual for collections to be predominantly domestic. If a piece is on the second-hand market, it is likely to have been used, so expect a few small surface scratches. Try to avoid anything with large dents or bruises, however.

Although many items are very ordinary, a number of stylish products have emerged over the years, from manufacturers and designers including Old Hall, Stelton and Alessi.

Other stainless steel items

Teak and stainless steel cruet set, 1950s–70s. £10–15

Old Hall Campden Range coffee set by Robert Welch, 1960s. £70–75

Taylors Eye Alveston cutlery, by Robert Welch, 1961. £150–180

Epic salad servers with resin handles, 1960s–70s. £15–20

The one to look for

Italian firm, Alessi, is renowned for its many great collaborations with leading designers.
Alessi stainless-steel Mickey Mouse teapot, designed by Michael Graves, limited edition, 1986. £80–100

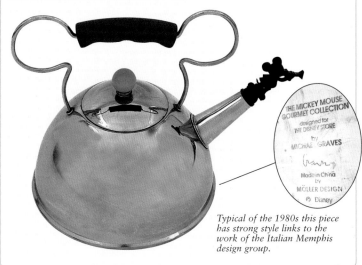

Typical of the 1980s this piece has strong style links to the work of the Italian Memphis design group.

Old Hall

Old Hall Alveston stainless-steel teapot, designed by Robert Welch, 1962. £80–100
Formed in 1893 by the Wiggin family, Old Hall was established to manufacture small-scale metalware items for the saddlery trade and, later, bathroom fittings with a chromium-plated finish. With the discovery of stainless steel the company changed production methods, using solely the new 'Staybright' material. They started with a small toast rack in 1928 and, in 1930, made the world's first stainless steel teapot.

Gense of Sweden stainless-steel fruit bowl, 1960s–70s. £50–60

Cylinda Line teapot, by Arne Jacobsen for Stelton, 1964–67. £120–145

Stainless-steel toast rack, 1972. £5–10

Polaris vase designed by Olay, No. 4585, 1960s–70s. £85–95

Brass & copper

The use of brass and copper is many centuries old and the earliest items were generally produced as everyday domestic pieces. During the 1970s and 1980s brass and copper wares were extremely fashionable in interiors, with many homes dressing fire surrounds with copper warming pans, stitch-back kettles and horse brasses. Recent years and changes in taste have seen a slow and steady decline in the value and interest of such items, however, making them both accessible and affordable to collect. The wane in interest seems to have arisen in response to modern living with a combination of simplified interiors and a basic lack of spare time to clean and maintain collections.

Brass *Early wares, predominantly from central Europe and the Low Countries, included functional items such as candlesticks and chandeliers as well as domestic wares such as jugs, bowls and cooking pans.*

The British market developed through the 17th century and saw simple designs made in small quantities and reflecting fashionable silver forms of the day. Such pieces are now highly sought after.

Brass candlestick by Christopher Dresser, c1880. £320–350

By the 18th century, many continental metalworkers had fled to the safety of Britain fleeing from religious persecution in Europe. With them they brought many new skills and styles. Areas including Bristol and Birmingham became centres for the production of small-scale items, such as novelties, cutlery and furniture mounts.

Following mechanization of the industrial age, the 19th century saw a huge boom in production which, for many, saw an all over cheapening of the product. Towards the end of the century, however, brass was once more taken up by designers who used simple and elegant designs in the Art Nouveau and Arts & Crafts styles.

When looking to collect brass, consider the age of a piece. Despite a downturn in the market, early pieces have retained a strong desirability with collectors and have a distinctive subtle patina built up over years of handling. Domestic pieces will have been polished many times, which adds to their rounded and soft appearance.

Brass stick stand, c1890. £250–300

Brass and iron trivet by W. & P., 1890. £20–25

*Kettle,
19thC.
£100–120*

Copper Like brass, copper has been an intrinsic element to domestic life for many centuries. However, unlike brass its use has been largely restricted to more functional wares such as kettles, measures and jelly moulds. The use of copper for decorative wares before the English Arts & Crafts period is unusual, brass having been by far the more favoured material.

Early copperwares were hand formed; the metal would be hammered against a forming tool with frequent returns to the heat to make the material soft. These pieces show distinctive hand-crafted traits, such as a soft pattern of hammer marks upon the surface.

*Newlyn inkwell with
fish pattern, c1900.
£600–650*

*Half gill
measure
with tin
lining,
c1915.
£35–40*

Beware if these appear even and uniform, as this may infer that the piece has been made by machine to simulate a handmade item. Often the body of a hand-crafted piece will have an irregular thickness, while machine-made pieces tend to be of a uniform gauge throughout the body.

Look at how a piece has been constructed. Early examples have distinctive features, such as a stitch seam where they have been joined. With a zip-like appearance, this is a time-consuming method of manufacture but provides a greater surface area to bond two pieces together. Often sought after in copper kettles of the 18th and 19th centuries, such pieces are referred to as 'stitch-back'.

Jelly moulds were also popular in the 19th century and come in many unusual shapes. They were often made using a mechanized stamping process. The most desirable tend to be castle-shaped and can change hands for three-figure sums.

Always consider decoration. Early wares tend to have simple punchwork or hammered floral patterns, revived during the Arts & Crafts period. Similar pieces were often made in large quantities by industrial makers, but will be of less value.

*Tin-lined
mould,
c1910.
£30–35*

Other metalware

Metal has many applications in the field of collecting, from humble domestic appliances to beautifully hand-crafted pieces made by members of major art guilds. The finished product can be cast, polished, plated or patinated, and might be pewter, bronze, iron, nickel or spelter. With such a broad scope it's difficult to suggest exactly where to start, but here are a few ideas.

Kitchenalia comprises many weird and wonderful objects created from the need to improve everyday life. These pieces were often created through casting or metal fabrication. There is a renewed interest in antiquated devices, as these can provide a talking point and, in many cases, might also still be in reasonable working order. Such items can be purchased for very modest sums, although condition can be poor, as they are likely to have been used as everyday objects and as such will probably have suffered at the hands of domesticity.

Other household items can prove more valuable, however, and fall into very distinctive areas of collecting. Wine and drinking-related collectables, such as corkscrews and bottle openers, are very popular, with early examples often fetching three-figure sums. Many companies in the 20th century recognized the potential of advertising using small items like this and, through basic casting processes, firms were able to embellish a simple device with a company logo or motto. These were often given away as promotional items and as such were seen as throwaway. Other drink-related wares to look out for include cocktail shakers, with cocktail memorabilia in general having a huge following among today's collectors.

Smoking-related wares are still popular, despite the change in views regarding smoking: ashtrays and lighters feature regularly among collections, with many fun novelty items having been produced during the course of the 20th century.

Methods of casting have improved over the years, and there have been many improvements in quality and detail. There are numerous affordable metalwares, from early neoclassical designs through to pieces in the Art Deco style. When looking for items in this field, always keep an eye out for the more unusual or novelty pieces, which will appeal to other collectors when it comes to selling.

Other metal items

Box iron with wooden handle and cockerel decoration, late 18thC.
£30–40.

Cast-iron double cherry stoner, c1900.
£180–190

Beatrice cast-iron coffee grinder, 1908.
£75–85

Chrome Juice-0-Mat orange press, c1950.
£30–40

The one to look for

The Württembergische Metalwarenfabrik (WMF) was established in 1880, following the merger of two existing companies. The firm was particularly renowned for its creations in the Art Nouveau style.

WMF pewter dish with figure of a lady, c1905.
£600–700

This dish is cleverly designed with a stylized female figure as the handle, surrounded by sinuous and stylized leaf forms. These motifs occur frequently on WMF wares and were a popular feature of the European Art Nouveau style.

WMF wares are usually well marked with either the letters or their famous ostrich motif. Other firms producing around the same time include Orivit, Kayserzinn and Gerbrüder Bing. However, WMF remains among the most valuable and sought after.

Chromed metal tabletop fuel cigarette lighter, c1950s. **£20–25**

Nickel-plated corkscrew, c1930. **£20–25**

Pewter half-pint tankard named to RMS Atlantis, c1930. **£25–30**

Painted spelter snuff holder, modelled as a dog, early 20thC. **£75–85**

Wood

Wood has been used for centuries to make everything from kitchen utensils to toys. Although cheap and readily available, its main disadvantage is that it is susceptible to rot and insect attack. For this reason it can be hard to find antique items in good condition – much depends on the environment in which they have been stored. Woods used for small items include ash, sycamore, fruitwood, pine, box and beech.

Small objects in wood are known as treen, which literally means 'of the tree'. Treen can be purely practical or very decorative and can include a whole array of small household objects; some examples were specially made for the tourist trade. American collectors were quick to appreciate treen and wooden bygones. In America these are often termed 'folk art' and generally fetch higher prices and are more desirable than their British counterparts.

Wooden items were often made by craftsmen for local use and were usually unmarked, although some may be carved with a date and sometimes other information. However, dating is usually a question of patination. Well-carved and decorative pieces will fetch more than plain ones. Turning on a lathe was a popular method of decoration and well-turned objects are more sought after than plain ones. Another type of decoration is poker work, in which hot pokers were used to create the designs.

Mauchline ware

Mauchline ware is a distinctive range of treen souvenirs made for the tourist trade by W. & A. Smith in the town of Mauchline, Ayrshire, and later in Birmingham, from the 1820s until the 1930s. Usually made of varnished sycamore and transfer-printed with various designs, products include boxes, needle cases, napkin rings and wooden eggs. The box on the left depicts Osborne House, Queen Victoria's residence on the Isle of Wight. It is a typical example of a piece made for the tourist trade.
Mauchline ware box, c1870. £50–60

Other items

Pan scourer,
c1900.
£20–25

Carved bear,
c1910.
£55–65

Mahogany knife
tray, c1915.
£65–75

Boxwood salt box,
c1920.
£45–50

The one to look for

One of the most celebrated makers of high-quality medical equipment was S. Maw of London and it is their name that helps to make these pieces desirable. They made everything from pill boxes to amputation sets and their pieces are usually marked. The firm also made Champagne taps, as Champagne was once prescribed by doctors as a tonic.

While this is an attractive piece in its own right for treen collectors, the link with S. Maw makes it equally appealing to collectors of medical items. Antiques related to the medical profession and to apothecaries have a loyal following.

Turned treen bottle box by S. Maw, London, with original glass bottle, c1910. £70-80

Tunbridge ware

Tunbridge ware is a decorative technique that was developed in the 19th century and, as its name suggests, was practised in Tunbridge Wells, Kent. Long sticks of different coloured woods were glued together in a block, with a pattern running through them, as in a stick of seaside rock. The blocks were then sliced to produce a series of sheets with identical patterns on them, which could then be applied to items such as this box.
Tunbridge ware box with carved knop, c1860. £80-90

Shortbread mould, c1930.
£10-15

Pull-along toy, c1950.
£40-45

Carved breadboard, with knife, c1950.
£25-30

Salt and pepper pots, 1950s.
£25-30

Moulds

During the 19th century, middle- and upper-class households enjoyed elaborate meals where presentation was important, and equally elaborate moulds would therefore be used for both sweet and savoury dishes. The most attractive and collectable moulds were made of copper – Benham & Froud being a major British maker – and Wedgwood creamware, but earthenware ones were also made.

By the early 20th century, commercially made moulds were being produced on a large scale by various makers and in many different materials, including tin. Names to look for include Swan Brand, Tala, and Nutbrown.

An important name in confectionery or chocolate moulds is that of Anton Reiche, a major producer of moulds in Germany, and another is Letang Fils of Paris. Important American makers include Schall & Co, who marked their moulds 'S & Co' and Eppelsheimer Co, both of New York.

The value of moulds depends on the medium, shape and condition. Copper moulds are always popular on both sides of the Atlantic, for their great beauty. Whatever the material, the more elaborate a mould is, the more desirable it will be. Always check for condition, and beware of rust on tin moulds. Also, look out for any maker's marks that can help to identify them. Many moulds are unmarked, however, but can still be collectable if they are of an appealing design.

Ice cream moulds

Ice cream moulds were commonly made from pewter. Old pewter moulds should never be used today because of their lead content. Lead was banned from the late 1860s because of its toxic nature, but any mould, regardless of material, should be checked carefully for damage if it is to be used. Ice cream moulds were usually made in two or three parts. The mix, made from ice, milk and eggs, would be packed into the mould, which would be placed in an ice house until needed. Pewter is often marked, so look for marks when buying.

Pewter ice cream mould, date mark for 1868. £200–220

Shapes & materials

Copper and tin jelly mould, c1900. £140–160

Tin-lined copper mould, c1910. £30–35

Tin chocolate mould, c1920s. £35–40

Galvanized metal chocolate mould, c1930. £15–20

The one to look for

Several firms made ceramic moulds and names to look out for include Spode, Copeland, Grimwades and Shelley. Animals were always popular, and Shelley made moulds in the form of chickens and rabbits among others.

Like most potteries, Shelley marked their products with the company name. This mark, with 'Shelley' inside a shield and 'Made in England', was used from 1912 to 1925, but there were different styles and they can be used to date Shelley wares.

Ceramic moulds should be in good, clean condition. Some suffer from a little creamy discolouration, which can be acceptable, but should be reflected in the price. Also, look for cracks and chips which, depending on their severity, can devalue a piece considerably.

Shelley ceramic jelly mould, in the form of an armadillo, made in three sizes, 1912–25. £200–220

Glass jelly mould, 1940s.
£5–10

Plastic jelly mould, 1940s.
£1–5

Plastic jelly mould, 1940s.
£1–5

Swan aluminium jelly mould, c1950.
£5–10

Bakelite & plastics

Bakelite, an early form of plastic, was developed between 1907 and 1909 and takes its name from its inventor, Belgian-American Dr Leo Baekeland. This new wonder material was embraced enthusiastically by the public, and was soon used in everything from telephones and radios to chess sets and cocktail shakers.

Predominantly made in dark colours such as black, brown or green, some Bakelite was also made in red, a particularly desirable colour. Catalin, a brand name for a cast Bakelite product with a different manufacturing process, was developed in New York in 1927. The resin produced was clear and could be made into different colours or even marbled.

Many companies, including the British firms Bandalasta of Birmingham and J. Dickinson of London, marked products with their names, but generally speaking, collectors are more interested in colour and style than makers. The wares of both these firms are popular with collectors. Aside from its use for items such as radios and telephones, Bakelite was widely used for making desk accessories, and its insulating properties made it useful for saucepan handles.

Bakelite quickly fell from favour after WWII, when it was superseded by new plastics. Post-war plastic, while lacking the kudos of Bakelite, has its admirers nonetheless, and storage jars and other kitchen items from the 1950s, '60s and later can still be collectable – Tupperware is a field in itself. As most people are still unaware that post-war plastic is collectable, it can still be bought cheaply. Collectors want items in good condition, so avoid scratched or faded items. Be aware that harder forms of plastic can crack easily and plastics can become brittle and sticky with age.

JONTY'S CHOICE

Michelin's iconic 20th-century advertising figure was inspired by a pile of tyres that resembled the human form. Bibendum's first appearance was in 1898 and over the years his shape has changed to reflect the different profiles of the company's tyres.

Bakelite ashtray, with a figure of Bibendum, c1935.
£165–185

Manufacturers & shapes

Tupperware bowl and cover, 1970s.
£1–5

Nally ware container, c1970.
£5–10

Crown Merton cassette tapes stand, 1970s. £5–10

Maxram pocket corkscrew, c1950.
£5–10

The one to look for

This very collectable table cigarette lighter is called the Silent Flame. It was made in the US for Parker of London, who were known for a variety of smoking accessories, including a range of classic pipes. At first sight it is difficult to identify it as anything other than an ornament, and this is part of its appeal. A flame is produced when a removable wand holding a wick in its black Bakelite base touches the metal figure, which is charged from two batteries in the base.

With its elegant figure, this lighter is the very epitome of Art Deco style. Lighters can form an attractive collection as they are often quite imaginative in design. Bakelite often becomes brittle with age, so beware of this when buying.

Chrome and Bakelite Silent Flame table lighter by Parker of London, 1930s. **£160–180**

Bakelite egg stand, 1930s.
£10–15

Tupperware lemon squeezer, 1970s.
£1–5

Bakelite pipe stand, 1930s.
£10–15

Plastigon Bakelite seed sower, c1950.
£15–20

Tools

Collecting tools is a relatively new field, but interest is growing. Craftsmen used to make their own tools as part of their apprenticeship and, while tools by anonymous makers are collectable, most collectors focus on known names as these are easier to date and to research. Name, quality, date and a sense of 'artistry' are important to collectors of tools.

Tools made before c1830 are generally more valuable, although rarity and quality are also important. The most sought after are those that come in boxes with fitted compartments and have all available accessories intact.

Lathes tend to attract the highest prices, especially if they are well equipped. Examples by John Jacob Holtzapffel are highly prized, as are those of his contemporary, William Jones Evans.

Planes, braces, saws and rules make up the bulk of the tool market. Wooden braces, especially of rosewood or box, are usually more desirable than metal ones, although there are exceptions.

The most popular tools among American collectors are those by Stanley. This firm has produced millions of tools from planes to saws and from rules to screwdrivers.

In Britain, Stanley is a well-known name, and 'Stanley knife' is used as a generic term for the utility knife or box cutter. More popular with serious collectors are the products of T. Norris & Son. Established in 1860 in London, this firm moved to New Malden, Surrey, where it continued to trade until 1944.

Planes explained

Plough planes are used for grooving and rebating, beading and tonguing.
Beech plough plane by John Moseley, London, c1860. £35–40

Smoothing planes are for general work. Collectors prefer more specialist tools.
Iron adjustable smoothing plane by T. Norris & Son, London, No. 51, c1920s. £35–40

Other tools

Mini drill, c1900. £45–50

Cast-iron bevel gear drill, with bits, c1910. £45–50

Steel wire gauge, by L. Partridge, early 20thC. £25–30

Set of six hacksaw blades, 1950s. £1–5

The one to look for

The Stanley No. 55 is a unique design and, because of its flexibility, has been described as the Swiss Army Knife of hand planes – it has a single body and scores of interchangeable blades. The excellence of its design ensured that it had a long production run, from 1899 until 1962. This example is complete with its original box and full set of cutters, which makes it very desirable.

Stanley hand plane,
No 55, 1920s.
£450–500

Chisel planes have no front housing, so the blade works the wood like a chisel.
Chisel plane by Stanley, No. 97, c1920.
£325–375

Chariot planes such as this were used for fine finishing work.
Rosewood chariot plane, stuffed with brass
bow bridge, c 1880. £180–200

Cast-iron and wood
brick hammer,
1930s. £15–20

Boxwood measure
with brass joint,
c1920. £15–20

Panel saw by
Disston, c1860.
£20–25

Wood-handled
spanner, early 20thC.
£10–15

Telephones

Alexander Graham Bell patented the telephone in 1876. The first models were bulky, mostly wall-mounted and made from wood; the early 'candlestick' design had a separate mouthpiece for greater clarity.

Bakelite phones with a composite handset appeared in the 1920s. These so-called 'pyramid phones' are design classics and were rented out to customers in Britain by the General Post Office. Initially only black was available, but by the 1950s and '60s there were eight colours to choose from. Strangely, the rarest today is black. It was not possible to buy telephones in Britain until 1982 and consumer choice was limited. Telephones supplied by the GPO carried a stamp or sticker on the base, indicating the type of telephone and ending in the year and month of installation. They were supposed to be collected and destroyed on the termination of a contract, so fewer old phones are now available to collectors.

Advancing technology made new designs possible. The Ericsson Ericofon of 1954 was a radical step forward, a one-piece design with a dial in the base. In Britain, the lightweight Trimphone was designed in 1964 and had a distinctive electronic warble instead of a bell. Although stylish and sleek, the Trimphone was not a great commercial success; as relatively few were made they are collectable today.

Wall-mounted telephones

Here are two very different telephones. The one on the left is a Swedish wooden wall-mounted phone, c1905, which was sold in the UK by the National Telephone Company and became known as the Post Office '59' model. On the right is the designer plastic wall-mounted Kirk Plusphone by Alcatel, dating from the 1990s. Each is typical of its era.

Alcatel Kirk Plusphone, 1990s. £35–40

National Telephone Co telephone, c1905. £35–40

Landline telephones

Bakelite 200 series telephone with bell stand, 1940–50. £300–350

Ericsson Ericofon plastic telephone, 1950s. £100–120

GPO 700 series plastic telephone, 1935–40. £35–40

Plastic Trimphone telephone, 1970s. £65–75

The one to look for

Mobile telephones emerged in the 1980s, and it is still early days as far as a collecting market is concerned. This means that it is possible to find genuine bargains. Early mobiles are often referred to as 'bricks', because of their size, shape and weight.

Motorola 8000X Dyna TAC mobile telephone, 1983, boxed. £270–300

This American model of the Motorola 8000x Dyna TAC series was the first to receive Federal Communications Commission approval in the US in 1983. Dyna TAC stood for Dynamic Adaptive Total Area Coverage.

The earliest models are generally the most collectable. For maximum value they should have their original boxes and any accessories. If they have never been used, so much the better.

Novelty telephones

Even relatively recent phones can be collectable; novelty phones are often of interest to collectors if they are attractive and unusual. All kinds of character and fun phones are now available, and as soon as they cease production, they become desirable and often increase in value.

Left: ACL plastic Snoopy telephone, c1990. £20–25
Centre: Plastic Winnie-the-Pooh telephone, c1970. £175–190
Right: Plastic Love Bus telephone, c2000. £20–25

Mobile telephones

Motorola 4500X transportable telephone, c1985. £135–150

Sony CM-HH333 mobile telephone, c1994. £45–50

Motorola MR501 Star TAC mobile telephone, boxed, c1996. £45–50

Nokia 2140 mobile telephone, c1996. £25–30

Cameras

The first photographic processes were developed in the 1830s and during the late 19th century photography became a craze. Folding mahogany and brass cameras of the 19th century are very collectable.

Cameras from the 20th century are collectable, although folding models are worth little unless they are unusual. Early 20th-century roll cameras lack aesthetic appeal, but can still fetch reasonable prices if in good condition.

The period from 1920 to the 1940s saw great technological innovation. Early models by Leica, Zeiss, Contax and Rollei, as well as Nikon and Canon are collectable, and interest in 35mm cameras by makers such as Canon and Nikon rose considerably in the 1990s, but prices have fallen in the wake of the digital revolution, so now is a good time to buy.

If buying for display, condition is important, so check for corrosion or damage to the case. However, many old cameras are still usable and enthusiasts like to use them.

TRADE SECRETS

- *Cameras with several high-quality lenses are more desirable.*
- *Repairs are expensive, so before you buy, make sure the camera works.*
- *Watch out for fungus – moisture trapped inside a camera makes an ideal breeding ground.*

Leica cameras

Leica IIIf camera, No.66752, with extra lens, mid-20thC. £120–150

Leica II No. 320126, with Leitz Elmar f3.5.5cm lens, c1940. £145–175

Introduced in 1932, the Leica II was the first Leica to have a built-in range-finder. The Leica IIIf, launched in 1950, incorporated a number of post-war refinements, including flash synchronization.

Other models

Kodak No. 4 cartridge camera, 1897–1907. £115–125

Zeiss Ikon Ideal folding plate camera, c1927. £115–135

Kamera Werkstätten Pilot reflex camera, 1930s. £135–150

Zeiss Ikon Nettar camera, c1949. £20–25

The one to look for

The firm of Voigtländer was originally founded as an optical company by Johann Christoph Voigtländer in Vienna in 1756, and is the oldest existing camera firm.

The Voigtländer Prominent is admired for the quality of its optics and solidity of construction – but not for its design. Ergonomically it was a disaster, being large, heavy and awkward to use.

Voigtländer Prominent camera, with interchangeable Ultron lens and 35mm range finder, c1953. £200–250

Sub-miniature cameras

Sub-miniatures are the smallest cameras. The Russian Narciss 16mm SLR (single lens reflex) camera shown here was the first sub-miniature SLR. Serious photographers dislike sub-miniatures because it is difficult for them to produce decent-sized photographs, but they have a cult following, partly because of their 'Cold War' image.

Narciss 16mm sub-miniature SLR camera, with Vega-M-1 lens, c1960. £100–120

Wrayflex II Unite camera, with Wray lens, 1950s. £500–550

Canon Dial 35 camera, 1960s. £55–60

Kodak Extra 22 camera, with box, late 1970s. £15–20

Nikon FE2 camera, No. 223582, 1983–89. £120–145

Radios

Radio broadcasting for entertainment purposes began in the 1920s and while crystal sets were the cheapest option, the 'wireless' soon became a part of the furniture in almost every home. In fact, many sets were made to look like traditional furniture, while others were more modern in design.

To the modern collector, the style of the case is generally more important than the workings and, sometimes, the maker. Relatively few examples from the 1920s survive and sets from the 1930s and '40s are very collectable, especially those designs influenced by the Art Deco style.

The material can also make a difference to price. In its day, Bakelite was cheap to manufacture and was used to make less expensive sets. Some radios were produced in both Bakelite and a more luxurious plywood version. Today, Bakelite examples are more valuable because it is a material that is very much 'of its time'.

By the 1950s, radios were being produced in vast numbers by makers including Bush, KB, Pye, Panasonic and many more. The advent of the transistor made radios portable and they began to colonise the whole house, including bathrooms and kitchens. They also appealed to the new and affluent teenage market.

In the 1960s and '70s, small pocket radios were made in plastic by firms such as Zenith, Emerson, Sony, Regency and many more. As so many were simply thrown away, surviving examples that are in good condition are collectable. Again, it is largely style that determines desirability. Pocket transistor radios of this era were not handled with care, probably because they were cheap and portable. However, they were simple and robust and therefore it is by no means unusual to find them in good working order.

JONTY'S CHOICE

Collectors regard this as a design classic. Gone were the heavy cabinet designs of the 1920s and '30s in favour of new rounded lines and sleekness of style. The case is made from Catalin (a form of Bakelite), which allowed for new, bright colours. This radio is often referred to as the Bullet or Streamliner, although neither name was used by the company.

FADA 1000 Bullet radio, in a Catalin case, c1945.
£350–450

Other models

Bush DAC90A radio in a Bakelite case, 1940s–50s.
£150–175

Delco radio in a Bakelite case, 1947.
£300–350

PYE P75 radio in a walnut case, 1951.
£35–40

Joseph Lucas gilt-metal and enamel radio/table lamp, 1950s. **£45–55**

The one to look for

Made by the firm of E. K. Cole, better known as Ekco, this radio is an acknowledged design classic and dates from 1935. Its round shape, created by architect Wells Coates, makes it unmistakable and it was one of a series of similar designs in the AD range – the first was the AD65, introduced in 1934.

Ekco AD36 radio in a Bakelite and chrome case, 1935.
£700–800

The AD76 was available in two finishes, a basic walnut and a black and chrome finish, as seen here. Both versions were made from Bakelite. The black and chrome examples were more expensive than the walnut and remain more valuable to this day.

Decca TPW 70 radio in a plastic case, c1961.
£40–45

Vesta radio in a Bakelite case, c1947.
£300–350

Hacker Herald radio, c1969.
£45–50

ITT RX75 Professional radio, c1979.
£10–15

Computers & technology

Computers were once huge beasts that filled entire rooms, but the microchip revolution of the 1970s and '80s revolutionized the way we used them and they became an important part of our leisure time. When the first Space Invaders machines were introduced, people queued up in arcades to play them, but games soon came into our homes.

The demand for computers and games consoles was such that large numbers were made, but the pace of technological change was such that they quickly became obsolete. Only dedicated enthusiasts held onto them. There are still old machines around, but very few are in perfect condition.

In the early 1970s, electronic pocket calculators began to appear and these now have a following among collectors. The earliest models and those that became acknowledged classics are sought after. Names to look for include Sinclair, Rockwell, Casio, Texas Instruments and Hewlett-Packard.

In the 1990s, computers became pocket-sized with the advent of the Personal Digital Assistant (PDA). Apple's Message Pad, known as the Newton, after its operating system, was launched in 1993. Way ahead of its time, it became notorious for its bug-ridden software. It was discontinued in 1998, but was so popular that many are still used today. They have a real cult following and there is a thriving market for used Newtons on eBay.

A look at Sinclair ZX home computers

Sinclair ZX81, 1980. £45–50 *Sinclair ZX80, 1980. £350–400*

The ZX 80, launched in 1980 by Sinclair Research of Cambridge, England, was the first computer in the UK to sell for under £100 and was sold in kit form or ready made. It was superseded a year later by the now much less valuable ZX81 which was produced for two years, before being replaced by the ZX Spectrum. The ZX80 was a breakthrough machine, but only 70,000 were produced. That, its crude design and tendency to overheat means that few have survived, which is why they now sell for much higher prices than the ZX81.

Other models

Casio FX 2000 calculator, 1977. £25–30

Namco Pac-Land hand-held game, with box, 1984. £10–15

Super Nintendo Entertainment System, 1989. £25–35

Comodore 64 Games System, 1990. £200–220

The one to look for

The Atari 2600 was launched in 1977; it popularized the use of microprocessor-based hardware with cartridges for the game code, rather than having dedicated hardware with games built-in. It simply plugged into the back of a television set to bring the arcade experience into the home. More than 40 million were made, but it is hard to find them in good condition.

Atari 2600 games console, 1977.
£70–80

There is a thriving collectors' market in Atari 2600 consoles. To achieve maximum value it should have its original box and packaging, as well as instructions. They originally came with one or two cartridges, but hundreds of games were released. There is also a strong market for the cartridges and, in fact, new games are still being produced by enthusiasts.

Nintendo Game Boy

The Game Boy, with its monochrome LCD screen and cartridge games was the first successful hand-held console. It was released by Nintendo in 1989 and was bought in vast numbers; together with its colour version over 118 million have been sold worldwide. Today they are not expensive to buy, but remain popular with collectors because they were the forerunner of modern hand-held consoles. The Game Boy line remained the leading hand-held gaming system until the introduction of the Nintendo DS in 2004.

Nintendo Game Boy, 1989. £10–15

Sega Game Gear portable video game, 1992.
£35–40

Bandai Tamagotchi virtual pet, 1996.
£10–15

Apple Message Pad, 1993–98.
£135–150

US Robotics Palm Pilot, 1996.
£25–30

Clocks

The subject of clocks is a vast one and covers an enormous range of styles, technology and makers. The very first examples, known as turret clocks, were built for church towers and clocks were not very accurate until the invention of the pendulum in the 17th century. It wasn't until the 19th century that clocks could be found in most homes, and then they were usually prized possessions.

There was a boom in clock making from around 1850 until the 1930s and a huge variety of styles emerged to suit all tastes and pockets. Cheap, mass-produced movements made clocks affordable to everyone, but quality varied considerably. As a general rule, the more complicated a clock is the better, and a clock that chimes and perhaps has a moonphase as well will be more desirable than one that merely tells the time.

Wooden mantel clocks of the 1930s are popular entry level items for many collectors. Fondly remembered from grandparents' mantelpieces, they are inexpensive and readily available. These clocks were made in large numbers, particularly by British and German makers.

The well-known British makers Smiths produced their first synchronous electric clock movements in the early 1930s,

known as the 'Smiths Sectric' clocks ('sectric' stood for 'synchronous electric'). In common with many makers, they produced a number of clocks in Bakelite, which is popular with collectors as a typical material of the early half of the 20th century. Particularly desirable names to look out for in electric clocks include the Eureka Clock Co, Synchronome Co and Ever-Ready.

Dedicated horologists will collect clocks for their movements and the quality of the movement is usually the most important factor in determining value. However, during the 20th century, form became more important than function and, as long as clocks were reasonably accurate, most customers would be satisfied. Clocks became canvases for the imaginative skills of the designer. Today, even relatively recent clocks appeal to collectors if there is something special about the design.

Design classics include the Jefferson Golden Hour clock, a so-called 'mystery clock' in the Art Deco style, which continued in production until the firm's clock division closed down in August 1991. These American clocks, made by the Jefferson Manufacuring Co, are easy to date as there is usually a date stamp inside the base.

Clock styles

Art Nouveau mahogany clock by W. A. Perry & Co. £200–235

Art Deco clock with quarter-cut walnut, 1920–30. £350–400

Goldsmiths & Silver-smiths Co marble and slate clock, c1930. £170–200

Smiths Bakelite clock, 1930s. £25–30

What to look for

Marble mantel clocks were very popular in the 1920s and 1930s and are popular with collectors today. This example, in variegated marble, is elegant and attractive. It has great 'eye appeal' and is typical of the Art Deco style.

A French marble mantel clock with silvered dial, surmounted by bronze and ivorene female figure, c1930.
£350–400

The elegant lady on top of the clock is typically Art Deco and is in the style of Demêtre Chiparus, a Romanian-born sculptor who lived in Paris. Chiparus became famous for using a combination of bronze and ivory in his creations and for influences that included Ancient Egypt and the dancers of the Russian Ballet.

Oak and chrome mantel clock, 1930s.
£40–45

Seth Thomas plastic alarm clock, 1960s.
£45–50

Marksman plastic alarm clock, 1960–70.
£40–45

Metamac chrome Starburst wall clock, 1970s.
£100–120

Toys & Dolls

During the latter part of the 19th century toys became more readily available to the expanding middle classes, largely on account of the technical achievements of the industrial revolution. Competition between toy manufacturers meant that consumers benefited from wider choices and keener prices. In the 20th century, developments such as hollow-cast processing, die-casting and the use of plastics led to further changes in manufacturing methods.

When I was young I was lucky to have a grandmother who ran her own toyshop, and nostalgia draws me back to this comforting area of collecting. I suspect this is the case for other collectors, too.

Of all collectables, it is arguably toys that have the greatest nostalgic appeal. Collectors who buy toys that were popular when they were young are buying a reminder of childhood days. Toys that are much older seem to evoke a simpler time when playthings were valued and treasured. Collecting toys is a pastime that has gained in respectability in the last 20 or 30 years, moving in to the mainstream of the collecting world.

Real, repro, or fake?

In the world of toy collecting, there are few out-and-out fakes, but a bigger problem is that of passing off a new, reproduction item as an original. Some originals have soared in price, so reproductions

Matchbox Regular Wheels London Trolleybus, No. 56a, with box, 1958–65. £60–70

Steiff mohair rabbit, 1950s. £100–120

provide the look without the price. There is nothing wrong with this and such toys are usually clearly marked by the makers and are often made in different sizes as well. That does not stop the unscrupulous from distressing or altering recently-made toys to make them seem much older.

Your best defence against this is knowledge. If you are concentrating on a specific area, make sure you are familiar with your chosen toy. Read as much as possible on your subject, and join a collectors' club where you can exchange notes with like-minded people. In particular, learn about every possible

known variant of a given toy. If you want to buy sensibly and often, it is important to visit good specialist toy fairs, dealers and auctions whenever possible to get a feel for the originals. Look at and handle as many examples as you can. There is no substitute for first-hand knowledge of the real thing; such hands-on experience is valuable and can save a lot of money.

Mint and boxed

Toys that are in mint condition and in their original boxes will always be more highly prized. Not only does the box often give valuable information about the toy and its maker, but the toy itself is more likely to be in good condition, with any accessories often still intact.

The fact that most children discarded the boxes (and still do) means that boxed examples of most toys are harder to come by. Occasionally there are discoveries of old toys stored in their boxes which, for one reason or another, never reached the retailer or remained in the shop's stockroom.

*Parker Brothers Q*bert board game, 1983. £15–20*

Toys as investments

During the 1980s and '90s extensive publicity about the value of old toys and record auction prices changed the nature of the market. It ensured that toys were taken seriously – the sale of a Steiff teddy bear for £110,000 in 1994, for example, showed that there was certainly serious money to be made.

Kenner Robocop *Birdman Barnes poseable figure, 1988.*
£5–10

Interest became so strong that people began buying toys for investment purposes, building up a portfolio of collectable examples. Today, there is a strong and continuing demand for toys generally, and if you want to buy for investment there are even specialists who will advise you. However, no form of investment can be assumed to be a one-way bet, and it is impossible to predict the future.

Some toys from as little as 30 or 40 years ago have so far proved staggeringly good value as investments, even if they were not bought for that reason. Some

toys that sold for loose change back in the 1960s and '70s now sell for three- and even four-figure sums. The best reason for buying toys remains pleasure, and any increase in value should be regarded purely as a bonus.

The future

The toy collecting market is constantly replenished as new toys are made and those who remember playing with them grow up and become nostalgic. For this reason, it is tempting to buy toys now with an eye to the future, and there are already people doing precisely this. It is also important to distinguish between toys that are made to be played with, and those made with collectors in mind. Modern-day toys aimed at the collector are likely to be kept in good condition, and it is probable that there will be many of them around 20 years from now. It is the toys that will be bought for young children, who will tear off the packaging and subject them to heavy use, that will be harder to come by in fine condition in the future.

Mattel Skipper doll, with box, 1963.
£100–120

Steiff

Steiff is, without a doubt, the best-known name in the world of teddy bears. Its products are also among the most desirable.

The firm was founded in 1880 by German seamstress Marguerete Steiff, although her first product was not a bear, but a pincushion in the form of an elephant.

The first bear was designed by Steiff's nephew, Richard, who took it to the Leipzig Toy Fair in 1903. Buyers seemed unimpressed, but shortly before the fair closed, an American buyer bought the entire stock of 100 and placed an order for another 3,000. At the St Louis World's Fair in the US the following year, Steiff sold no fewer than 12,000 bears.

Steiff continues to make bears for the adult collectors' market. The appeal of the bears, and the high prices they command, lies in their making. The firm established rigorous standards for quality and used modern marketing skills to promote the toys.

Steiff bears set the standards in the collecting world and, not surprisingly, it is a Steiff that holds the world auction record for a bear – a 1904 example that sold for £110,000 in 1994. While this was an exceptional price, Steiff bears do sell at the upper end of the market and early bears are expensive, so most collectors start with post-WW II bears, which are more affordable.

How to spot fakes

Many high-quality traditional-style bears have appeared on the market in recent years made by several firms, including Steiff. These reproductions are perfectly legitimate. However, some have been passed off as originals by the unscrupulous, who distress the fur using a wire brush. The resulting wear is too even to be natural wear through play. The felt pads on the feet can also be a giveaway, as they look too new. There have even been cases of mohair bears from the 1950s having their kapok stuffing replaced with wood wool to make them seem more authentic. Such fakes will even have the right 'old bear smell'.

Steiff toys

Steiff bear, with mystery button in ear, 1906–08.
£2,000–2,400

Teddy bear with button in ear, c1907.
£1,100–1,300

Jocko chimp, with button, 1910–15.
£250–300

Molly dog, 1925–35.
£150–180

The one to look for

Early Steiff bears, from around 1905–1910 are the most sought after of all. They look more like actual bears, or bear cubs, than later teddies. The earliest bears have a seam running across the top of the head, from one ear to the other.

Characteristics of an older Steiff bear include a humped back, a pronounced muzzle and long limbs, with curved, spoon-shaped paws to the arms and large feet.

Steiff bear with shoe-button eyes, c1908. £300–350

Steiff buttons

Steiff bears were not only of the finest quality, using the best materials, but they were also distinctive, and readily recognized by a metal button bearing the firm's name, which was sewn into the bear's ear. It is not unusual for these buttons to become detached over years of wear, leaving a small hole. Some bears had not only a button in the ear, but also a tag. One or both of these may be missing, which could hinder the instant identification of a Steiff bear.

Tom cat, with button, ear tag and chest tag, 1959–67. £100–110

Teddy bear, 2000. £175–200

Scottish bear, limited edition, 2000. £180–200

Barle bear, 1904 commemoration replica, 2004 only. £175–200

Teddy bears

While Steiff remains the most celebrated maker of teddy bears (see pages 136 to 137), similar toys were made by many other companies in a bid to cater for the bear craze that swept the world in the early 20th century. Many of these bears are very collectable today and fetch high prices. However, good-quality replicas of early bears also exist, so some caution is necessary: a bear may have been distressed and 'aged' artificially. Look for signs of wear that you would expect to find on a toy of any age – thin or worn patches, minor repairs, missing buttons or labels – and smell it: old bears and soft toys in general have a distinctive smell that is impossible to reproduce.

Chad Valley The Birmingham firm of Chad Valley made many collectable bears, among them this mohair bear with a 'growler'. It dates from the 1940s–50s. Chad Valley bears can be recognized by their large ears and bulbous noses, often said to resemble a piece of coal. The firm was granted a Royal Warrant in 1938 and a white label attached to the feet read 'By appointment toy makers to HM The Queen'. After the Coronation of Elizabeth II in 1953, the wording was changed to read 'Queen Mother'.

Mohair growler teddy bear, 1940s–50s. £300–350

Farnell This bear dates from the 1920s; jointed and stuffed with a wood wool filling, it was made by London company J. K. Farnell. Farnell is credited with making the first English teddy bear in 1906 and early Farnell bears share many characteristics with German bears, including pointed muzzles, long limbs and humps on their backs. From 1926 until 1945, an embroidered blue and white label reading 'Farnell's Alpha Toys' was fixed to the foot.

Plush teddy bear, c1920. £550–650

Chiltern The firm of Chiltern, established in Buckinghamshire in 1915, made some appealing bears, including this 1950s bellows musical teddy bear. It contains a 'growler' which, in this case, plays a tune when hugged. Like most Chiltern bears, this one has large, brown glass eyes. Chiltern noses are distinctive, with long, upwards stitching at either end. Plastic, moulded noses were used from the very end of the 1950s, but didn't feature widely until the 1960s.

Bellows musical teddy bear, 1950s. £250–300

Schuco This is a Yes/No bear, so-called because its nods and shakes its head. The bear has a small tail, and moving this operates the mechanism. Schuco was the trade name of Schreyer & Co, who made the first yes/no bears in 1921. This one dates from the 1950s. After WWII, they were reintroduced as the 'Tricky yes/no bear' and have distinctive downturned paws; they were available in seven sizes and a range different coloured mohair.

Yes/No teddy bear, 1950s. £200–220

Tara Toys In 1938, the Irish Government established a new toy industry in order to create jobs. It included a factory in Mayo, known as the Elly Bay Co, for teddies and soft toys. It traded under the name of Erris Toys until 1953, when it changed its name to Tara Toys. They were well made with distinctive stitching on the nose. Up until 1949, bears bore a 'Made in Eire' label, but from 1950 onwards, the label read 'Made in the Republic of Ireland'.

Plush teddy bear, c1950. £100–120

Hermann Zotty The 'Zotty' bear was a design produced by both Steiff and Hermann, a German firm that was founded in 1907 and made this bear. The first Zotty bears were produced in 1951 and have an innovative, open-mouthed design. They have a cheerful, optimistic expression, reflecting the post-war mood. They also have long hair, as economy was no longer paramount and more expensive materials had become available. The name Zotty is derived from the German 'zottig', meaning 'shaggy'.

Bear with glass eyes, c1950. £130–150

Soft toys

Soft toys for children have been made for many centuries. Originally, they were crafted by hand in the home from scrap material, and it wasn't until the 19th century that a soft toy industry developed.

Early toys were usually made from mohair and stuffed with excelsior, which is made from wood shavings. Such toys are easy to recognize, because they make a crackly sound when squeezed. After WWII, synthetic fabrics were more widely used.

Post-war shortages meant that the natural materials favoured for a toy's fur were hard to come by. Toys often came fully clothed, therefore, and used cheaper, more readily available materials for fur.

The most famous maker of soft toys is Steiff (see pages 136–137), although Farnell, Dean's, Chad Valley, Knickerbocker, Chiltern Toys and Schreyer & Co are all names worth looking out for. Don't dismiss unmarked toys out of hand if they are attractive and well made, however. Toys of an unusual design, even if unmarked, can still be collectable. Good condition is important; look for moth damage, fading and poor-quality restoration – all will reduce value. Soft toys do not attract the attention of teddy bears, so there are genuine finds to be made and, with interest growing among collectors priced out of the teddy bear market, the are opportunities for those with an eye.

Labels

From 1926 to 1945, Farnell bears had a blue and white 'Farnell's Alpha Toys' label attached to the foot. It was replaced by a satin label with 'Alpha' inside a shield.

A Merrythought label; embroidered labels were used pre-war, along with celluloid buttons for identification. After WWII, printed labels were used.

Other soft toys

Chad Valley rabbit, with glass eyes, c1920.
£170–200

Deans Rag Book Co Mickey Mouse, c1930.
£175–200

Deans Rag Book Co Pluto the Dog, c1930.
£350–400

The one to look for

In the interwar years, soft toys based on characters from stories, comic strips or films became very popular, and makers vied with each other to secure licences to produce them. Bonzo was a bull terrier pup who featured in a cartoon in the now defunct British newspaper the *Daily Sketch*. He became a phenomenon and many related collectables were made.

This rendition of Bonzo the bull terrier was made with printed detail and jointed limbs by the British firm Dean's Rag Book Co.

Dean's toys are easily identified as they were printed with the company name, usually around the neck or under the foot, on swing tags or printed labels.

Dean's Bonzo with printed detail and jointed limbs, 1920s.
£350–400

Farnell Mumbie elephant, 1930s.
£250–280

Merrythought pyjama case, 1930s.
£90–100

Merrythought Dougal plush toy, c1966.
£100–120

Bisque dolls

Doll manufacturers started to use bisque in the 1830s. Bisque is a fired, but unglazed, ceramic that made a useful, if relatively fragile, material for doll manufacture and was typically used to make a doll's head and hands, while her body and limbs would be made from tougher materials such as cloth or composition.

The big advantage of bisque was economy, since dolls cost less to produce than those made from wax, the other dominant material at the time. The big disadvantage was that bisque was easily broken; today dolls are often found with cracks, chips or missing fingers.

Germany led the bisque doll market, with firms such as Armand Marseille, Simon & Halbig, Kämmer & Reinhardt and Kestner among the best-known names. The dolls were well made and good value for money; they were also widely exported. French makers such as Bru and Jumeau began to challenge the Germans from the 1860s onwards, producing high-quality bisque fashion dolls and *bébé* dolls. The latter were dolls made as idealized versions of young girls, with chubby limbs and rounded stomachs. Early examples, which usually featured closed mouths and fixed wrists, are especially popular among collectors. In 1899, French makers formed the Société Française de Fabrication de Bébés et Jouets (SFBJ) in an attempt to compete together against German imports. French dolls are often marked with these letters.

When buying bisque dolls, condition is important, as is the quality of moulding and painting. Looks are also significant, and sheer visual appeal should be considered. Watch for hairline cracks and signs of restoration. Old bisque will usually feel rougher than its more recent equivalent. Original clothes and hair are always desirable and if the clothes are not original, they should at least be appropriate to the age and style of the doll.

Collectors in this field are demanding and are increasingly looking for exceptional examples. Many will buy the best (and most expensive) they can find, leaving aside lesser dolls. This does mean that there are bargains to be had at the lower end of the market.

Other dolls

François Gaultier bisque-headed doll, c1860.
£1,500–1,800

Jumeau bisque-headed doll, 1886–89.
£3,500–4,000

Jumeau bisque-headed doll, 1890.
£250–300

Kestner doll, No. 171, c1900.
£550–600

The one to look for

Kämmer & Reinhardt was one of the top German doll manufacturing firms founded in 1886 by model maker Ernst Kämmer and entrepreneur Franz Reinhardt. The doll has a mohair wig and sleeping glass eyes that open when standing and close when lying down.

An appealing, well-painted face is essential. It should have its original paint and the 'blush' should be even. This is a good example, but watch out for poorly-executed repainting or 'touching up' around the eyelashes and lips. Sometimes, sleeping eyes have been reset so that they are fixed. This can be acceptable, but will be reflected in the price.

Leading makers liked to mark their products, usually on the back of the head. This doll is clearly marked with the initials 'KR' and the trademark six-pointed star symbol. Dolls were also marked with a mould number; rarer numbers command the highest prices.

Kämmer & Reinhardt bisque-headed doll, with composition jointed body, c1890. £500–550

Bahr & Proschild doll, c1892. £550–600

Jumeau bisque-headed doll, 1890s. £1,400–1,600

Kestner toddler doll No. 260, c1910. £600–650

Kämmer & Reinhardt soldier doll, c1920. £1,000–1,200

Fabric & composition dolls

Bisque and china dolls were relatively expensive, but fabric and composition dolls were cheaper alternatives, and were made in both the United States and Europe. Composition is made from paper or wood pulp, reinforced with other ingredients that might include rags, bones and eggshells. Wood and plastic were often used in the mix for American dolls. European dolls tended to follow the style of their bisque and china counterparts and sometimes even used the same moulds.

German firms dominated the market and exported their dolls in large numbers all around the world. It is therefore possible to find German examples in many countries today. The finest of all German dolls were made by the early 20th-century maker Marion Kaulitz. She made made top-quality dolls modelled on real children and with hand-painted faces. These dolls were only made for a short time and are very hard to find today. Consequently they are of high value.

While German firms were market leaders, American composition dolls are especially collectable and are often more valuable than their German counterparts. Collectable American makers include Ideal and Effanbee (which stood for Fleischaker & Baum) whose dolls are highly regarded. British firms to look out for are Pedigree, who also are also known for plastic dolls (see pages 146–147), and Palitoy. Affordable fabric and composition dolls can still be found quite easily, sometimes with their original clothing which is always more desirable. Some examples also incorporate musical movements into the bodies and this adds interest and charm.

The Italian firm of Lenci is very popular with collectors. Dolls produced by Lenci were sophisticated and primarily intended for adults. The golden age of Lenci was 1920–40, when typical characteristics included an expressive pressed felt face and a somewhat sullen expression.

It is quite difficult to find composition dolls in good condition. This is mainly because they were hard to clean, as they were easily damaged by water. They were also vulnerable to flaking and crazing.

Other dolls

Cameo Doll Co Kewpie composition doll, 1925.
£130–150

Cameo Doll Co Skootles composition doll, 1925.
£150–170

Arranbee Nancy composition doll, 1930s.
£85–95

E. I. Horsman Rosebud composition doll, 1930s.
£115–130

The one to look for

The American firm of Effanbee became known for its portrait dolls and this is one of a series of six 'American Children' dolls for a 1936 toy show. They were designed by Dewees Cochran, arguably the greatest doll artist of the 20th century. Her creations resembled children and matched the proportions of their young owners.

This doll has separated fingers, an interesting feature that means it could wear gloves. A few incorporated a magnet, enabling them to hold kitchen utensils.

This doll bears the 'Effanbee American Children' mark, and 'Effanbee/Anne-Shirley'. Later dolls were marked just 'Effanbee'. The dolls were made in two sizes, 17in (43cm) and 20in (51cm), and came dressed in the popular fashions of the time.

The doll has painted eyes and, as an added touch of realism, the wig is manufactured from real human hair, rather than mohair.

Effanbee Shirley Anne composition doll, 1936. £450–500

Shirley Temple paper cut-out doll

Paper cut-out dolls were the simplest and cheapest of dolls and came complete with a cut-out paper wardrobe. In the 1930s, child film star Shirley Temple became a world-wide phenomenon. She still has many fans today and related merchandise of this era is very collectable. Owing to the nature of the material, survivors are comparatively rare.

Shirley Temple cut-out doll and clothes, 1938. £40–45

Norah Wellings Mountie cloth doll, 1930s. £70–80

Pedigree composition doll, 1930–40. £70–80

Madame Alexander composition doll, 1937. £135–150

Cabbage Patch cloth and vinyl doll, 1978–82. £20–25

Plastic dolls

Plastic was regarded as something of a wonder material, and had many advantages for doll makers. It was easier to clean than composition, which also suffered problems of crazing and flaking.

Celluloid, the first entirely synthetic plastic, was used for dolls in Germany from 1873, and subsequently in France and the US. However, it was flammable and had a tendency to crack and fade. Such dolls have a glossy sheen. Well-known firms include Kestner, who made googly-eyed dolls.

Hard plastic began to replace celluloid in the 1940s and 1950s, initially in the United States, but production was relatively short-lived. By the mid-1950s, vinyl had largely superseded it, being softer and more durable, if a little prone to fading. Vinyl dolls had the advantage of rooted hair, rather than wigs or moulded hair.

Collectable plastic dolls include 'Ginny', launched in 1951 by the American company Vogue, and products of America's Alexander Doll Company, whose range included many walking and talking dolls wearing the latest fashions. Popular British firms to look out

for include Pedigree, who also made walking and talking dolls.

Original boxes always add value, as do original hair and clothes, and condition is important. Dolls can suffer from hard plastic disease, which disfigures them. Symptoms include dry, brittle looking hands with a grey tinge and a vinegar odour.

Buy or Sell?

The Amanda Jane Doll Co was founded in 1952 and made high-quality dolls' clothes and shoes. In the late 1950s, it produced its first doll, known as 'Jinx'. This Amanda Jane 'Party Dress' doll has her outfit and box. The Amanda Jane factory suffered a fire in 1965, in which all the patterns and most of the records were destroyed. The company started again and is still going today, based in South Wales. Amanda Jane dolls are popular with adult collectors, and still quite affordable. As an early example, this is one worth keeping.

Amanda Jane Party Dress doll, c1960.
£50–60

Other plastic dolls

British National Dolls Dolly Walker, 1950s.
£130–145

Italian Furga doll, 1950s.
£10–15

Ideal Ted vinyl doll, brother of Tammy, with box, 1964.
£90–100

Palitoy French Foreign Legion Action Man, 1970s.
£40–45

What to look for

Pedigree was the brand name of a range of dolls made by the Lines Brothers, who also made Tri-ang toys. The name suggested quality, and that is certainly true of this example. The hair, though moulded, is well detailed and her complexion and lips still have their original colour.

Lines Brothers Pedigree doll, with original dress and shoes, c1955. £140–155

These dolls were marked at the back of the neck or across the shoulders with 'Pedigree' in a moulded script and 'Made in England'. This was the marking used from 1953; before that, 'Pedigree' was marked in small capital letters.

The presence of the original outfit is clearly an advantage. Pedigree made a variety of outfits for their dolls during the late 1950s, and these could be bought separately under the Mamselle Boutique label. Knitting and sewing patterns were also available.

Pedigree walker doll, 1950s.
£100–120

Roddy hard plastic walker doll, 1950s.
£10–15

Rosebud doll, with moveable arms, 1950s.
£10–15

Zapff soft-bodied plastic doll, 1970s–80s.
£25–30

Barbie

Barbie, the teenage fashion doll, was launched by American toy firm, Mattel, in 1959. More of a phenomenon than a doll, she was created by Mattel's founders Ruth and Elliot Handler, who named her after their daughter, Barbara. Barbie made her debut at the New York Toy Fair in 1959 and it was clear from the start that the doll would be a hit. She was unusual in that most dolls at the time were of babies and toddlers, rather than teenagers – although the German Bild Lilli doll was a forerunner.

Barbie was made from vinyl; the earliest dolls were mounted on stands, and therefore had holes in their feet. Such is the value of collectable Barbies that these holes are sometimes faked to add value. Later, Barbie had a stand that fitted under the arms, so holes in the feet were no longer necessary.

Adult collectors of Barbie dolls are usually only interested in pre-1972 dolls, which are considered 'vintage' and are therefore the most collectable. These dolls are subdivided into two groups: those from the 'ponytail era' (1959–66), owing to the prevalent hairstyle at the time, and those from the 'Mod era' (1967–72).

Passionate collectors will buy anything to do with Barbie. She has always had a good wardrobe and dolls dating from the early 1960s were especially stylish, with outfits designed by Balenciaga, Dior and Givenchy. Barbie also had plenty of accessories, from dolls' houses to related toys and even records and record players – all collectable in their own right.

Buy or Sell?

The Twist n' Turn Barbie could not only turn at the waist but had bendable knees as well, making her more poseable than previous Barbies. She also had a more youthful look with sideways glancing eyes and vibrant make-up to match her new wardrobe. Fashions changed rapidly in the 1960s and Barbie had to keep up. Mattel introduced a retro-style Barbie in the 1990s, based on the 1960s originals, complete with Twist n' Turn waist. This in itself says a lot about the popularity of the originals, which are now highly desirable.
Twist n' Turn Barbie, boxed, 1960s.
£50–60

Barbie & friends

Mattel Barbie dress pattern, with sewing book, 1961.
£5–10

Mattel Bubble-Cut Barbie, with box, 1962.
£180–200

Mattel No. 6 Ponytail Barbie , with box, 1962.
£160–180

Mattel Midge, with box, 1964.
£450–500

The one to look for

Barbie dolls made from 1959 to 1962 are marked 'Barbie', while dolls from 1963 to 1965 are marked 'Midge/Barbie'. Nail varnish is important and the doll should have all fingers and toes. Look for fading or rubs to the original facial paint. Boxes are important, so watch for damage. Splits, tape, dents and ink marks are all too common.

She has the original top-knot ponytail hair wrap and lower elastic, but unfortunately also has slight green staining at the earring holes, caused by the tarnishing of the metal earring posts.

Her fingertips have the original red nail varnish.

This maker's mark is on the doll's bottom, and is referred to in America as the 'butt mark'.

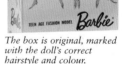

Mattel No. 5 Ponytail Barbie, with box, 1967.
£300–350

The box is original, marked with the doll's correct hairstyle and colour.

Mattel Talking Stacey, with box, 1967.
£340–380

Mattel Hawaiian Ken, with box, 1979.
£100–120

Mattel Tropical Barbie, with box, 1985.
£25–30

Mattel Baywatch Barbie, with box, 1994.
£20–30

Puppets

Puppets have a rich history, but it was not until the 19th and 20th centuries that they were used for children's entertainment. In the 1950s, characters such as Muffin the Mule and Sooty in the UK and Howdy Doody in the US became big television stars. Toy makers signed deals to produce replicas, which became big sellers.

Names to look out for include Chad Valley, Dean, Steiff, Fisher Price, Peter Puppet Playthings and Pelham, whose puppets are considered to be the finest of all.

There are three basic types of puppets: glove puppets, rod puppets and marionettes. When buying puppets, always check for signs of damage and general wear and tear. Rarity is not necessarily a guide to value in this case, as many puppets that are hard to find are not worth as much as older examples; age (the older the better) and maker are more important. Materials can be a guide to age, as older puppets were often made using army surplus material from ammunition cases and kit bags.

Pelham Puppets Minipups

Minipup horse, with card header, 1952–53. £55–65
To complement their larger marionettes, Pelham Puppets introduced a smaller and more affordable range known as Minipups in the 1950s. Designed with younger children in mind, they were operated with just two strings. These puppets were packaged not in a box but in a simple cellophane bag with a card header, printed with a message from the firm's founder, Bob Pelham. Minipups with headers are worth a lot more – as much as five times the value of a Minipup without the card.

Other puppets

Fairylite Flower Pot Man glove puppet, 1954–55. £45–50

Lesney Muffin the Mule finger puppet, with box, 1955. £80–90

Pelham Twizzle string puppet, c1960. £180–200

Pelham, Kermit the Frog string puppet, 1970s. £180–200

The one to look for

Pelham were greatly admired by puppeteers and collectors alike for their sheer quality. The firm was founded in England by Bob Pelham in 1947. Expensive in their day, they were sold at such well-known stores as Hamley's in London and F. A. O. Schwartz in New York.

This rare King puppet has a yellow box, but brown ones were initially used. The earliest boxes have the trade name 'Wonky Toys', but it was dropped after only a year.

Pelham King string puppet, 1963.
£200–250

Pelham are best known for their marionettes and all are very collectable. The company went into receivership in 1992, but replicas have been made recently. All are signed and dated to avoid confusion with older examples.

Chad Valley Parsley glove puppet from The Herbs, c1970s.
£45–50

Pelham Zebedee string puppet with original box, 1972.
£100–110

Pelham Mickey Mouse string puppet, c1980.
£65–75

Four Sapro Magic Roundabout hand puppets, 1992.
£15–20

Dinky

The firm of Dinky was founded in England by Frank Hornby, who also invented the construction toy, Meccano. He was inspired by the example of Tootsie Toys of Illinois in the US, who successfully produced die-cast toy cars. Initially, Dinky made sets known as 'Modelled Miniatures', which were intended as accessories for the Hornby model railway sets that Liverpool-based Meccano sold. Made to a 1:43 scale, this was originally known as the 22 series, and included a sports car, delivery van, tractor and an army tank; this series is highly sought after today.

In April 1934, the models became known as Dinky toys and were sold as toys in their own right. The Dinky toys were so successful that Hornby opened an additional factory in France; toys were freely imported and exported between the two countries to meet demand. The name Dinky is from a Scottish word 'dink', meaning fine, neat or small – Frank Hornby was himself of Scottish descent. The very first toys were made from lead but then a magnesium-zinc alloy known as 'mazac' was used. Early models made from this alloy were vulnerable to metal fatigue and it is hard to find them in good condition. The alloy was improved after WWII and fatigue ceased to be a problem.

Very early models were simply generic vehicles, but Dinky soon began to produce accurate replicas of popular production models. They were produced in a range of colours, although occasionally they are found in a colour that was not normally used. The reason for this is simple: Dinky sometimes ran out of the usual paint towards the end of making a batch and would use whatever was available to finish. These colour variations make the toys much more desirable.

A range of larger scale Dinky toys was launched in 1947. Called Supertoys, they came at the start of a collecting craze that lasted throughout the 1950s. During this time all Dinky toys were hugely popular in Britain, France, the Netherlands and Belgium, but much less so in the United States. Supertoys were prized possessions then and are popular with collectors today.

Dinky collecting is now a mature market and genuine finds are hard to come by as they are so well known. The most valuable examples often have their original boxes. There are companies that sell replica laser-printed boxes that are quite flimsy and come apart easily. The type of card used is a giveaway, as is the quality of the print, although the latter is improving. These do not increase the value of the toys, however.

Other models

Junkers JU90 airliner, No. 62N, with box, 1930s.
£270–300

Esso petrol tanker, 25 Series, 1930s.
£200–240

Oldsmobile 6 Sedan, 1947–50.
£90–100

Ford Sedan, No. 675, 1950s.
£200–240

The one to look for

This flat truck is an example of the Dinky Supertoys, introduced in 1947. Many of the Supertoys were vans bearing advertising transfers – the Weetabix van, made only from 1952 to 1953 is the most valuable of the range. Early issues of these toys are known as the 500 series.

Dinky Toys Guy Flat Truck, No. 512, 1950s. **£220–250**

As with all Dinky toys, the original box increases value and could in fact double it.

Golden age

Most collectors consider the period from 1958 to 1964 to be a 'golden age'. From the mid-1950s, the firm introduced new colours and models and a new range of commercial vehicles, including this Heinz van. It is not to be confused with the rarer and smaller Guy Warrior Heinz van from 1960, which combined a Guy Warrior chassis and box van from the earlier Guy Otter lorry; only about 1,000 were made.
Big Bedford van, No. 923, 1955–58.
£300–350

Maserati racing car, No. 231, with box, 1950s.
£50–60

Ford Anglia, No. 155, with box, early 1960s.
£50–55

AA patrol service Mini van, No. 274 with box, 1964–73.
£130–150

Ford Capri, No. 2162, in unopened packaging, 1973–76.
£90–100

Corgi

The Corgi factory opened in Swansea, South Wales, in 1948 and was built by Mettoy. Products were at the high end of the market and boasted a variety of features. Vehicles had plastic windows, unlike those of their competitors, and spring suspension was added in 1959. From 1963, vehicles were made with opening doors and bonnets, as well as folding seats. One of Corgi's most popular models, the Chrysler V8 of 1963, even featured a little corgi dog.

In 1969, Corgi introduced 'golden jacks' for its Hillman Hunter rally car (winner of the London to Sydney rally); this allowed wheels to be changed. Corgi produced several rally cars in the wake of British racing successes, and was known for TV and film tie-ins, including Batman and James Bond.

JONTY'S CHOICE

In 1957 Corgi introduced a new range of models of larger commercial vehicles known as Corgi Majors. The first of these was the Big Bedford tractor unit, which was coupled with the Carrimore car transporter and the Mobilgas petrol tanker. The Corgi Major range continued to showcase beautifully produced commercial vehicle models until the Majors name was dropped in 1969.

Corgi Major racing car transporter, with original box, 1961. £360–400

Prices compared

Austin A60 De Luxe Saloon Motor School car, No. 236, with box, 1960s. £80–90

Austin A60 De Luxe Saloon Motor School car, No. 236, with box, 1960s. £45–50

The values of these cars is determined by the condition. The item on the left is in very good condition; that on the right is used. While a box does add to value, its condition will influence the combined value of the car and box.

Other models

Smiths Karrier Bantam mobile shop, No. 413, with box, late 1950s. £80–90

Austin Healey sports car, No. 300, with box, c1960. £110–125

The Green Hornet's Black Beauty car, No. 268, with box, c1967. £130–150

The one to look for

Original packaging is important. Not only does it complete the toy, but toys in their boxes are more likely to be in good condition. The box must be correct; reproductions can usually be identified by the type of cardboard and the quality of the printing.

Tour de France Gift Set, No. 13, with Paramount film unit, Renault 16 with camera mand and a cyclist, with original box, 1960s. £140–170

Several Corgi models came with accessories such as plastic figures, and the value of the set is seriously reduced if they are missing or broken.

Below are two examples of a Corgi Toys logo as it appeared on the box. The logo on the left is an early version from the late 1950s; the one on the right appeared in the 1970s.

James Bond Aston Martin, No. 270, with box, 1973. £170–190

Rocket Firing Batmobile, with Batboat and trailer, with box, 1967. £1,125–1,250

Magic Roundabout Dougal's car, No. 807, 1971. £110–125

Hotwheels

The world of die-cast toy cars in the US was revolutionized when the American company Mattel introduced Hotwheels in 1968. With fanciful designs inspired by hot rods and dragsters, they were very different from anything made by competitors such as Matchbox.

Originally designed to run on a plastic track, they have plastic wheels that run on thin axles, allowing them to go further and faster when pushed along. Their success prompted other manufacturers to introduce similar ranges – Matchbox responded with 'Superfast' in 1969 and Corgi introduced 'Whizzwheels' in 1970.

Collectors consider vintage vehicles to be pre-1980, although for most, the 'golden age' was 1968–73. Hotwheels have a date on the bottom, but this can confuse collectors, as it refers to the date of the design, not the date of manufacture: a car dated 1968 could actually be more recent.

Hotwheels were produced in a wide range of colours, and some are rare. Cars in 'hot pink' are sought after as few were made; it was thought that pink cars would not appeal to boys.

Speed Demons Torboa,
No. 2061, 1986. £5–10

How to spot a fake

White 'All American' Firebird, No. 9518, 1960s–70s. £20–30

This is a later colour and transfer variation of the No. 2014 Hotbird, made in 1977. Later versions like this were made in Hong Kong and have blue tinted windows; they also lack the 'redline' wheels of earlier Hotwheels models. Check the underside of models in case there are signs that the rivets holding the car together have been tampered with; it is not uncommon for models to be repainted in order to give the impression of a rare variation.

Other Hotwheels

Green redline
Silhouette, No.
6209, 1968.
£15–20

Purple redline
Custom Fleetside,
No. 6213, 1967.
£15–20

Turquoise
Stripteaser, Firestone
transfer, No. 6188,
1971. £40–60

Green Ranger Rig,
replaced wheels,
1975. £20–30

The one to look for

This Mattel Hotwheels rendition of the Dodge Deora in a metallic lime green Spectraflame finish is from the first or possibly second year of production. Spectraflame was an attractive finish achieved by polishing the bare metal and then coating it in a clear, coloured lacquer, allowing the brightness of the metal to shine through. This model is not in the best condition, but does at least retain its original surfboards, which are often missing.

Mattel Hotwheels 'redline' Deora with surfboards, No. 6210, 1968. £40–50

Damage to the paintwork reveals the bare metal underneath. Normally, Hotwheels collectors are choosy about badly chipped vehicles but if it is an early and desirable model, damage may be forgiven. Impressive though the Spectraflame paintwork was, it has a tendency to bloom and tarnish with age.

The early years of Hotwheels production are referred to by collectors as the 'redline' era, because of the red line that was etched around the wheels from 1968 to 1977. Some early models were reissued in the 1990s as collectors' items, but the red lines were printed, not etched.

Orange Splittin' Image, No. 6261, 1969. £20–30

Purple Sand Crab, No. 6403, Crane Arms decal, 1970. £10–20

Blue redline Cement Mixer, No. 6452, 1970. £20–30

Burgundy redline Snorkel, No. 6020, 1971. £35–50

Other die-cast toys

As well as the best-known manufacturers such as Dinky and Corgi, there were many other makers of die-cast toys. Almost every industrialized country produced die-cast vehicles at some point; the 'slush cast' process of pouring molten metal into an open mould was fairly straightforward.

Wherever they come from, die-cast toys are usually easy to identify, since the makers stamped their names on their products. Collector interest remains strong: Europeans tend to be most interested in European makes, while Americans prefer collecting US firms such as Tootsie.

Tootsie Toys *Founded in Chicago, Illinois in 1906 by the Dowst brothers, the first product was a miniature model T Ford. The 'Tootsie' name came from the nickname of a grandchild. In 1918, Tootsie began producing cars in mazac, which was much safer than lead. From the mid-1920s, Tootsie models included detail such as recessed lines around the engine compartment and doors.*
Ambulance, c1920. £45–50

Chad Valley *This firm is known for tinplate toys, board games and soft toys but it did produce an admirable range of high-quality die-cast vehicles from 1932 to 1955. These are popular with collectors and easy to date, since the date was usually stamped on the number plate – eg 'CV 1949' stood for 'Chad Valley' and the year 1949.*
Clockwork Wee Kin cable layer, 1949–53. £80–90

Crescent Toys *The company was founded in London in 1922, but subcontracted the manufacture of its die-cast toys to a firm called Die-Casting Machine Tools (DCMT). In 1950, production moved to Wales where various toys of excellent quality were made. Today they are more valuable than their Dinky equivalents. This is one of ten die-cast racing cars made.*
D-Type Jaguar, 1956–60. £115–130

Mercury *This Italian firm was founded after WWII. Mercury used a system known as high pressure die-casting, which required expensive steel moulds. Quality was good, but needed large production volumes to offset manufacturing costs.*
Ferrari Dino, 1950s. £45–50

Solido *This company is the most famous of the French die-cast manufacturers and was founded in 1932. Solido's quality was outstanding, rivalling and sometimes even exceeding that of Corgi. Not surprisingly, their toys are very desirable. Although they did produce an extensive collection of civilian vehicles, the firm is best known for its range of military vehicles, which was first launched in 1961.*
M-47 tank, 1960s. £45–50

Matchbox *These toys were made by the British firm Lesney, founded in 1947. Introduced in 1953, the toys were designed to be affordable and pocket-sized – they sold in their millions. This steamroller is one of the earliest models; the name 'Moko' on the box was used from 1950 to 1959. It refers to the Anglo-German firm Moses Kohnstam Ltd, which had the exclusive rights to sell them.*

No. 1 Steamroller, with box, 1950s. £30–35

Tri-ang *The 'Spot-On' range was introduced in 1959. Their 1:42 scale made them slightly larger than Dinky and they had innovative features such as 'flexomatic suspension'. The range of commercial vehicles was only made from 1960 to 1963. The combination of quality and rarity makes them sought after, and boxed models are especially prized.*
E.R.F. 68g dropside lorry, 1960, with box, 1960s. £175–195

Tinplate

Tinplate began to replace wood as the material of choice for toy makers during the 19th century, thanks largely to the new technology of the Industrial Revolution, which made it cheaper. Tinplate is tinned sheet steel, and is particularly associated with European (especially German) and, later, Japanese production. America had its own tinplate toy industry but this was smaller, as cast iron was generally preferred. The German firms of Märklin, Lehmann, Bing and Tipp & Co are among the biggest names.

Early tinplate toys were hand painted but, from the late 19th century onwards, lithographic printing became the preferred method of decorating tinplate toys. Production methods also changed. Initially, toys were soldered together from components stamped out on presses. In the 1890s, Bing of Nuremburg used a lighter gauge of metal with a system of tabs and slots that fitted together to secure the components in place. This method of manufacture eventually became commonplace throughout Europe, and was referred to as 'the Nuremburg style', after the place where it was originally pioneered.

Condition and rarity, rather than age, are important, as some older toys were produced in large numbers and many have survived.

Rust is the greatest enemy of tinplate, so beware, and be prepared to reject anything that is severely affected. Look out for damage to the tabs that hold these tinplate toys together, and look for flaking or fading of paint (the former is more significant than the latter). While condition is important, tinplate toys are especially vulnerable to dents, and a few minor ones will not make too much difference to the value.

The larger and more elaborate toys were naturally more expensive in their day, and tend to be more valuable now. It's not hard to see why – they were relatively costly to make and were made in smaller numbers for a more exclusive market. Because they were expensive, they were prized possessions and treated with care, so many of them have survived in reasonable condition.

Gradually, tinplate fell from favour, partly because of the availability of new and cheap plastics but also because of safety concerns – their sharp edges consigned them to toybox history. However, a nostalgia-fuelled collectors' market has emerged and replica tinplate toys, usually made in China, are popular with adult collectors. This has in turn encouraged a greater interest in the originals and prices are beginning to reflect this.

Other shapes

Lehmann clockwork van, 1900.
£1,000–1,200

Distler Mickey Mouse Organ Grinder, with original box, c1930.
£8,000–12,000

Tipp & Co military ambulance, late 1930s.
£500–700

The one to look for

Founded by brothers Ignaz and Adolf Bing in 1863, the Bing factory originally made kitchen utensils but went on to become the largest toy factory in the world. Bing's products ranged from trains to teddy bears, and all their lines are sought after today.

Bing tinplate clockwork U-boat with detachable flag, 1930s. £450–550

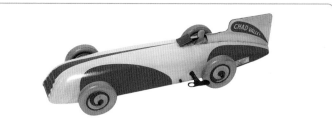

Before around 1923, the letters 'GBN' marked Bing toys, and stood for 'Gebrüder Bing Nürnberg'. Later toys used a 'BW', which stood for 'Bing Werke' (Bings Works). This boat has suffered some damage with missing masts and rudder, but it remains desirable nonetheless.

State of the market

This car has a lot going for it in the current market. It has a transport theme, which is popular with collectors, and is by a well-known maker. It is also in excellent condition, which is very important, as lithographed tinplate is difficult to restore and a bad restoration job seriously detracts from the value of a toy. Collectors are demanding, but the market is still buoyant for good tinplate toys. The number of collectors is growing and there is a finite supply of old toys, so now is a good time to buy.
Chad Valley clockwork racing car, c1935. £220–250

Bucket decorated with anthropomorphic dogs playing on a beach, c1940. £30–35

Mechanical clown bank, c1920. £700–800

Fort on a wooden base, 1920–50. £50–55

Post-war tinplate

Not surprisingly, toys during WWII were considered non-essentials so toy factories across the world – including those making tinplate toys – were adapted for military production. After the war, toy production resumed and, in the case of Japan and Germany, was encouraged by the victorious allies as it was clearly desirable for both nations to rebuild their economies with peaceful industries. After WWI, military subjects fell from favour (although Japanese firm Tomy enjoyed great export success with a B-29 bomber) but transport themes were generally popular.

Germany, a traditional world leader in tinplate toys, found new challenges as industries had developed elsewhere in Europe and there was some consumer resistance to German products. Japan was also emerging as a serious rival. Few new companies appeared after the war, but established firms such as Märklin and Schuco continued to make good-quality toys that were commercially successful.

Most German toys in the 1950s were still powered by clockwork; batteries came later. German motorcycle toys are particularly collectable, not least because they appeal to motorcycle enthusiasts as well as toy collectors.

Japanese toy makers enjoyed access to American markets and consequently a lot of their cars were modelled on American vehicles; many were surprisingly detailed and often included a clever use of motors to add play value. Names to look out for include Yonezawa, Masudaya, Nomura and Yoshiya. As science fiction became popular with the dawn of the space age, so too did space toys and robots, of which the most sought after of all are members of the 'Gang of Five' by Masudaya (see page 171).

In Britain, the tinplate toy industry reflected a general decline. True, many good-quality products were still made, especially by firms such as Tri-ang and Chad Valley, but there was a gradual slip in quality and competition from plastic. The advantages of this material eventually won the day, partly because it was safer, as it lacked sharp edges and also because it was cheaper to produce. During the late 1950s, many toys incorporated both plastic and tinplate into their designs.

For collectors, tinplate toys with car or transport themes have been increasing in value in recent years, as opposed to 'novelty toys', which have become less popular.

When valuing tinplate toys remember that condition is important – as is having the original box which, ideally, will be in good condition too.

Other toys

Louis Marx clockwork police motorcycle, with siren, 1950s.
£160–180

Alice in Wonderland *paint box. 1955–60.*
£25–30

Battery-operated Super Flying Police Helicopter, 1960s.
£100–125

The one to look for

Tomiyama is the trading name of a Japanese toy firm founded by Eiichiro Tomiyama in 1924. It became known as Tomy in the 1950s and still exists today as the world's fifth largest toy manufacturer. The firm became known for its innovation and patented a number of ingenious motor designs for its toys.

Tomiyama Firebird Race Car, 1950s. £400–450

This battery-operated car has a stop/go action and even emits smoke from the exhaust. The driver also moves his arm as the vehicle drives. The car's relative complexity makes it harder to find an example in good working order.

The Japanese influence

The Japanese seized much of the market from the established European makers after WWII and Japan became a centre of innovation and imaginative design. Japanese makers perfected the manufacturing techniques of earlier European makers and produced toys that were notable for their range of bright colours and for their actions. They were also affordable and were marketed through catalogues and promotional brochures that have now become collectable in their own right.

Tinplate and plastic jet car, 1965–75. £20–25

Clockwork fire engine, West German, 1960s. £15–20

Clockwork motorcycle and rider, 1965–75. £30–50

Volkswagen Beetle, 1970s. £55–65

Lead figures

Most people imagine toy soldiers when they think of lead figures. Although the production of toy soldiers was an important part of the toy maker's repertoire, other figures were also popular, such as those inspired by the zoo, the farm or cartoon characters. This was especially true immediately after WWI, when there was something of a reaction against military toys and many parents looked for a range of alternatives for their offspring.

Continental production led the way until 1893, when William Britain Junior developed a method known as 'hollow casting' in the UK. This enabled the manufacture of hollow figures that were lighter, and used less lead than their solid European counterparts, which saved significantly on production costs. A British home-grown industry quickly emerged, and the firm of Britains had produced over 100 different sets of figures by 1900.

In the 1920s, Britains introduced the 'Home Farm' range. Unlike its military counterparts, the toys were a success with both boys and girls. Vehicles included a farm waggon with carter (see opposite), a shepherd and his sheep, and a plough with ploughman. After 1927, even a 'village idiot' was added to the Home Farm series, after Queen Mary said this was the only thing missing.

Lead is, of course, a toxic metal, and its use in toy manufacture was banned in the 1960s, but the 'golden age' of lead figures had passed by then. Pre-WWII figures by Britains are the most collectable, owing to their quality and the wide range available.

Other names to look out for include John Hill & Company, who produced hollow-cast lead figures in a similar style and scale, although their figures tend to have a less rigid pose. Heyde of Dresden, whose toys were most commonly imported into the UK before the dominance of Britains, and Charbens, in production from 1920 to 1955 are also key names.

Many figures are more likely to be found in their country of origin, and collectors' interests today tend to lie with the products of their own countries. An exception to this is America, where Britains figures are well known, having been exported to the US in large numbers. As a result of this they are now very collectable on both sides of the Atlantic.

Other figures

Britains Household Cavalry, 12 pieces (gun team shown), 1950s.
£300–350

Figure from Britains Home Farm series, 1920s–50s.
£1–5

Britains boxed set of Boy Scouts, 1950s.
£400–500

The one to look for

This is one of the larger pieces in the Home Farm series, and is therefore more desirable. Britains sold small and large pieces, so that children could buy the occasional figure with their pocket money, while the more costly pieces like this were bought for them on special occasions, such as birthdays.

Britains Farm Waggon, 1920. £100–150

The Farm Waggon was quite a versatile toy, as the horses could be removed from the shafts and played with independently. Unfortunately, horses, carts and carters have sometimes become separated – a stray figure or cart may have belonged to this set.

At Britains, figures were still being hand-painted in fine detail, which adds to their appeal. Colours of figures may vary and while this cart is green, there was also a blue version.

Britains Zoo set, complete and pieces in mint condition, 1950s. £250–300

Pixyland & Co Pip, Squeak and Wilfred, after characters in the Daily Mirror newspaper, 1920s. £30–40

American military lead figure, early 20thC. £10–15

Games

Games of one sort or another date as far back as the dawn of civilization. Many modern board games have their roots in antiquity – Ludo, for example, is a simpler form of the ancient Indian board game, Pachisi.

Board games were first produced commercially in the mid-18th century, but surviving examples today are more likely to date from the mid-19th century onwards. The development of colour lithography meant that attractive games could be made and printed in large numbers and at a relatively low cost. Games from the late 19th century onwards typically came on a folding board made from cardboard, rather than being mounted on canvas as was previously the case.

The best-known makers include the American firms of Parker Brothers and Milton Bradley, while worthwhile British firms are Spears, Waddingtons and Chad Valley. Brooks & Co, Thomas Varty, Carrington Bowles and John Betts, who also produced puzzles, are among the 19th-century makers to look out for.

Games are more desirable if they are bright and colourful, so artwork is always important; faded colours resulting from exposure to strong sunlight will reduce the value. Reject any games with signs of mildew or insect attack. Beware of games that have been stored in poor conditions. They should be stored vertically if possible, never stacked on top of each other. Using rubber bands to secure box lids can cause damage and this should always be avoided. Similarly, gluing or taping a board game or puzzle to its backing board will dramatically reduce its value.

In today's market, dedicated collectors of games are relatively thin on the ground. However, this does mean that there are plenty of opportunities to buy at a reasonable price, as games are often overlooked. Board games produced between 1880 and 1914 are particularly sought after, as this is regarded as the 'golden age' of chromolithography and the standard of printing was very high at this time. It is also worth remembering that some games have a specialist interest – for example, a collector of travel-related antiques might be interested in a game with a travel theme. The same is true for science fiction, military and sport-related collections. In such cases, the discovery of an appropriate game may well make up for other potential shortcomings, such as an unknown maker.

Most games have many components, which must be present to make them collectable and valuable.

Other games

Set of Scottish, ceramic spongeware carpet balls, c1880.
£50–60

Magic set, original box, c1880.
£550–600

Domino set in a tin, c1910.
£35–40

Chad Valley Stumpy Joe Quoits game, with box, c1930.
£15–20

The one to look for

Snakes and Ladders was a Victorian invention, although it may have been inspired by much earlier games. It would certainly have been a relatively recent game when this example was produced. It is in excellent condition for its age.

Snakes and Ladders game, c1910. £20–25

To be of value a game needs to have its original dice, counters and any other playing pieces, as well as the instructions. This game is complete, so it is a rare find.

Parker Bros & Monopoly

Parker Brothers launched Monopoly in 1935 and Charles Darrow is credited as its inventor. Its origins, however, date back to a 1904 game called The Landlord Game, by Lizzie J. Magie. Initially, Darrow's game was rejected by Parker Brothers as being too complex, but it proved to be an instant hit and the game has since sold more than 100 million examples worldwide. It is estimated that at least 750 million people have played it. Because different versions

have been produced for various markets, and now numerous collectors' editions are available, some games collectors focus solely on Monopoly.

Waddington's Totopoly, 1960s. £100–125

Standard Toy Craft Supercar Road Race Game, 1960s. £180–200

Ideal Rubik's Revenge cube, 1980s. £15–20

Nintendo Game & Watch Multi Screen game, with box, 1982. £80–90

Trains

The earliest toy trains appeared in the mid-19th century, as the railways themselves spread across Europe and America.

Early European models were fairly crude and generic, bearing little resemblance to any actual locomotives in use at the time. However, by the late 19th and early 20th centuries more realistic trains were beginning to emerge from a number of producers. The German firm of Märklin introduced standardized gauges at the Leipzig Toy Fair of 1891, after which this innovative company became a market leader. It did so not only by making quality products, but also by introducing, and then constantly adding to, an impressive range of rolling stock, stations, figures and accessories.

German manufacturers in general found ready buyers in Britain, a prominent maker being Bing. There are many German-made trains to be found in the UK today. French companies included Dessin and Favre, who made lightweight, tinplate 'carpet' trains, while America had a toy train industry of its own. American makers included Lionel and Ives, as well as American Flyer of Chicago, who first made clockwork trains and later 0 gauge electric trains. British makers to look out for include Hornby and Bassett-Lowke – the latter subcontracted design and toymaking and also collaborated with Bing.

Trains from the interwar period are especially sought after, as this is regarded as something of a 'golden age' of model trains. During this time, smaller gauges were introduced in Britain; smaller houses were being built at the time, and down-sizing the toys made them more practical for the average home. Although German products became less popular after WWI, Germany remained the dominant manufacturing nation for trains.

Collectors of model trains are both demanding and knowledgeable, so only good-quality examples in good condition are of interest. Collectors are also quite unforgiving, so any kind of damage will have an adverse effect on values. This applies equally to metal fatigue, which is often a problem that occurs with wheels: although it is accepted, it will always be reflected in the price.

Mechanisms should be original and springs should be intact. Clockwork trains were often converted to electricity and if this is the case, the value will be reduced. The presence of a winding hole is a giveaway. If an electric train has had its motor replaced, this may still be acceptable, as long as the replacement motor is of the correct type for the train.

The presence of accessories is always advantageous and the more there are, the better.

Other models

Bing 4-4-2 tank engine, 1920s.
£350–400

Hornby 4-4-4 tank engine, early 1930s.
£450–550

Hornby clockwork 4-4-0 tender locomotive, 1930s.
£400–450

The one to look for

The Flying Scotsman became a legend to rail enthusiasts and model versions of this famous locomotive were put into production by several firms. This rendition became the most admired of Bassett-Lowke's products in the interwar years, and was designed by managing director, Robert Bindon-Blood.

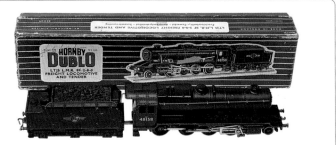

Bassett-Lowke Flying Scotsman, 1933.
£1,000–1,500

The 0 gauge locomotive has an electric mechanism and pulls a rake of coaches designed by Edward Exley. It was still being produced well into the 1950s. The Bassett-Lowke Flying Scotsman was superior to its competitors because of its attention to detail. It is a highly accurate model of the original train and its overall appearance is much finer.

Hornby's 'golden age'

In 1938, Hornby launched its Dublo range, designed to compete with the 00 gauge sets of competitors such as Märklin. This is widely considered to mark the dawn of a 'golden age' for Hornby. The Hornby Dublo trains were of very high quality, well designed with detailed diecast bodies and were very successful. They were also technically very innovative, using a magnet mechanism that enabled trains to change direction without the need to change the motor polarity and without mechanical switching. The range is popular with collectors today, although pre-WWII examples in good condition are hard to come by.
Hornby Dublo tank engine, 1950s. £50–60

Hornby 0-4-0 tank engine, 1950s.
£140–175

Bassett-Lowke 4-6-0 tender locomotive, 1950s.
£800–900

Pair of Tri-ang Emu powered and non-powered motor coaches, with boxes, 1950s.
£100–120

Sci-fi & fantasy

Science fiction and fantasy toys are mainly a post-war phenomenon, with very few surviving examples from the pre-war era. That is not to say, of course, that the genre did not exist before then, as any H. G. Wells or Flash Gordon fan will testify, but the post-war years saw the advent of atomic power, the Space Race and numerous, well-publicized UFO sightings. All of these provided inspiration for writers, film makers and toy makers.

While there are many generic science fiction toys representing spaceships, robots and the like, the toy industry in this field received much of its impetus from comics, films and, later, television, with toys based on popular characters. As a general rule, the more colourful and fantastic a generic toy is, the more popular it will be with collectors. Japan led the way in affordable but imaginative space toys during the 1950s and 1960s.

Robots and ray guns are science fiction staples and both, especially the former, attract dedicated collectors who specialize in them. Robots of the 1950s and 1960s are always popular, but increasingly hard to find in good condition. Sometimes, 'warehouse finds' are made, as in the 1990s when a quantity of Japanese Yoshiya 'Action Planet' robots was discovered – good news for those wanting an original, but it did drive prices down for a while.

As for toys based on comics, TV and film, interest is largely dependent on the characters. Dan Dare of *Eagle* comic fame was a part of the childhood of many Britons, but he is less well-known in America – although a new computer-animated series of his adventures has recently aired on American television. *Thunderbirds* (and other Gerry Anderson shows), *Dr Who*, *Batman*, *Star Trek* and *Transformers* are among the 'franchises' with devoted followings – and in the collecting world, *Star Wars* is a global phenomenon (see pp254–255).

As well as the Japanese makers, firms such as Corgi and Dinky made toys based on sci-fi and fantasy characters and these are very collectable. Again, interest varies depending on the characters, but there is a hard core of dedicated collectors.

Collecting action figures has become a major field in its own right and variations of figures were made for different markets. For this reason, a European edition of a *Star Wars* figure can be more desirable in the US because of its comparative rarity, and vice versa.

Science fiction toys

Ingersoll Dan Dare pocket watch, 1951. £250–300

Thunderbirds cloth hat, 1960s. £25–30

JR 21 Toys battery-operated plastic Thunderbird 5, 1960s. £220–250

Corgi Batmobile with red tyres, early 1970s. £50–80

The one to look for

In the 1950s, the Japanese firm of Masudaya made a series of robots with a similar 'skirted' design known as the 'Gang of Five'. This is the rarest and most valuable; a 1958 version sold for £19,000 in a New York auction in 2000. It is battery powered with a 'bump n' go' action and flashing eyes, ears and mouth.
Masudaya 'Gang of Five' Machine Man, 1950s.
£25,000–30,000

Reproductions of these popular toys were made by Masudaya in the late 1990s. They are much smaller, however. An original stands at 38cm (15in) tall.

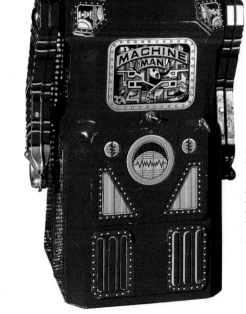

Owing to their motion and because many designs were top heavy, robots often fell over and suffered damage. Slight damage is acceptable, but should be reflected in the price. Masudaya toys were usually marked with an 'MT' logo – this stood for 'Modern Toys'.

Marx Toys Dr Who *battery-operated Dalek, with box, 1960s.* £70–80

Space 1999 *bubble gum cards, trade box, 1970s.* £60–70

Mego Star Trek Captain Kirk action figure, American, 1979. £65–75

Takara Transformers Cybertron Commander Convoy, 2002. £25–30

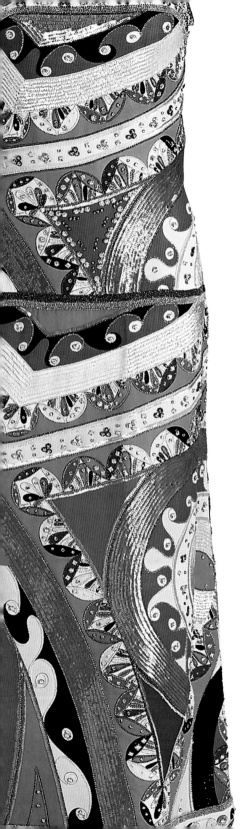

Fashion & Jewellery

Clothes tend to reflect the mood of the people and the times in which they live. The elegance of the Edwardian era, the decadence of the 1920s and '30s, the austerity of the Second World War and the confidence of the swinging Sixties all influenced the fashions of the day. It was not just the clothes either; take a look at the accessories that accompanied them, such as hats, shoes, handbags and even make-up.

Vintage fashions and accessories bearing designer names and iconic styles can fetch large sums. However, the keen collector can still find many a bargain when rummaging through charity shops, boot fairs and garage sales.

FASHION & JEWELLERY

Vintage fashions epitomise the era they were made in, whether a 1930s clutch bag, 1950s prom dress, or 1980s power suit. If you are looking for designer chic, vintage clothes offer plenty of style – often at very little cost. If you are happy to shop for pieces which have the look without the designer label you can often find a bargain. Both established collectors and casual buyers can be found looking for vintage fashions and it is possible to find something for every budget with stylish items changing hands for as little as £1.

Plastic clutch bag, decorated with simulated pearls, c1960.
£20–25

How to get the look

The secret is to look for items that are typical of their time, in good condition and robust enough to withstand some, if not daily, wear. You will often find that vintage clothes are better made than many of those sold

Foale & Tuffin Liberty Varuna wool tunic and culottes, late 1960s.
£280–320

today and made from beautiful fabrics, some with exquisite beading and lace details. Check the seams, labels and any decoration for indications of quality. Check out vintage fashion magazines for clues as to what to look for and how to wear it (the magazines themselves can be collectable, so make room in your shopping bag for them, too).

Couture outfits by the likes of Coco Chanel, Elsa Schiaparelli, Emilio Pucci and Vivienne Westwood will always be popular but may not be common finds. Similarly, pieces by the big names of the 1960s and '70s, such as Mary Quant and Biba, are rare and valuable finds. Instead look for period pieces inspired by these and other designers. Details such as zips and washing instructions can help with dating. Many synthetic fabrics were not developed until the 1950s, so an item labelled nylon, polyester or acrylic is likely to have been made at that time or later. Remember that vintage fabrics may be fragile, so careful handwashing is safer than machine washing, despite what any care labels may say. If in any doubt, seek advice from a specialist dry cleaner.

Knitted wool Cowichan-style cardigan, 1960s.
£35–40

Shoes and handbags

Iconic shoes such as 1950s winkle pickers, 1970s platform boots and 1980s trainers are worth searching out, as are vintage handbags such as leather clutches from the 1930s and Lucite box bags from the 1950s. Check shoes and bags carefully for wear – a little is acceptable but tears, missing beads or other visible faults may make something unwearable.

Jewellery

Vintage costume jewellery has become highly collectable over the past 20 years. Signed pieces from the 1930s, '40s and '50s by the likes of Trifari, Hobé, Dior, Schiaparelli, Miriam Haskell and Stanley Hagler have grown in popularity and value. Check the back of a piece for a designer's name, make sure that the clasps and clips still function and that none of the stones are missing. However, pieces from the 1960s and '70s are worth buying as they offer value for money, as do unsigned pieces which are well designed and made from quality materials. Plastic and Bakelite jewellery of the 1930s continue to be desirable.

Precious jewellery can often be spotted among fake pieces if you know what to look for. The late 19th and 20th centuries saw many inexpensive silver and even gold pieces on the market. If the fashions of the late 19th century are not to your taste, look for stylish pieces from the 1950s and '60s which make a statement without leaving a hole in your purse.

Trifari brooch with paste stones, 1940s. £100–120

Other accessories

Accessories such as hats, scarves, sunglasses, fans, ties and cufflinks are all worth checking out. They can lift an outfit and give the wearer the cachet of wearing vintage without having to take the plunge into a complete ensemble.

Smoking accessories such as lighters, cigarette and Vesta (match) cases and cigar cutters are all popular collectables today, possibly because smoking is no longer fashionable.

Other items you may find are powder compacts and fountain pens, which are no longer a necessity of daily life. Writing with a fountain pen can turn paying bills into a stylish event, while powder compacts

Patent leather handbag, 1960. £20–25

make an elegant usable collection.

The past two years have seen a popular revival in wristwatches, the trend being led by fashion designers who have suggested a smarter look for men. As well as new and vintage models by the top brands, many men are looking for vintage 'fashion' watches that have an immediate visual appeal and period style.

1950s Fashion

The look most readily associated with the 1950s – long, full skirts with nipped-in waists and tailored jackets – actually began in 1947 with Christian Dior's revolutionary 'New Look'. By the 1950s the style had defied post-war rationing and shortages and was being worn by women young and old.

Clothes inspired by Dior – and other talented French designers such as Yves Saint Laurent – are worth looking out for. These outfits came with wide-brimmed hats, gloves and stiletto heels. While wearing the whole ensemble may be daunting, wearing just one item – a jacket, skirt or hat – will always look stylish. An original Dior suit might be worth as much as £800–1,200 at auction and an evening dress up to £5,000. While these may may be hard to come by, period imitations can often be found.

Other designers worth looking for include Coco Chanel, who re-launched her classic, straight-skirted suit in the 1950s. Such suits can now command £600–800 at auction and outfits inspired by them have been made ever since.

For designer leisurewear, look out for Italian Emilio Pucci's signature swirling patterns on 'ski slacks' and cropped Capri trousers.

The mid-1950s marked the beginning of fashion clothes for the young. With circle skirts, ankle socks and penny loafers for teenage girls and denim jeans and white T-shirts for their male contemporaries, the under-20s helped to inspire the street style of the late 20th century.

These clothes are still relatively easy to find. Expect to pay a premium for quirky designs featuring poodles – the ultimate fifties symbol. Also worth seeking out are the petticoats needed to keep skirts and dresses looking their best. Swimsuits, summer frocks and prom dresses remain stylish while sunglasses and Hawaiian shirts from the decade have a nostalgic charm.

It may be possible to replace the lenses in vintage glasses and sunglasses, which makes them a realistic buy. Check that any decoration – such as diamante – remains intact, as it may prove hard to replace or restore.

Clothes & accessories

Printed cotton day dress with acrylic button detailing, 1950s. £70–75

Levis 501XX jeans with capital E on the red tab, selvedge, and watch pocket. 1950s. £400–450

Ruched rayon swimsuit, 1950s. £40–45

The one to look for

Prom or party dresses are usually in good condition, their original wearers having kept them as souvenirs for many years and are usually highly typical of the era. With their tight bodices and gathered skirts, they are still wearable today.

Labels often record manufacturers and stores that have been closed for some time. Get to know the top-end stores that once supplied special occasion dresses in your neighbourhood and you'll be able to spot superior party wear easily.

Look closely at the stitching and any fastenings on these dresses, as they help to decide the quality of a piece. Poor fabrics, detailing and poorly finished seams are a sign of a cheap dress.

THIS GARMENT IS FITTED WITH THE
Ricci Michaels LTD.
"FLEXICRIN" Petticoat
INCORPORATED BRIT. PAT. SPEC. NO. 720577

Ricci Michaels ruched evening dress, 1950s. £230–260

Howe Street Hawaiian shirt, 1950s. £55–65

Pair of Bective Chiquita shoes, with diamante decoration, 1950s. £145–160

Pair of plastic sunglasses, with diamante decoration, 1950s. £30–35

1960s Fashion

Fashion in the 1960s was diverse. It was as much about a hippie trip to Marrakech as a mission to the moon. Inspired by America's lunar programme, Parisian couturier André Courrèges clad his sci-fi heroines in trouser suits, miniskirts and white go-go boots. He used new synthetic materials such as wet-look vinyl in his stark and angular designs. Elsewhere in Paris, Pierre Cardin made helmet hats, jumpsuits, and tunic dresses. Cardin is also credited with geometric cut-outs and circular zip fastners. A-line dresses and denim jackets are also among the clothes that characterize this era.

Fabrics such as Tricel were among the innovations of the decade and clothes made from this and other new synthetics will often boast it on the label.

London became a mecca for 1960s fashion. Carnaby Street and the King's Road were the hip places to be, with clothes that became the epitome of style. Having opened her first boutique, Bazaar, on the King's Road, British fashion designer Mary Quant produced inexpensive fashions that were bright and well-coordinated. Besides promoting the miniskirt, she unveiled the first range of British coordinates with sleeveless and pinafore dresses. Barbara Hulanicki's Biba store sold floaty fashions, feather boas and handbags. In the 'Swinging Sixties', boutiques that sold clothes with an individual stamp, such as Quorum, were fashionable.

The Beatles had a big influence on men's fashion – from the tailored suits of the early years to the Edwardian-style military uniforms of *Sergeant Pepper* and the hippy look of *Let It Be*.

Italian Emilio Pucci's tunics, kaftans and harem pants featured in 1960s *Vogue* photo shoots. His clothing combined futuristic and hippie styles and his printed fabrics were widely copied. Ossie Clark rejuvenated the bias-cut of the 1930s. From 1965 to 1974, he created floral gypsy dresses and peasant blouses. Printed fabric designs by his wife Celia Birtwell are also worth looking out for. All the designs were mimicked by high street stores, so look for the style as well as the name.

Clothes & accessories

Acetate summer dress, 1960s. £45–50

A Foale & Tuffin Liberty Varuna wool tunic and culottes, late 1960s. £280–320

A pair of Riviera GTX woven cotton trousers, 1960s. £20–25

The one to look for

Biba – said to be more a 'happening' than a store – started as a mail-order business but soon became a chain of boutiques. The romantic, retro look came to define late 1960s and early 1970s fashion for many young women. This jacket and cap have a retro baker's boy feel.

Biba cord jacket and hat, 1960s. £160–180

Biba clothes were inexpensive and often not particularly well made but are highly sought after by collectors today. A matching jacket and hat like these will always command a premium.

The Biba label appeared on clothes, make-up, jewellery and shoes. On early clothing the logo is printed on a large brown satin tag. On later pieces the label is smaller and the logo embroidered with yellow thread.

Kant & Co Beatles-style two-piece suit, late 1960s. £85–90

Marks & Spencer cotton skirt, 1960s. £25–30

Pucci-style Tricel trouser suit, 1960s. £50–55

1970s & beyond

The key looks of the early 1970s were characterized by British fashion designer Ossie Clark's wraparound dresses and Bill Gibb's colourful layered dresses. This 'sophisticated peasant' look prevailed for much of the decade with floaty cheesecloth skirts and embroidered kaftan tops. Parisian Yves Saint Laurent unveiled chic trouser suits – those made for the evening are referred to as 'le smoking' and were made famous by celebrities such as Bianca Jagger.

Wraparound dresses were also taking off in the US: designer Diane Von Furstenberg made the look her own and, following her recent renaissance, originals are highly sought after by collectors today. American designer Roy Halston's halter-neck dresses, kaftans and jumpsuits were widely copied. Manufacturers such as Max Mara and Jaeger produced imitations of the best designers, which offer the same style at a fraction of the price.

This tailored style was challenged in the late 1970s, however, when British designer Vivienne Westwood and her partner, Malcolm McLaren, promoted punk and bondage styles on the catwalk. An iconic bondage suit from this time can fetch around £500–600 while a cheesecloth 'Destroy' or 'Anarchy' shirt can command £300-500.

In the 1980s, Karl Lagerfeld reproduced the classic 1950s Chanel suit in many pastel shades of tweed. The suit was copied by a number of manufacturers and, if you cannot find the real thing, good-quality examples, are wearable and represent real value for money. The Italian designer Giorgio Armani created masculine 'power suits' for women which symbolized the decade's affluent mood. Pieces influenced by these designs often feature severe shoulder pads and have glitzy ornament such as gilt buttons and heavy braid.

When the 1980s fashion set weren't in the office they were relaxing in batwing sweaters with geometric patterns, stonewashed denim and the latest trainers. Limited edition footwear by firms like Nike is very collectable, if in good condition.

Unwanted designerwear from the 1990s and early 2000s is certainly worth looking out for. The key designers of the past 20 years include Stella McCartney, Versace, Dolce & Gabbana and Chloe, all of whom will have collector fans in years to come – and may still be wearable today.

Clothes & accessories

Maxton stretch acetate blouse, 1970s. **£25–30**

Pair of leather hotpants with bib, 1970s. **£50–60**

Pair of A. R. Sons leather platform boots, 1970s. **£125–140**

The one to look for

Mainstream fashion produced stylish yet
practical clothes for the modern woman.
Flattering and comfortable to wear they were
made by lesser-known designers, and for
department and chain stores.

*New, stretchy man-
made fabrics were
the precursors of
today's Lycra and
offered easy care and
easy-to-wear clothes.*

*Dresses such as this
were inspired by
New York designer
Roy Halston, who
relied on fabric and
cut to make stylish
outfits for working
women. They may
appear simple, but
the techniques used
to design them were
anything but.*

*Fabrics such as this
were inspired by
the swirling
patterns of the Art
Nouveau movement
of the early 20th
century, which
became popular in
the 1970s.*

*Giovanozzi printed
stretch-jersey maxi
dress, 1970s,
£50–55*

*Screenprinted cotton
sleeveless T-shirt, 1970s.
£35–40*

*Pair of PVC trousers,
1990s.* **£40–45**

*Paul smith printed cotton
shirt, 1990s.
£50–55*

Handbags

Handbags have come a long way since the turn of the 20th century, when women were financially dependent on men and only needed small bags. Floral-patterned beadwork bags from this period – currently worth £100–200 in good condition – had metal clasps and chains. Metal mesh bags command similar prices, although you should expect to pay more for gold and silver. The American manufacturer Whiting & Davis has been making mesh bags from 1876. Its patterned bags from the 1930s can be valuable today. The firm's disco bags from the 1970s also have a firm following with collectors.

By the 1920s, with women smoking and using cosmetics, larger daytime bags became the norm. Bags from this time, whether made of cloth, leather or beadwork, were often decorated with Art Deco patterns.

In the 1930s, clutches – bags without handles – offered women interior divisions to organize their necessities. Standard clutches may be valued up to about £50 but those made of fine-quality materials, such as snakeskin, can fetch more, especially if the design is typically Art Deco.

During WWII, bag production was curtailed, and many were made using old clothes. In the 1950s, however, the novelty bag arrived. These ranged from wicker bags with felt fruit to rigid Lucite (a form of plastic) box-shaped bags in bright colours. Some of the names to look for from this era are Wilardy, Dorset Rex and Llewellyn.

In the 1960s and 1970s, tote and shoulder bags became practical alternatives to the briefcase – and many are valued at less than £50. Novelty examples may be decorated with painted, beaded or sequinned designs. The American designer Enid Collins made wooden box and cloth bags embellished with painting, faux jewels and sequins, popular on both sides of the Atlantic.

Gucci handbags and Prada rucksacks became status symbols in the world of business during the 1980s and 1990s, with women buying them to complete their expensive outfits. Today such bags sell for more than £80–100.

A Judith Lieber crystal-covered metal bag is a good example of a handmade evening bag and can command £1,000 or more. Lieber's bags were recently named the most wanted by American women.

Mass-produced bags inspired by designer classics – such as the quilted Chanel 2.55 – have been popular since the 1980s and will have many years' use left in them.

Handbag styles

Cut-steel evening bag, 1918.
£200–230

Bakelite clutch bag with stainless steel detail, 1920s.
£200–230

Leopard print handbag with Bakelite handle, 1940. **£165–185**

Wilardy Lucite handbag, 1950s.
£165–185

The one to look for

The name Hermès has been associated with glitzy, high-quality bags since the 19th century. The Hermès Kelly bag – named after movie star Grace Kelly – is possibly the most luxurious bag in the world, with originals fetching more than £2,000. Other Hermès bags may not be worth quite as much money but their timeless quality makes them a great buy.

Many designer bags are copied and even faked. Genuine bags usually have the maker's name stamped on the metalware and a reference number marked on the inside lining.

Hermès baby crocodile skin bag, 1960s. £1,350–1,500

Hermès bags are handmade from the finest materials. Look carefully for any wear, as this will affect value.

Basketweave bag, with appliquéd felt decoration, 1950s. £25–30

Plastic 'telephone coil' clutch bag, early 1960s. £75–85

Union Jack handbag, 1960s. £50–60

Suzy Smith Chanel-style padded leatherette handbag, 1980s. £25–30

Perfume bottles

The first specially designed commercial bottles for perfume emerged in the early 20th century. Before then, ladies had a number of decorative bottles with silver or glass stoppers that they took to a chemist for refilling. Both types are collectable. The value and

desirability of early bottles mostly depends on the design and maker. Bottles from Bohemian glassmakers are popular for their attractiveness and the quality of the designs, while bottles by great glassmakers such as Lalique and Boucheron are collected for their designer name as well.

The collectability of commercial 20th-century bottles depends largely on the maker and the rarity of the bottle or perfume. One famous example is L'Air du Temps by Nina Ricci; the bottle, designed by René Lalique's son Mark, features two doves representing love and peace (shown below). Classic perfumes such as Guerlain's Mitsouko (shown left) are also sought after, especially early bottles dating from the 1930s.

A bottle containing its original scent and with its original box is often worth more than an empty one.

Novelty perfume bottles

By the 1920s and '30s it had become acceptable for a woman to apply her make-up and perfume in public, rather than in the privacy of her own bedroom. The result was a plethora of novelty forms from a number of leading manufacturers. Among them was this range of teddy bears and monkeys from the German toy firm, Schuco. Designed for a lady's handbag, the heads of these little figures could be removed to reveal either a perfume bottle, a compact or a manicure set.

Mohair bell-hop chimp perfume bottle, 1920s. £135–150

Other bottles

Double overlay glass bottle, with brass top, 1880. £350–400

Oval-shaped glass perfume bottle, with silver top, 1880. £200–220

Heart-shaped cut-glass perfume bottle, with silver top, 1880. £225–275

Le Narcisse Bleu perfume bottle, 1920–1930. £85–95

The one to look for

Schiaparelli created a number of ground-breaking fragrances in the 1930s and '40s. Her fragrance Shocking is possibly the most famous and sought after by collectors. The box may be faded but the Shocking name is so popular with collectors that its condition does little to detract from the value.

The perfume bottle is in the shape of a dressmaker's dummy and inspired by the Surrealist movement.

This bottle is decorated with a bunch of flowers and sits on a pedestal. The pink box is lined with padded pink satin. This shade of pink – shocking pink – was created by Schiaparelli.

Shocking perfume by Elsa Schiaparelli, c1936. £155–175

Bohemian glass bottles

For centuries the glass makers of Bohemia, now eastern Germany, made some of the finest glass in the world. The perfume bottles that glassmakers created in the late 19th century are testimony to the proficiency and creativity of the craftsmen who made them. In many cases, layers of coloured and clear glass were cut into spectacular shapes and decorated with enamel and gilding. Values of these pieces today depend as much on the quality of the workmanship involved as the complexity of the design and the condition of the bottle.
Bohemian cased glass perfume bottle, 1890. £130–150

Elizabeth Arden Blue Grass perfume bottle, with box, c1934. £130–160

Enamelled crystal perfume bottle with silver rim, 1930s. £200–250

Green perfume bottle, 1950s. £120–150

Worth Je Reviens eau de cologne, bottle by Lalique, c1950s. £5–10

Powder compacts

It first became acceptable for women to apply make-up in public in the 1920s, after which time, compacts – small cases containing face powder and mirror – fast became fashion accessories.

Early examples are decorated in a typical Art Deco style. The 1930s were memorable for an upsurge in the production of compacts and most were made of silver plate, chrome plate or gold plate. By the 1950s compacts were larger and some could even play music. Coty, Kigu and Stratton are maker's marks worth looking for.

Compacts lost their allure in the 1970s, although recent limited editions by cosmetics' manufacturers such as Christian Dior, Estée Lauder and Yves Saint Laurent have proved popular.

Buy or Sell?

A compact in mint condition and with its original powder puff is always going to command a premium. The 1950s charm and quality of this Elgin compact decorated with an elegant Victorian boot set with garnets will have great appeal for collectors, especially as glass was usually used instead of semi-precious stones. Condition is very important – any wear will reduce value.

Brass and silver-plated compact, c1950. £120–140

Compacts compared

Faux guilloche and enamel compact, 1950s. £50–60

Enamel and paste compact, 1940s. £200–220

It is important to inspect the condition of enamel as it is difficult and costly to repair. If damaged the value of a piece is considerably reduced. Also, the compact above left may look enamelled but the metal base has simply been covered with plastic. The compact on the right is decorated with enamel and, as a result, is worth almost four times as much.

Other compacts

Celluloid and tin compact, 1920s. £150–165

Coty Airspun loose powder, 1913. £5–10

White metal, enamel and marcasite compact, 1920s. £60–70

Bakelite Chicago World Fair powder compact, 1939. £100–120

What to look for

The enamelled top features flamingos standing in a pool of water. The detailing of the wings and feathers and the ripples in the water all indicate high quality.

Gold, colour-enamelled compact by Stratton, c1950. £45–55

There is no obvious wear around the catch – a sign that this compact is likely to be in mint or near mint condition.

Good-quality compacts often contained more than just a mirror, powder and puff. This example also has an internal lid that separates the puff from the mirror to keep the latter free of smudges.

Manufacturers often marked their compacts on the inside rather than the outside. Look closely for maker's marks – or even hallmarks or the word 'Sterling', which suggest the piece is made from silver.

Evans gold enamelled powder compact, 1950s. £100–110

Enamelled and petit point powder compact, 1930s. £80–90

Kigu metal, faux pearl and diamanté powder compact, 1950s. £25–35

Kigu enamelled brass compact, 1950s. £45–55

Gents' accessories

While today's gentleman rarely leaves home without his car keys and mobile phone, 80 to 100 years ago the necessities of daily life were quite different. Cufflinks and tie or stick pin, lighter and fountain pen were all essential accessories that many men live without today.

Cufflinks may be solid gold or silver, or plated base metal. Plastic 1930s sets often came in novelty shapes such as dice, while in the 1960s metal and plastic cufflinks might be shaped as cars or bowling pins.

Those decorated with engravings or enamel – especially sets decorated with the four 'vices': drinking, gambling (horse racing or cards), smoking and women – are particularly sought after today.

Collectors might focus on a particular jeweller, such as Tiffany or Cartier, or on a style, such as Art Deco. While some finely made precious material items can be worth up to £1,000 or more, early 20th century gold-plated cufflinks that carried printed scenes under clear glass or plastic can be bought for anything from £10–50 depending on the quality of materials and scene.

Smoking items, such as lighters, matchboxes (vesta cases) and cigarette boxes have recently become popular with collectors while the habit they supported has fallen out of fashion.

Silver boxes might be engraved, embossed or decorated with enamel – look for everything from erotic scenes featuring scantily clad women to hunting scenes.

Portable lighters were made from the early 20th century and the most collectable were made by Dunhill. Sleek silver examples were common but – perhaps surprisingly – it is the novelty plastic 'Aquarium' lighters that command a premium. Look out for lighters with extra functions, such as a watch, which are always worth more than standard ones.

Fountain pens by names such as Montblanc, Parker and Waterman were first made in the early 1900s, although those from the 1920s–30s are particularly sought after. In all cases, check that the plastic is in good condition and that sets consisting of a pen and pencil match correctly. Metal overlaid pens, particularly those with engraved designs, are likely to be a good investment, although engraved initials or a name may reduce value.

The Parker 51 is highly sought after by collectors. But more recent pens, such as the Parker 75, which came in many versions – are also collected. Look for pens in mint condition in their original boxes.

Other accessories

Art Deco enamel and silver gilt cufflinks, c1930. £130–140

Celluloid and gilt cufflinks depicting greyhounds, c1930. £20–25

Ronson Mastercase chrome lighter and cigarette case, boxed, 1930s. £90–100

Trout fisherman's lighter, cufflinks and tie pin set, 1950s. £45–55

The one to look for

The Parker Vacumatic began life as the 'Vacuum-Filler' and was advertised as holding 102% more ink than other pens. It was launched in 1933 and was an immediate success. Parker continued to make the pen for 15 years.

Parker Vacumatic Maxima pen, 9ct-gold nib, 1939.
£270–300

The Vacumatic was made in a number of limited edition designs, including a Holy Water Sprinkler and a Doctor's set which included a thermometer case. The luxurious Imperial Vacumatics had solid gold or gold-plated caps.

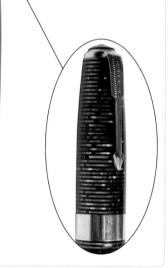

The original two-colour 9ct-gold nib is in excellent condition. It is engraved with Parker's new arrow trademark. This design was only made for a few years.

The amount of ink left in the pen could be seen through the transparent stripey barrel, which was made of a unique laminated plastic.

Dunhill silver classic lift-arm lighter, c1960s.
£220–250

Parker Victory Mark V pen, boxed, c1960.
£40–60

Silver-mounted tusk double cigar cutter by Sampson Mordan, c1910. £180–230

Enamelled tie stick pin, depicting a dog, signed WB Ford, 1872. £380–450

Luggage

Methods of travel have changed considerably over the decades and, so too, has the type of luggage required. Long gone are the days of The Grand Tour of the late 18th and early 19th centuries, when the wealthy had numerous servants to move the numerous, heavy boxes that contained their clothes and accessories as they travelled around Europe.

The coming of the railways meant that practical cases and carpet bags joined sturdy leather trunks as necessities of travel. Carpet bags were fashionable among ladies, who used them to carry their essential items.

Trunks – often specially fitted out to hold clothes on hangers and with all manner of compartments for hats, shoes and other accessories – were a feature well into the 1930s and epitomized the glamour of first-class travel by boat and the new aeroplanes.

Alongside these larger pieces of luggage, travellers needed a plethora of smaller pieces. Gentlemen's collars were separate from their shirts and required their own cases. The studs that held the collar to the shirt, and often fastened the shirt instead of buttons, also needed a storage box. Jewellery, hats and cosmetics all travelled in their own cases. Travelling writing sets contained bottles of ink as well as storage for pens and paper.

A lady's travelling case might hold glass bottles and a number of silver accoutrements including nail scissors, manicure sets, hair and clothes brushes and a mirror. Look out for sets with hallmarks or by known makers such as Asprey, which command a premium – more, if the contents of any given set are complete.

The popularity of the motor car and advent of package holidays meant that luggage needed to be easier to carry and store in the boot of a car or overhead locker in an aeroplane. Pieces from the 1950s and 1960s feature colourful leatherette on suitcases and vanity cases. These smaller pieces make useful handbags today.

Luggage by luxury makers such as Louis Vuitton, Tanner Krolle and Connolly command a premium among collectors. Vintage pieces by companies such as Samsonite may also prove a wise investment if they are typical of their era.

Leather top hat box by E. Goyard, 19thC. £550–650

Other luggage

Edwardian bucket leather hat box. £120–140

Crocodile suitcase with brass fittings, c1910. £250–300

Fitted leather vanity case, 1910. £50–60

Tanned leather collar box, 1920s. £35–45

The one to look for

In the late 1800s, Louis Vuitton designed the first stackable trunks – until then they had domed tops. By 1875 he was making fitted wardrobe trunks with a theft-proof lock that is still used by the firm today.

Canvas, leather and brass case by Louis Vuitton, c1920.
£2,000–2,500

Vuitton's bags are very good quality and some are still used today; others are used as decorative pieces. Special commissions, such as gun cases, were also made and can be valuable.

Picnic sets

From the early 20th century, and with the growth in popularity of the motor car, picnic sets became an essential part of a summer weekend. Originally made for just two people, they soon contained enough equipment for up to six to dine in style. Early examples are in wicker or leather; later ones are in leathercloth and, later, leather-look plastic. Contents may be china and glass or plastic, depending on age and quality. Makers to look out for include Drew, Mappin & Webb, Coracle, Brexton and Vickery.

Brexton Picnic case, retailed by Harrods, 1950s. £45–55

Black leather attaché case by Harrods of London, 1930s. £50–60

Lady's travelling vanity case, Mappin & Webb, c1941. £100–130

Pair of cowhide suitcases, England, 1950. £70–80

Red vinyl-coated vanity case, 1960s, £20–25

Jewellery

Jewellery has been worn as an adornment and as a display of wealth for many centuries. It has also been given as a token of love. Until the mid-19th century, however, only the very wealthy could afford precious and semi-precious metals and stones. This all changed in the mid- to late-19th century, with the growth of the middle classes. This, together with advances in technology – which allowed for mass production – and the discovery of silver and gold in North and South America, meant that beautiful jewellery became affordable for more and more people. Many of the pieces that were made during this time became treasured possessions and a good number of these jewels survive today.

Nineteenth-century bangle *Bangles were popular early in the 19th century when broad bands of gold and silver were decorated with precious stones and closed with decorative clasps. The advent of Bakelite in the 1920s and 1930s saw women wearing several colourful bangles at the same time. A late 19th-century fashion, revived in the 1930s, was wearing a snake or serpent bangle on the upper part of the arm.*

Victorian 15ct gold bangle set with half pearls.
£1,100–1,300

Sentimental brooch *The late 19th century saw a new fashion for sentiment, resulting in jewellery being imbued with romantic symbolism. Entwined hearts, flowers (which each had their own meaning), love birds, anchors (a symbol of hope) and cupids were common. Stones were also used to add meaning: a combination of ruby, emerald, garnet, amethyst, sapphire, diamond spelled out REGARD.*

Victorian gold, ruby and pearl locket brooch.
£900–1,000

Hardstone brooch *The 19th century saw a fascination for historical revival reflected in everything from furniture and architecture to jewellery. Brooches based on Iron Age originals set with Scottish hardstones such as agate and granite satisfied this interest and the enthusiasm for Scotland inspired by Queen Victoria's love of Balmoral.*

Streaky agate brooch in a brass and copper setting, 1920s. £40–45

Turquoise earrings In the 19th century earrings tended to be long and delicate to set off an elegant hairstyle and low-cut gown. Few of these survive intact because of their fragility. As 20th-century fashions changed, so did jewellery – with smaller, less fussy earrings which sat on the earlobe. Earrings from the mid-20th century are often pavé set with precious stones – this means dozens of tiny stones are set very closely together.

Pair of 15/18 ct gold and turquoise earrings, 1870–80. £1,000–1,100

Moonstone necklace Heavy, ornate necklaces were fashionable in the mid-19th century. They are not generally considered to be wearable today and so are less desirable than lockets and chains of the same era. Late-19th and early-20th century necklaces tend to be more fashionable and feature semi-precious stones such as opals, moonstones, peridot and garnets set in gold or silver. Look out for 'parures': a set with necklace, earrings and bracelet.

Edwardian moonstone necklace. £450–550

Cluster ring Rings have been used as tokens of betrothal and as symbols of status since ancient times. Cluster rings, set with a larger stone surrounded by a number of smaller ones, have been made since the mid-19th century. Other common styles include half-hoop rings set with a row of stones, and gypsy rings, containing two or three stones set flush with the metal.

Gold, opal and diamond ring, late 19thC. £650–800

Costume jewellery

Costume jewellery – pieces usually made from base metals and non-precious stones – has been popular for centuries. However, wearing fake jewels did not become fashionable until used by fashion designer Coco Chanel and the glamorous film stars of the 1930s.

Chanel saw jewellery as a means of decoration rather than a display of wealth, and her fake pearls and gilt chains helped to define the style of much 20th-century fashion jewellery. Meanwhile in Hollywood, both on and off the screen, stars such as Joan Crawford wore costume jewellery by the latest designers – a fashion their fans wanted to copy.

In America the Wall Street Crash resulted in a number of jewellers turning their backs on precious materials and designing with paste and crystals instead. Probably the most famous of these was Alfred Philippe who was head designer for costume jeweller Trifari from 1930 until his retirement in 1968. He had previously worked for prestigious firms such as Cartier and Van Cleef and Arpels and continued to create elegant jewellery for his new employers using high-quality Swarovski crystals. One of his masterpieces sold recently for £700.

Other companies making fashionable and affordable jewellery throughout the 1930s, 1940s and 1950s included Hobé, Coro (Corocraft), Joseff of Hollywood, Hattie Carnegie, Marcel Boucher, Vendôme and Weiss. Individual names to look out for include Elsa Schiaparelli, the flamboyant Italian designer who worked in Paris and New York, Frenchman Christian Dior and New Yorker Miriam Haskell.

The latter made exquisite handmade jewelley using fine gold wires to form extravagant, three-dimensional assemblies of beads and crystals. The detail in her jewellery is more important than when a piece dates from, with the best pieces worth £1,000 or more.

Costume jewellery from the 1960s and 1970s has gained popularity with collectors over recent years, particularly as prices for earlier pieces have risen significantly. Jewellery from these two decades remains affordable, with pieces by big names such as Dior and Trifari costing at least a third less than 1940s and 1950s examples. At the same time the value of a number of well-designed unsigned pieces has also risen, especially those that are typical of their period and of good quality.

Other pieces

Coro Duette Horse brooch, 1940s.
£225–250

Christian Dior paste choker and earrings 1950s. £270–300

Dior set of bead brooch and earrings 1967. £90–100

Miriam Haskell glass bead, faux pearl and paste bracelet, c1950. £300–325

The one to look for

Vendôme was renowned for its many innovative designs which were executed with quality materials and by skilled craftsmen. The name – taken from the Place de Vendôme in Paris, centre of the city's jewellery trade – was designed to bring French chic to post-war American women.

Vendôme paste necklace, 1950s. £250–270

The iridescent finish on the rhinestones is known as Aurora Borealis. The effect, named after the Northern Lights, is created using a metallic coating. Here, the stones have been prong-set in a silver-plated setting, which helps them to catch the light. The Vendôme label has been fixed to the back of the setting.

Miriam Haskell brooch set with faux pearls c1960. £220–250

Pair of Trifari Indian papier-mâché style earrings, 1937. £450–500

Trifari bracelet 1950s. £50–60

Pair of Vendôme paste flower earrings, 1960. £45–50

Bakelite & plastics

Bakelite proved the perfect material for fashionable jewellery in the 1920s and 1930s. As the streamlined, geometric, Art Deco look gained popularity brooches, bangles and necklaces made from the 'material of a thousand uses' were both chic and affordable. These pieces fell out of favour by the 1950s, but attitudes changed in 1988 when Andy Warhol's collection sold at Sotheby's, New York. Since then prices have risen and a number of pieces have become scarce.

Following the Wall Street Crash of 1929, many women could no longer buy precious jewellery. The new Bakelite pieces allowed them to buy the latest fashions at prices they could afford.

The material proved perfect for jewellery makers, as it could be made in a wide range of colours and could be moulded or cut into spectacular shapes. Typical colours include black, brown, red, yellow and white, often combined in one piece and/or embellished with rhinestones, brass or paint. Chrome settings are also typical of Art Deco examples.

Pieces made from clear plastic – Lucite – are highly collectable, as are those made to resemble tortoiseshell. Bright vibrant colours and innovative shapes are popular with collectors and tend to be worth more. Large bangles and novelty brooches – from Scottie dogs to bunches of cherries – command a premium.

Lea Stein

Parisian designer, Lea Stein, began making costume jewellery in 1969 using laminated layers of coloured rhodoid. This plastic can be cut and moulded into three-dimensional shapes. Created by her husband, this material could also be combined with metal elements and fabrics, such as lace, to seemingly limitless effect. Until 1981, Stein mostly made brooches, although bangles, rings and earrings can also be found. Favourite shapes included cats, dogs, birds, flowers and stylized native American chiefs and flapper girls. However, it is the fox pin that has become her signature piece. Although Stein stopped making jewellery in 1981, she started again in the late 1980s to meet demand from collectors. All pieces are marked 'Lea Stein Paris' and it can be hard to tell an early piece from a later one.

Cellulose acetate brooch, 1970s. £35–40

Other jewellery

Heat-set rhinestone hat flash/lapel brooch, 1920s–30s. £20–25

Bakelite bangle with carved decoration, 1930s. £115–125

Translucent marbled Bakelite necklace, 1930s. £100–110

Plastic, pearl and diamanté bangle, 1950. £80–90

The one to look for

In the 1920s and 1930s, plastic was a new and exciting product rather than the cheap, mass-produced material it is perceived as today. As a result, designers embellished plastic and Bakelite jewellery with hand carving and metal mounts. This rare chess-style piece, shaped as a bishop, is embellished with faux pearls and simulated onyx. It is part of a set that included a king, queen and knight.

Chess-style Bakelite clip brooch. £400–500

The deep cutting and angular features of the head and crown are typical of Art Deco Bakelite jewellery from the 1930s. The chain and pearls around the neck were fragile and at risk from wear or breaking. The fact they are intact adds to the value of the piece.

In the 1930s some jewellery designers turned to games for inspiration. Jewellery was made in the form of playing card kings and queens.

Bakelite dagger brooch, 1930s. £250–280

Gilt metal and plastic bead necklace, 1950s. £55–60

Bakelite multicoloured bangle, 1960s. £90–100

Cherry brooch, reproduction, 2006. £75–80

Pocket watches

Technological advances and the growing middle classes saw an increase in the number of watch factories during the 19th century, paving the way for the evolution of pocket watches. Before 1800, they were mainly used by members of court and wealthy merchants. Now, after 1800, the lower and middle classes could afford them and relied on them when working on the railways.

As well as a fundamental change in the class of owner, the start of the 19th century saw a change in the general construction of the pocket watch, which had remained largely unchanged since the late 17th century. Watches became slimmer and, by the mid-19th century, the keyless watch had been introduced, with winding as an inbuilt mechanism. By the 1870s, almost all pocket watches were keyless. Look out for decorative enamelled cases from this time, and novelty cases in the shape of violins, beetles, pistols and snuffboxes.

Many watches from the 19th century had several subsidiary dials, whereas before 1800 their most notable feature was the champlevé dial, which was made of metal inlaid with black wax.

A watch from this period may also have a hunting case or a half-hunting case. The former is a pocket watch with a solid flip lid and the latter is one where the flip lid has a viewing window. Another popular watch was open-faced, which had a glazed front and a hinged back cover.

Today, the most collectable watches are those with chronograph stopwatch mechanisms, repeating mechanisms, moonphases and calendars. Values lie in the quality and complexity of the movement, the materials used and the name of the maker. In Britain, Thomas Tompion and George Graham were among the most renowned makers, while France boasted Abraham-Louis Breguet and Vacheron & Constantin. Elsewhere, Swiss makers introduced innovative changes at the end of the 19th century, such as repeating mechanisms that sounded the hours, quarter hours, and sometimes also the minutes.

Expect to pay between £30 and £200 for standard pocket watches from the late 19th century to the early 20th century. Complicated and precision watches – often regarded as one-off pieces or scientific instruments – represent a striking contrast to the more standard, everyday pocket watches and are well worth adding to a collection.

Other pocket watches

Consular-cased verge pocket watch, John Ward, 1784–99.
£450–500

Gilt pair-cased verge pocket watch, c1790.
£1,800–1,950

Gilt verge hunter pocket watch by Delonra, London, c1800. **£630–700**

18ct gold pocket watch by John Taylor, London 1825. **£1,000–1,150**

The one to look for

Interesting very ornate pocket watches by prolific makers such as Waltham can offer good value for money. This example is an open-faced watch, the edges of the case engraved with flowers and a filigree design. The condition of this watch is exceptional – it still has the original glass and the original label in the back of the gold filled case. These are often lost or replaced.

Open face Waltham pocket watch, 1893. £350–400

The back of the case is engraved with a stag surrounded by a border of foliage. There is very little evidence of wear on the gold case. This pocket watch is an unusually ornate example from this maker.

The white porcelain dial has black Arabic numerals, a subsidiary seconds dial and blued steel hands. Inside, the gilt keyless wind movement appears to be in excellent condition – as good as new.

18ct-gold cylinder
pocket watch
by Robert Whatley,
1828. £1,250–1,350

18ct gold half-hunter
pocket watch
by Robert Webster,
1859. £1,250–1,350

Early 20th century
pocket watch.
£225–275

14ct gold Omega
pocket watch,
c1940. £300–330

Wristwatches

The early 20th century saw a boom in the manufacture of wristwatches, as both traditional clock and pocket-watch makers and new companies fed a growing market. Among these companies a handful have become synonymous with luxury and include Rolex, Omega, Patek Philippe, Longines and Piguet. Such is their prestige – new or vintage – that their value is high and fakes are common. Get to know the 'real thing' before gambling on a bargain that looks too good to be true.

The brand, movement, materials and functions of a watch help to indicate its value so inspect these closely. Within a brand certain 'iconic' models are more desirable, such as Cartier's 'Tank'. The quality of the movement is important, and should be correct for the watch. While the metal of the watchcase and its bracelet should be considered, most of the value of a watch lies in its movement – the more complex the mechanism, the more valuable the watch is likely to be.

Unfortunately, the value of gold and silver cases is often limited to their scrap value, platinum cases are particularly sought after. Ladies' gem-set watches are viewed as items of jewellery in their own right and their value should be estimated accordingly.

Association with events and famous people can also increase value and collectability. Military wristwatches are a popular area of collecting, particularly if those designed by eminent makers like Longines, I.W.C. and Omega. The backs of such watches usually have marks that identify for whom they were made. For example, an arrow was used on watches made for the British Ministry of Defence during and after WWII.

Watches featured in films are also very collectable. James Bond, in particular, has helped popularize many watches, including the Rolex Submariner, whose standard models can fetch £3,500–5,500, and the Omega Seamaster, whose standard models from the 1960s and 1970s can fetch between £100 and £500. Another well-known Omega model is the Speedmaster, the official watch of NASA, worn by astronauts like Edward White and Neil Armstrong.

Look out, too, for Rolex Oyster watches, with the world's first waterproof case. Be sure to have any waterproofing checked, as serious damage can occur if the watch is worn in water without its proper sealing.

Also, whichever watch you buy, remember that its sales material, with any details of restoration work, always add value.

Other wristwatches

Very rare Omega Waterproof wristwatch, c1945.
£1,500–1,650

Omega Seamaster automatic wristwatch, 1950s.
£230–250

Steel Jaeger le Coultre reverso wristwatch, late 1940s. £1,800–2,200

Omega De Ville Gentleman's Wristwatch, c1970.
£380–460

The one to look for

Rolex designed the Oyster – the world's first water-resistant watch – in 1927. It had a screwed-down back and winding crown and the cushion shape was typical of the fashionable designs of the time. However, don't expect a vintage example to have the water resistance of a new one.

Rolex 9ct-gold cushion-shaped Oyster wristwatch, 1930s. £2,200–2,450

Check inside the case for the quality of the gold: the watch was made in a number of metals. The case on this example bears British import marks, showing the gold case met British hallmarking standards. It is also numbered, which can help with dating.

Oyster Royal stainless-steel wristwatch, 1930s. £250–300

Longines 9ct-gold wristwatch with seconds dial, 1930. £1,100–1,200

Longines waterproof wristwatch, c1943. £1,800–2,000

Waltham wristwatch, c1930. £1,000–1,250

Wristwatches

If you like the look of vintage watches but don't want to pay the price of prestige examples, watches by well-known makers from the 1930s to 1960s can start from as little as £50. The style of watch can help with dating, but vintage styles are popular with modern makers, so always check carefully. As a general rule, small, round 'pocket watch' shapes with wire lugs are usually early 20th century. Rectangular watches, or simple circular watches with clean-lined designs usually date from the 1930s. From the late 1940s onwards, watches became highly stylized and more innovative in shape, often taking on the styles of contemporary jewellery.

Watches from the 1950s are amongst the most popular today owing to their simple, yet classic styling. Fine-quality watches by names such as Rolex or Longines can often be found at lower prices than contemporary examples, sometimes even in precious metals. 1960s–1970s watches are particularly in vogue at present. Cases tend to be large and heavy, with futuristic designs in coloured plastic and stainless steel. Check the dial carefully, as it may have been replaced.

A calendar mechanism with a moon-phase indicator can add to value. For example, one of only three platinum-cased calendar, moon-phase watches ever made by Patek Philippe of Geneva – which had cost £180 in 1933 – sold for a record price at auction in 1990.

The style of the case and other factors can affect price. A Buler wind-up wristwatch – its face shaped like a TV – can fetch £70–100. A Vulcain lady's wristwatch, on a gold-plated bracelet with its original tag, can command £50-80.

Hamilton designed the first digital watch in 1970. Early ones had light-emitting diode (LED) displays, which needed a lot of power, and so the screens only lit up at the push of a button. The numbers became permanently visible with the introduction in 1972 of the liquid-crystal display (LCD).

The majority of digital watches keep time by sending an electric current through quartz crystals. Examples made in Japan tend to be inexpensive and accurate, and have dominated the market for years. It can be hard to locate original batteries to fit vintage digital watches, although modern equivalents are usually available.

A final word of warning when buying any digital watch is always to check that it is in good working order and that there is no sign of battery leakage.

Other wristwatches

Hamilton Deco-style gold wristwatch, 1930s. £150–180

Casio SA-70, 1980s. £120–130

Citizen LCD Digital Watch, c1983. £45–50

18ct gold Ingenieur IWC wristwatch, c1959. £3,500–3,850

The one to look for

From the late 1970s, digital watches were sometimes combined with other features, such as calculators. Seiko's speaking watch, from the late 1980s, is a classic of the form: push the button and a female voice tells you the time. The speaker grille takes up the majority of the watch face, with the time and 'speak' button tucked away at the base. The watch also had an alarm and chime feature and advanced models allowed the wearer to choose the language it 'spoke' in.

These multi-function watches are particularly evocative of the period and eagerly collected by many.

Speaking Watch by Seiko, c1988.
£135–150

Swatch watches

The first 12 Swatch watches were launched in 1983 as a fun, inexpensive range of watches in plastic cases. Such was their success that within a year over one million had been produced. Today, the most sought-after Swatches are those conceived by fashion designers and artists such as Keith Haring, Kiki Picasso, Vivienne Westwood and Christian Lacroix.

18ct Le Coultre wristwatch with backwind, c1930.
£5,550

LED wristwatch, c1974. £25–30

Seiko RC-4000 wristwatch, 1985. £85–90

Jaeger-Le-Coultre Automatic 9ct gold wristwatch, c1970. £280–340

DON

TH
S
BUSIN

his prov

encount

Books & Comics

Collecting modern day literary first editions or comics can become incredibly addictive. Books signed by the author, first editions and early comics in good condition will always find a ready market among enthusiasts who have a particular affinity with an author or character. Film and TV adaptations can also generate huge interest.

My advice to the novice would be to start by building up a collection of authors or genres that you enjoy, regardless of the current collecting trends. You never know, they may well prove to be a good long-term investment.

The American writer and poet David McCord once wrote: 'Books fall open, you fall in'. Although he was referring to books in general and the lure of reading, it is also true of book collecting. The beauty of books is that they potentially appeal to everyone. Non-fiction, for example, offers everything from cookery books with exotic recipes to gardening books that tell us how plants were nurtured without the benefit of modern technology. Travel books cannot fail to fascinate with their vivid accounts of places as they were in days gone by.

Comics have long been the poor relation of books, but they are now recognized for their worth as documents of social history as well as for the skill of

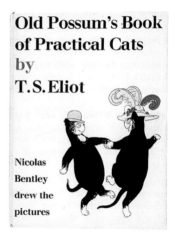

T. S. Eliot, *Old Possum's Book of Practical Cats, 1st ed, 1940. £700–850*

copies of *Wuthering Heights* in different languages, including Icelandic and Japanese. Paperbacks have been largely ignored until recently, because they were cheap, but certain paperback editions from the 1950s and '60s are now collectable. 'Pulp fiction' crime novels constitute a niche market.

Whatever you collect, there is a need for some kind of focus to avoid a random and incoherent jumble. With comics, it is technically possible to amass a continuous run of issues from the very first to the present day; with some titles, this will obviously be more difficult – and expensive – than others. For a

A Sugar Smacks promotional Superman comic. 1955 £50-80

their illustrators and writers.

One thing that should be borne in mind is that the vast majority of both books and comics, even if old, will be worth very little. Only the rare, unusual and interesting titles are valuable, and finding such a gem is the dream of every collector.

How to collect

Books are often collected by subject, but also collected by author, so you could aim for a first edition of each of your favourite author's works. One Emily Brontë fan has amassed

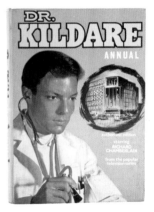

Dr. Kildare Annual, *by Dell Publishing, 1962.* £5–10

slightly broader collection, you might want to focus on a character, since some appeared in more than one publication. Artists and book illustrators also have a following and you may wish to augment your collection with an example of original artwork.

Where to collect
Antiques centres, fairs, markets, auctions and car boot sales are all good sources. Specialist book fairs are excellent places to go, not only to buy, but also to meet dealers. They are very useful contacts and you can enlist them to help you track down any specific volumes you may be looking for. Remember, these people do this for a living, so use their expertise.

For comics and annuals it is hard to beat the specialist fairs that are devoted to comics. There are also fairs dedicated to cult TV and science fiction memorabilia which should not be overlooked, as these events usually feature a good selection. Also, don't overlook your local charity shop. These days you are unlikely to find an unnoticed treasure there, since so many now use local dealers or auctioneers to 'screen' donated stock, but you might fill a gap in your collection of annuals.

Storage
Because they are made of paper, books and comics are naturally fragile. Their greatest enemies are strong light and damp, which can encourage mildew and

'foxing', which appears as brown spots on pages. Ordinary bookshelves are fine for storing all but the oldest and rarest of books, which need special attention.

Star Wars comic, No. 1, by Marvel, 1 July 1978. £15–20

Never pack books tightly onto shelves, and never remove them by pulling them out from the top of the spine – this is a common cause of damage.

Make sure your hands are clean when handling books, as grease marks can cause damage. When handling old and delicate volumes it is a good idea to wear cotton gloves. Comics should be stored in a cool, dark place. Ordinary cardboard boxes are not recommended as they may contain acids that will react with the paper. Similarly, plastic bags may contain harmful elements. Special acid-free comic storage boxes and bags are available; Mylar is the trade name of a plastic that is widely used.

Agatha Christie, By the Pricking of My Thumbs, 1st ed, 1968. £2,000–2,400

Children's books

It is not easy to find children's books in really good condition, and it is not difficult to see why. They were read with sticky fingers by their young owners, who coloured in illustrations, wrote their names inside and occasionally fought over them with siblings. Consequently, examples in mint or near mint condition are prized.

Some authors are more desirable than others. Beatrix Potter's books are always collectable, especially with their original glassine covers – glassine is a waxy paper, similar to greaseproof paper. A. A. Milne, Dr Seuss, Enid Blyton and books such as *Babar the Elephant* with attractive illustrations are also popular. Roald Dahl is another collectable name and the *Biggles* books by Captain W. E. Johns continue to surprise critics who believe interest in his books should be in decline by now. First editions of works by contemporary authors such as Philip Pullman and Lemony Snicket are certainly well worth considering.

Sometimes, books are as important for their illustrations, and works illustrated by big names such as Arthur Rackham are prized. Modern illustrators are not yet achieving top prices, although original artwork by Quentin Blake does well in the salerooms and galleries. Well illustrated volumes in good condition will always be saleable.

Film and TV tie-ins are always interesting and likely to attract fans of the film or show. It can be worth buying first editions of recent books that you feel are likely to be made into films. This is rather a gamble but pays off handsomely if you can spot the next *Harry Potter*. Be aware that interest in such books can fluctuate with the popularity of the film or TV shows.

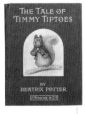

JONTY'S CHOICE

First editions of Beatrix Potter's books are extremely rare and difficult to spot. Dark brown boards and a small dot inside the letter O on the front cover are two ways to identify first editions.
If a date is printed inside the book or on the dust jacket it will be a later edition.

Beatrix Potter, The Tale of Timmy Tiptoes, *1st ed*, *1911*.
£100–150

Popular authors

Enid Blyton, Five Have Plenty of Fun, *1967*.
£10–15

Richmal Crompton, William the Detective, *1967*.
£15–20

Roald Dahl, James and the Giant Peach, *1st ed, 1973*.
£20–25

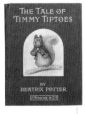

C. S. Lewis, The Lion, the Witch and the Wardrobe, *1st ed*, *1950*. *£5,000–6,000*

The one to look for

The Dr Seuss books are fondly remembered by adults and are still good sellers today. In recent years, both *How the Grinch Stole Christmas* and *The Cat in the Hat* were made into films, thus stimulating interest and values. A new film based on *Horton Hears a Who* is to be released in 2008.

Dr Seuss is the pen name of Theodor Seuss Geisel. As well as being a first edition, this book has its original dust jacket and it is signed by the author. An author's signature will always add value. Almost all Dr Seuss books were initially printed in New York, so a first edition should state this.

Dr Seuss, How the Grinch Stole Christmas, signed, 1st ed, 1957. **£1,800–2,200**

Ladybird books

Ladybird books, the pocket-sized books for children, first appeared in 1940 and were an immediate success. Pre-1960 volumes are the most sought after, but editions from the 1960s and '70s with illustrations by Martin Aitchison, who also worked on *Eagle* comic, are very popular.
Left: Read and Write, 1965. **£20–25**
Right: London, 1961. **£20–25**

A. A. Milne, The House at Pooh Corner, *1st ed, 1928.* **£1,500–2,000**

David Pelham, A Piece of Cake, *pop-up book, 1998.* **£15–20**

Philip Pullman, Count Karlstein, *signed, 1st ed, 1986.* **£40–50**

J. K. Rowling, Harry Potter, *boxed set of first four books,* 2001. **£15–20**

Annuals

Most of us remember receiving an annual for Christmas, based on a favourite comic, TV show or character. By definition, annuals are easy to date, as they were timed for the seasonal market and generally published in the autumn before the year on the cover.

Annuals are something of a specialist market and tend to be looked down upon by some mainstream book collectors, although attitudes are beginning to change. Of course, the fact that annuals are not taken as seriously as they might be means there can be real bargains to be had. At auctions, you will often find several annuals being sold together as one lot and there may be some gems among them.

Collectors look for good, clean copies but, as with many children's books, they are hard to come by. Damage is common, particularly to the spine which is a vulnerable area, and the corners of the cover. Another problem is that annuals were made to be used, so they frequently included crosswords and other puzzles that are likely to have been completed by their young owners. Ideally, the puzzles should not have been filled in but, if they have, it may not matter too much if the annual is especially rare or unusual.

Annuals often had their price printed in a corner of one of the inside pages. As they were intended as gifts, the price could easily be cut off without any serious damage to the book. Unfortunately, this is regarded as damage by collectors and will affect the value. Collectors refer to such books as 'price clipped'. Unclipped examples will always be more desirable.

Many annuals were designed as TV or film tie-ins, so their popularity and therefore value can vary according to that of the character, series or programme featured. Among the most collectable are annuals relating to the TV shows of Gerry Anderson, whose productions included *Thunderbirds*, *Stingray* and *Captain Scarlet*. Annuals from Gerry Anderson's early productions, such as *Four Feather Falls*, a puppet Western series first shown in 1960, are rare.

Some annuals are perennials in the sense that they always seem to find a ready market. A good example is that of the *Eagle* annuals of the 1950s and, of course, the *Rupert Bear* annuals. There is certainly public interest in old annuals, hence the success of facsimile editions of classics such as *The Beano* and *Oor Wullie* in recent years.

Other annuals

Blackie's Children's Annual, *1923*. £20–25

Mickey Mouse Annual, *1948*. £40–45

Bonzo's Annual, *1952*. £45–50

Young Marvelman Annual, *No. 1*, *1954*. £50–60

The one to look for

Rupert Bear was created by Mary Tourtel. He first appeared in the *Daily Express* in 1920 and continues to do so today. Rupert annuals, which first appeared in 1936, are still published. For collectors, the pre-1960 examples are the most desirable.

Rupert Annual, *published by the* Daily Express, *1949.* *£130–150*

When failing eyesight forced Mary Tourtel to retire as Rupert's illustrator in 1935, Alfred Bestall took over and continued on the newspaper strips until 1965 and for several years after that on the annuals. Bestall's work is much admired by aficionados.

Stingray Annual, 1966. £10–15

Z-Cars Annual, 1968. £10–15

The Dalek Pocket Book *and* Dr Who Annual, *1970s.* £25–30

Pinky and Perky Annual, *1974.* £5–10

First editions

There has been something of a boom in collecting first editions in recent years, with modern first editions by authors such as Agatha Christie, Ian Fleming, John Le Carré, Virginia Woolf and Graham Greene leading the way. A 'modern first edition' in this context is one from the 20th and 21st centuries. Generally speaking, for a book to be collectable it should be a first edition, unless there are exceptional circumstances.

Strictly speaking, a first edition is the first impression (print run) of the book. If it is a subsequent printing it should say so on the title page or title verso. In order to achieve maximum value, condition is important, as is the presence and condition of the dust jacket. Not so long ago, dust jackets were routinely thrown away when damaged, so it is not always easy to find books that still have them.

Many modern first editions are not that rare in themselves, so it is always worth looking out for anything that makes a book special. Signed copies, or books that have been owned by someone or associated with the author such as a family member or colleague.

It is a good idea to buy books that you enjoy reading, and perhaps start by limiting your collecting to a particular field such as crime, science fiction or travel. Books by contemporary authors such as Terry Pratchett, Sebastian Faulks and Ian McEwan are also worth considering and likely to remain collectable for the forseeable future.

Film tie-ins

Books that have been made into films attract film buffs as well as book collectors. Graham Greene is collectable in his own right but several of his books have been filmed, twice in the case of *The Quiet American*. Truman Capote's *Breakfast at Tiffany's* is actually better known as the film starring Audrey Hepburn.

Graham Greene, The Quiet American, *1955. £750–850*

Truman Capote, Breakfast at Tiffany's, *1958. £325–375*

Other authors

Julian Barnes,
Flaubert's Parrot,
1984.
£250–300

H. E. Bates,
The Flying Goat,
1939.
£200–250

Agatha Christie,
The Adventure of the
Christmas Pudding,
1960. £30–40

Seamus Heaney,
Door into the Dark,
1969.
£250–300

The one to look for

First editions of Ian Fleming's novels are always popular, thanks to the global appeal of his most famous character, James Bond. Over the years the various films have helped to keep interest in the books alive.

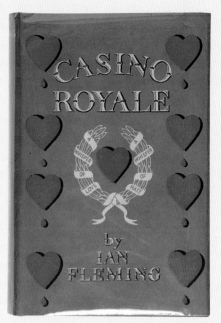

This first edition of Casino Royale *is complete with its dust jacket. As the first ever Bond novel it has obvious appeal, and the recent film starring Daniel Craig also helps to sustain interest.*

Ian Fleming, Casino Royale, *1953.*
£11,500–12,500

Thomas Keneally, Schindler's Ark, *1982. £40–45*

Sebastian Faulks, Charlotte Gray, *1998. £20–25*

Ian McEwan, Atonement, *signed, 2001. £100–135*

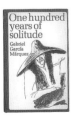

Gabriel Garcia Márquez, One Hundred Years of Solitude, *1970. £200–250*

Ian Rankin, The Flood, *signed, 1986. £500–550*

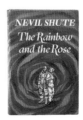

Nevil Shute, The Rainbow and the Rose, *1958. £35–40*

John Steinbeck, The Winter of Our Discontent, *1961. £100–130*

Cookery & travel books

Cookery books and travel books constitute specialist markets, but both have a large following. These two subjects are among the most popular and collected of specialist books. As with most books, a first edition is particularly desirable and, although collectors are very particular, they are prepared to pay for a book in pristine condition. First editions of the oldest travel books, especially if they are well illustrated with maps or engraved plates, such as the two volumes by Captain Franklin shown below, can fetch large sums. However, there is still a lot of interesting material from the late 19th and early 20th centuries that remains well within the reach of the average collector.

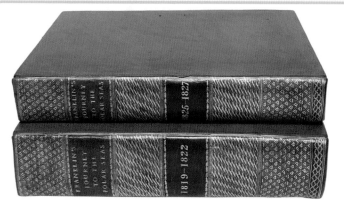

Travel Above: Captain Franklin was a polar explorer who mapped much of the northern coastline of North America. This is a contemporary account of his first expedition in 1819 and the second in 1823.
Captain John Franklin, Franklin's Journey to the Polar Seas, 1st ed, 1823 and 1824, 2 vols. £5,500–6,000

Right: The Baedeker guides are probably the best known of all travel guides. They are very collectable, especially the 19th- century volumes.
Baedeker's Rhine, 1892. £25–30

Left: Travel books don't have to be very old to be valuable. This was Chatwin's first book and is hailed as a landmark in travel writing. For many critics his style, which weaves historical information and anecdotes into the story of his travels in Patagonia, succeeded in redefining the travel writing genre.

Bruce Chatwin, In Patagonia, 1st ed, 1977. £250–300

Cookery Below: Mrs. Beeton's Book of Household Management was first published in 1861 as an indispensable guide to all aspects of running a household. It includes advice on etiquette, dinner parties and employing servants. Good copies are not easy to come by, partly because they were so prized that they were handed down through generations. This edition was published by Ward Lock, who took over publication from the author's husband, Samuel Orchard Beeton.

Mrs Isabella Beeton, *Mrs Beeton's Household Management*, c1930. £145–160

Above: This book was published in the United States, although guides to cooking and running a home became popular on both sides of the Atlantic during the 19th century. It contains recipes and advice on home management, promising 'the best results with the least expenditure of time and money'.
Virginia E. James, *Mother James' Key to Good Cooking*, 1892. £30–40

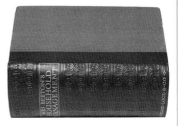

Right: World War II is a popular era with collectors of cookery books. This is partly because nostalgia for the period is still strong, but it is also because the books themselves were so inventive, creating ingenious, nutritious recipes that minimized waste. This copy of *Cooking on a Ration, or Food Is Still Fun* was published in the United States in 1943. Its author, Marjorie Mills, was a very well-known newspaper columnist and radio personality in New England.

Marjorie Mills, *Cooking on a Ration, or Food Is Still Fun*, 1943. £25–30

British comics

Comics have entertained children for more than 130 years. In Britain, early comics such as *Funny Folks* from 1874, and *Magnet* and *Gem*, which appeared around the turn of the 20th century, were followed by such titles as *Wizard* and *Hotspur* in the 1920s.

In the 1930s, the most famous of all British comics, *The Dandy* and *The Beano*, appeared. Later collectable titles include the *Eagle* from the 1950s and *The Victor*, launched in 1961. Names to look out for in girls' comics include *Bunty* and *Jackie*, currently enjoying a nostalgic vogue.

While these titles do have a following, do remember that most old comics are worth very little. Special editions, such as a first ever issue, and those that came with a free gift and still have it, are more likely to be collectable and command the highest prices. Discerning collectors also look for good examples with bright, strong colours.

Comics rarely survive in good condition, partly because they were roughly handled by their readers. They were also disposable as most children simply threw them away when they had finished reading them.

The Beano compared

The Beano, *No 36, 1930.* £100–120

The Beano, *No. 74: Xmas Number, 1939.* £300–330

Pre-war Beanos are generally the most collectable, not least because so many went for paper recycling during the war. The comic on the right is worth more than the one on the left because it is the Christmas 1939 edition, and collectors generally like special seasonal and landmark issues.

Other comics

The Beezer, *with free gift, 1958.*
£15–20

Buster, *No. 1, with free gift, 1960.*
£60–70

The Dandy, *No. 2, 1937.*
£800–850

Giggle, *No. 1, with free gift, 1967.*
£35–40

The one to look for

The Victor comic for boys was published by DC Thomson of Dundee, who also published *The Beano* and *The Dandy*. It was launched in January 1961 and ran for 31 years, carrying a mix of adventure and war stories. Many comics came with free gifts, especially the first edition and, if present, value can be enhanced by up to five times.

The Victor, *No. 1, with free gift, 1961.*
£85–95

Jackie, *with free gift, 1968.*
£5–10

Mandy, *No. 1, with free gift, 1967.*
£65–75

The Topper, *No. 4, 1953.*
£20–25

Wizard, *No. 4, 1953.*
£5–10

US comics

American comics are almost synonymous with the superhero, as this has been the dominant comic genre in America. Collectors divide US comics into three distinct 'ages'. While the exact chronological boundaries are a matter of debate, the Golden Age is generally considered to be from the late 1930s, the Silver Age from 1956 to 1969 and the Bronze Age from the early 1970s to the mid-1980s. Some authorities refer to a Platinum Age, before 1938, but such comics are so rare that they are not readily accessible to collectors.

In practice, most collectors start with Silver Age comics, as they are easier to come by than those of the Golden Age. Collectors often focus on favourite characters, such as Batman and Superman (both of them starting in the late 1930s) or Spiderman, whose stock has risen thanks to recent film adaptations.

The big names in US comics are DC (Detective Comics), who published *Superman* and *Batman*, and Marvel, who gave us such characters as Hulk, Spiderman, Daredevil and Silver Surfer.

As well as characters, collectors follow particular comic book artists. Comics illustrated by Steve Ditko and Jack Kirby are especially admired.

Iron Man

Tales of Suspense, *No 39*, 1963. *£350–450*

The Avengers, *No 1*, 1963. *£750–850*

Ultimate Iron Man, *No. 1*, 2005. *£1–5*

Iron Man, the alter ego of industrialist Tony Stark, made his debut in 1963 and first appeared in *Tales of Suspense*. His armour was initially grey; a golden look was adopted for his second story, and the familiar red and gold appeared in December 1963. In September 1963, he appeared in the first *Avengers* comic, as part of a superhero team. An Iron Man film is due for release in 2008.

Other comics

The Vault of Horror, *publisher's file copy*, 1952. *£850–950*

The Amazing Spider-Man, *No. 2*, 1963. *£600–700*

Daredevil, *No. 1*, 1964. *£600–700*

Batman, *No. 199*, 1967. *£5–10*

The one to look for

The Fantastic Four debuted in 1961 and gained their superpowers by accident after being exposed to radiation during the test flight of a new spacecraft. They decide to use their new found powers to protect the Earth from threats that are beyond the abilities of conventional armed forces. The characters are among the most popular of the Silver Age heroes and this first issue of the comic is especially sought after.

Fantastic Four, *by Marvel Comics, No 1, 1961.* £700–800

Transmetropolitan, *2002.*
£1–5

Giant-Size X-Men, *No. 1, 1974.*
£1,200–1,400

V For Vendetta, *Vol. 1, 1988.*
£5–10

Superman, *1993.*
£1–5

Coins, Medals & Ephemera

Most people have all sorts of bits and pieces languishing in the back of a cupboard; old coins, for example, that were once in daily use but are now obsolete, and medals that honoured the gallant men and women of the two World Wars.

Ephemera such as autographs of famous people, along with memorabilia connected with brands such as Guinness – remember the Toucan? – and Coca-Cola all have a market. Check them out before selling them off cheaply at the next car boot fair as they might just be worth more than you think.

Coins, medals and ephemera make very personal collectables. Coins have been used every day and carried in the pockets of millions of people for thousands of years. They are valued, and yet commonplace. Medals are very personal reminders of participation in conflicts that have become a part of history. Ephemera, which has been defined as 'those minor transient documents of everyday life', is a huge and varied field, ranging from autographs to packaging.

Huntley & Palmer's Showman biscuit tin, c1893.
£220–250

the finest creative minds to promote their products. Perhaps this is why so many collectors focus on these famous brands today.

The world of advertising has given us many memorable images, not to mention slogans and catchphrases. Advertising signs and posters were for many years just a part of the background of everyday life and few people thought to collect them; yet they were designed to provoke a personal response, if only that of buying the products.

The people behind such famous products as Coca-Cola and Guinness were particularly inventive and employed some of

Starting a collection

A good way to start a collection is simply to ask around the family. Most families will have had one or more members that have seen military service within living memory. Although many medals are not likely to be worth much they will have value as part of your family history, and this will be of interest to collectors. If you decide to sell your medals, include related material, including photographs of the recipient in uniform.

Most families will also have a bag of old coins, even if it is just a matter of a few foreign coins from a holiday. They are not likely to be worth anything, but always check very carefully before disposing of them, just in case. It is also worth taking them to an auctioneer or specialist dealer, who will be able to spot anything unusual or significant.

As far as packaging is concerned, items that are connected with another collectable, such as a character or a popular product like Coca-Cola, are more likely to have been spared the dustbin than the packaging of a more mundane product. However, it is surprising how many interesting items can emerge from the back of granny's larder.

If you should be lucky enough

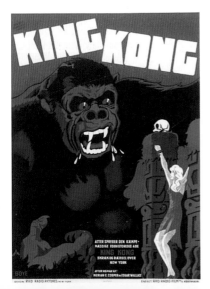

Poster for King Kong, *1948.*
£750–850

Coca-Cola advertising sign, 1934.
£115–135

to inherit a family member's collection of autographs, you will probably know the history of how they were obtained. Unfortunately, autographs have been widely faked, so this is one area where you really need to do your homework if you are buying. Signed photographs are always more interesting than signatures in a book, and they are also better for display purposes; other items of memorabilia signed by a star can provide added interest.

The need to focus

Some of the fields included in this section are so wide ranging that the choice is bewildering. You can start with a broader approach until you get a better feel for the subject, but it really is desirable to focus on one area. For instance, with posters, one might choose the work of a particular designer, or go for a specific theme, such as travel. It is then possible to focus on a particular country, a mode of transport (rail, ships, aircraft, motoring), or another theme, such as skiing, which is especially popular at the moment. Even if you start out with a broadly-based collection, it is likely that you will begin to specialize as you learn more about the subject and your interests develop.

Most collectors of coins prefer to focus on a period. There are further specializations, such as ancient coins, but most people will narrow their collecting to the reign of a particular ruler. Others collect by country, by monarch, or as many variants of a given denomination as possible. In the case of medals, specific conflicts provide an obvious starting point, although WWI and WWII involved such a vast number of people, and so many medals were issued, that most are worth very little. This does, of course, mean that medals issued during the two World Wars are readily available for a reasonable price. As with all collections, you should start off in a small way and build as your knowledge improves and you feel able to commit more time and money to your hobby.

Lifebuoy Health Soap box, 1950s.
£1–5

Coins

Not everything that is old is valuable, and this is as true of coins as anything else. Ancient Roman coins that are 2,000 years old may be worth very little, especially if they are of a base metal. One of the reasons for this is that coins were usually made in large numbers, were very durable and were rarely thrown away.

Early coins were worth the value of the gold, silver or copper they were made from, and many old coins are still only worth their bullion weight; they must be special to be worth any more.

Because silver coins were actually made of silver, 'clipping' was widespread – part of the edge of a coin was trimmed off

and melted down. In 1662, coins with a milled edge were introduced to discourage this.

Collectors grade coins according to wear, and any scratches or dents will detract from value. Sometimes, coins are used for making jewellery and the resulting damage, such as drilled holes, will seriously affect a coin's value.

It is worth noting that coins have been faked since ancient times, and that it takes an expert to spot fakes in most cases. Modern reproductions are different, and are fairly obvious. Coins should be handled as little as possible, and should never be polished or cleaned.

Pennies compared

Copper Elizabeth II one penny coin, not issued for circulation, 1970. **£10**

George VI one penny coin, 1950. **£20**

While condition is generally considered of paramount importance, other factors can be even more significant in determining the value of a coin. The penny on the left dates from 1970, the last year before decimal coinage was introduced in Britain and is uncirculated. It is collectible and worth about £10, but the 1950 penny on the right is worth twice as much, the reason being that only about 240,000 of these coins were minted.

Other coins

Roman bronze sestertius coin, Antonius Pius, AD 146. **£120–140**

Henry VIII groat, 1544–47. **£350–400**

French 40-franc gold coin, 1817. **£140–160**

Empire Tientsin dragon dollar, Chinese, year 3, 1911. **£150–180**

The one to look for

The brass 12-sided 'threepenny bit' was introduced in Britain
in the 1930s because of the growing unpopularity of the small
and fiddly silver threepenny coin. The 'brass' was actually an
alloy of mostly copper, with 20% zinc and 1% nickel.

*George VI
threepenny coin,
1949. £5–10*

*George VI threepenny
coin, 1937. £135–150*

*The inscription on the coin changed slightly after 1947, with
India's independence. It no longer declared George VI to be
Emperor of India, so the letters 'IND IMP', which denoted this
title, were removed. Early coins with the letters are more valuable.*

*The design of the 1937 coin shown on the right continued until
1949, although during WWII the shape changed slightly in that the
corners became rounded. The 1949 issue continued until the King's
death in 1952.*

*Ten Korono coin,
Hungary, 1912.
£30–35*

*US silver 'Peace' $1
coin, 1928.
£650–750*

*Lincoln one cent
coin, 2000.
£580–700*

*Library of Congress
$10 coin, 2000, one
of only 12.
£1,900–2,300*

Banknotes

The Chinese were the first to use paper money, in the 7th century, but it did not reach Europe for another thousand years. The first fully printed notes appeared in Britain in 1855. Before then, cashiers filled in the payee's name and signed each note individually.

Collecting banknotes only became a serious hobby from the mid-20th century. As with stamps, collectors often start with examples from many different countries, before choosing to specialize. Again, as with stamps there are opportunities for themed collections, such as animals, transport and famous people, or a collection could be chronological, concentrating on the notes of a particular historical period.

Values of notes vary considerably according to many factors, such as date, signature and condition.

JONTY'S CHOICE

These two green banknotes have consecutive numbers. Issued with a metal security thread to deter counterfeiters, this version of the £1 note was issued for just two years between 1948 and 1950, bearing the signature of the then cashier K. O. Peppiatt. Two uncirculated notes with consecutive numbers are very desirable and are becoming harder to find.

Two Bank of England £1 notes, 1948. £25–30

Notes of interest

This American five-dollar bill is from a series known as the 'Pioneer Family', after its subject matter. It is an appealing subject for collectors with an interest in American history or memorabilia, and it is well illustrated. In general, illustrated notes like this make good collectables and many collectors specialize in such examples.

United Stated $5 note, 1907. £100–150

Other banknotes

Norwegian 10 kroner note, 1939. £5–10

French WWII Allied Liberation currency 100 franc note, 1944. £15–20

Croatian WWII, 5,000 Kuna note, c1940s. £3–5

Jordanian 1 dinar note with King Hussein c1960s. £5–10

The one to look for

This version of the £5 note was introduced in 1971 and bore a portrait of the Duke of Wellington on the reverse. It continued in circulation for 20 years. This 1970s note would be worth £5–10 with its usual facsimile signature as intended.

Bank of England £5 error note, 1970s. £90–100

What makes this note worth considerably more than a normal one, is that it is an 'error note' – the usual cashier's signature, which is shown on the right, is missing.

Notes of interest

This note has a portrait of Napoleon on both sides as well as the Arc de Triomphe. More a work of art than a banknote, it is not difficult to see why this note appeal to collectors. It is superbly printed in full colour, with an elaborate and highly detailed design. If you do come across one it may well be worth putting aside as examples are becoming scarce and are expensive in mint condition.

Bank of France 100 new francs note, 1962. £20–25

New Zealand £1 note, 1960s. £20–25

Bahamian 10 shilling note, 1960s. £90–100

Bank of Malta £5 note, 1968. £90–100

Bank of England £5 note first issue, A01 prefix, 1981. £90–100

Medals

The last century or so has been a turbulent period in history, with conflicts in many parts of the world, not to mention World Wars I and II. Because of this, medals of one sort or another are found in many homes today, having belonged to a family member in the recent past.

On the other hand, because many medals are common, they are often of low value, although they may be of great interest to an individual for reasons of personal family history.

Most medals awarded during WWII were not impressed with the name of the recipient – a fact that caused considerable resentment at the time. Today, this makes it difficult to identify the owner of a

given medal, unless it is part of a group that includes a medal that was routinely engraved, such as the Military Medal. By contrast, although the WWI victory medals were suitably inscribed, they are also generally worth little, because millions of these medals were awarded.

Medals should come with their ribbons, although many are now faded or tattered. Replacement ribbons can be bought for display purposes, but keep the old ones, as they have some value. Bars on the ribbon with the names of campaigns will always add interest for collectors, and if the ribbon bears a small oak leaf, it denotes that the recipient was mentioned in dispatches.

Groups of medals

General Service Medal with clasp for Somaliland, WWI trio of Bronze Star, Silver War Medal and Brass Victory Medal and a George V Naval LSGC (Long Service). *Group of five, with paperwork. £350–400*

WWI trio of a Bronze Star, Silver War Medal and Brass Victory Medal, plus a Military Cross. This last makes the group especially interesting and valuable. *Group of four. £1,000–1,250*

Orders & medals

Waterloo medal, awarded to George Windus, c1815. **£1,350–1,500**

Crimea medal, with Sebastopol bar, 1854–56. **£270–300**

World War II German war merit cross, 1939. **£25–30**

Order of Burma, one of three awarded for heroism, 1946. **£2,700–3,000**

The one to look for

This impressive group comprises no fewer than eleven medals to a member of the Royal Medical Corps. It includes a Member of the British Empire (MBE) medal, a Distinguished Conduct Medal and Military Service Medal; they were awarded between 1914 and 1945.

This group is in excellent condition and contains several medals that are desirable in their own right.
Group of 11 Royal Medical Corps medals, 1914–45. £3,000–3,500

The group comprises an OBE (military), 1939–45 Star, France and Germany Stars and War Medal with oak leaf clasp and Defence Medal.
Group of five, with paperwork. £350–420

The group comprises a Distinguished Flying Cross, 1945 Italy, Africa Star, Italy Star, 1939–45 War Medal, South Africa Overseas Medal and 1953 Coronation Medal.
Seven-medal group, with paperwork. £2,600–3,000

South Korean war medals, 1950–53. £70–85

An American Legion of Honor Nile Temple medal, 1937. £80–100

Kuwait issue 1st Gulf War medal, in box, 1991. £10–15

Kosovo NATO medal, with box, 1994. £15–20

Posters

While posters are now more widely collected than they used to be, many affordable and attractive examples are still available. Posters attract not only admirers of artwork and graphic design, but also collectors whose interests lie in a specific subject, such as with travel, sporting or film. There are also many niche markets, such as theatre or advertising memorabilia.

Generally speaking the designer, visual impact and age are the most important factors, and the older a poster is, the better. For maximum appeal, it should also have good quality artwork and interesting graphics and the print quality must be high.

Art Nouveau and Art Deco posters are among the most collectable, partly because of the general popularity of the Nouveau/Deco era, but also because of their striking designs. Collectable designers from this period include Alphonse Mucha (his posters are the epitome of Art Nouveau design and fetch high prices), Jules Chéret, Adolphe Mouron Cassandre and Romain de Tirtoff, better known as Erté.

Because their designs are so popular, many have been reproduced in recent years. A good way of telling most reproduction posters from originals is to feel the quality of the paper. As they were originally expected to be torn down after use, originals are printed on a thinner paper than their modern equivalents. Colour can also help; if you can see the dots that make up the colour under a magnifying glass, it is probably a reproduction.

Those who wanted a collection of quality posters in a smaller format could subscribe to the *Maîtres de l'Affiche* (Masters of the Poster), an art publication that ran from 1895 to 1900 in France. Jules Chéret, regarded as the father of the modern poster, chose the collection, published in an 11 x 15in (28 x 38cm) format. More than 90 artists were represented, and they are as collectable today as their larger format counterparts.

Condition is an essential criterion with posters, and since paper is such a flimsy, easily perishable material, it can be hard to find old posters that are wholly undamaged. Some crease marks might be acceptable if a poster is a sought-after example, but if the printed surface has worn away along the creases, it will have an adverse effect on value. The same applies to any marks. Common posters need to be in perfect condition, as collectors have more choice.

Other posters

Fap'Anis, by Delval, 1920s.
£145–170

Eat More Oranges, 1935. £300–330

Paris 1937, by Jean Carlu. £150–180

National War Bonds, by A. J., 1939–45. £40–50

The one to look for

Barnett Freedman was taught by Paul Nash at the Royal College of Art. He illustrated numerous books and posters for Harold Curwen's clients.

London Underground poster, Circus, designed by Barnett Freedman, 1936. £650–800

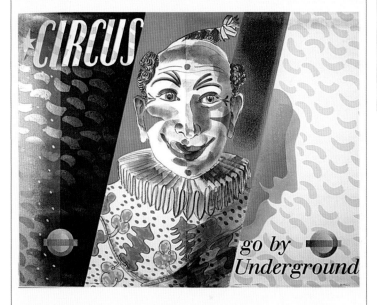

The colourful poster is printed on Japan paper, which is thin and has a satin finish, but is also resilient. It is a good-quality paper that is absorbent and lends itself well to colour printing, achieving excellent results.

IBM poster, printed by M P Lavore, 1965. £550–650

Olympic Games poster, by Jean Brian, 1967. £250–300

Woodstock Music and Art Fair, America, 1969. £350–450

Paul McCartney concert, by David Singer, 1990. £70–80

Travel posters

Travel posters represent one of the most important fields in poster collecting. The development of the railways and, later, the advent of air travel led to huge advertising campaigns to promote rail companies and airlines and so lots of different designs were produced. Shipping lines tempted the public with the glamour of an ocean voyage, while oil companies were keen to promote their fuels as private motoring became more affordable. Seaside resorts and other tourist attractions also invested in poster campaigns to persuade people to spend their holidays there.

The standard of artwork, use of colour and quality of printing was high. Many striking images from the first half of the 20th century have become famous through later reproductions; in such cases, the value of the original is usually enhanced. The market is fed by nostalgia for a 'golden age' of travel, and the new and modern forms of transport emerging in the 1920s and 1930s. The lure of faraway places is always a bonus and posters depicting interesting and exotic locations are among the most collectable.

Factors that will make a poster collectable include a strong design with good 'eye appeal', an interesting location, and a famous company, such as the Great Western Railway or BOAC. Posters relating to skiing are very popular, and rail posters will always attract a ready market among train buffs. A number of collectors like to concentrate on a particular theme, such as geographical location, or mode of transport.

Any design that epitomizes the age in which it was produced is appealing, and in this respect, it is hard to beat the art of influential Adolphe Mouron Cassandre, whose Art Deco era designs included a striking image of converging rail lines for a train company and his most famous design, which was for the luxury cruise liner *Normandie*.

Condition, as ever, is of great importance in this field, and while some minor creasing may be acceptable if it is a sought-after image. Posters with losses and tears to the image are best avoided; others will be available elsewhere and might be in better condition. Look after your posters by keeping them away from strong light, which will fade the print, and extremes of heat and humidity. Never fold them, but store them flat, wherever possible, or rolled.

Other posters

Cote d'Azur, by Adolphe Willette, c1905. £150–180

Rodeo Parade, by Edward Vincent Brewer, c1920. £170–200

Modena Express, 1925. £300–350

Paris-Lyon, by E. A. Schefer, 1935. £450–550

The one to look for

This poster was produced for the New York Central Lines, which produced a number of attractive posters to publicise its destinations.

New England, by Anthony Hansen, c1920. £600–700

The poster has great visual appeal. It is well-designed and conveys a strong sense of nostalgia.

Shell posters

Some of the most attractive travel posters were produced for the Shell oil company in the first half of the 20th century, and some of the leading artists of the day were recruited to work on them. They were mounted on the sides of petrol tankers and can be harder to find than, say, railway posters. This one is from the Landmark series.

Chanter's Folly and Dry Dock, Appledore, by Clifford and Rosemary Ellis, No. 491, c1937. £350–420

LNER poster, by J Bateman, 1937. £450–550

Blue Star line poster, 1950. £150–180

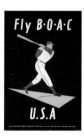

BOAC poster, by Aldo Cosomati, 1953. £100–120

Holland-America Line poster, by Frank H. Mason, c1955. £120–140

Autographs

Interest in autographs is high, and demand is strong in most areas. Value tends to depend on the fame of the individual, and collector interest also fluctuates according to the current popularity of the person.

It is important to remember that autographs are not difficult to fake, so beware. Also, stars often had secretaries or members of their entourage autograph pictures for them. It's worth noting, however, that in some cases these are collectable in their own right. Autographs on photos are always appealing, but the signature should be crisp and clear, and should not obscure the face of the celebrity. Letters are always interesting for content as well as signature.

JONTY'S CHOICE

James Stewart is one of the great Hollywood stars of all time, and his autographs are sought after. Autographs with personal dedications are always interesting, and doodles or illustrations are even more collectable.

Signed and titled drawing of Harvey the rabbit by James Stewart, c1950.
£700–780

Politics or pop?

Here are two signed images of 1960s icons, from the worlds of politics and pop. On the left is a signed invitation for John F. Kennedy's Inaugural Concert in 1961, framed and mounted with a photograph and worth c£3,500. On the right is a set of four genuine autographs of The Beatles, with an informal snapshot of Paul McCartney outside the Birmingham Hippodrome. It sold with autographs of other popular entertainers such as Gene Pitney, for £2,200.

Other autographs

Enid Blyton, a signed letter.
£100–125

Autographed photograph of Stephen Fry, 1980s.
£5–10

Photograph of Tony Curtis, signed in 2002. £45–50

Matt Lucas and David Walliams, framed and glazed, 2006. £65–75

The one to look for

The Seven Year Itch was first performed at the Fulton Theatre, New York, from 21st March 1955. The programme cover features the play's two stars in a scene from the production: Tom Ewell (who would reprise his role in the film version) and Louise King.

Signed programme for the original stage production, mounted with a photograph of Marilyn Monroe from the film version, framed and dated 1955. £3,000–3,500

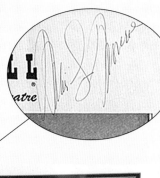

Marilyn Monroe has iconic status, so her autographs are very collectible. The film version of The Seven Year Itch won huge acclaim. The image is good and clear, as is the autograph, in blue ink, and it does not deface the image. This is a very desirable piece, in fine condition.

Michael Schumacher, Rubens Barichello, and Russ Braun, 2004. £275–325

Frank Sinatra autographed That's Life *LP, 1966. £200–250*

The Rolling Stones, framed with colour photo of band, 1960s. £250–300

Star Wars, Return of the Jedi, *signed photo, Bossk, Boba Fett, 2001. £65–75*

Coca-Cola

Coca-Cola was invented by pharmacist John Pemberton in 1886 and is now among the most familiar brands in the world. During the second half of tthe 20th century, it was exported globally, and became one of the first branded food products to be associated with a particular culture and way of life.

Over the years, countless Coca-Cola related items have been produced, and are avidly collected. They include clocks, cuddly toys, advertising signs, calendars, pens, badges, watches and more, and have come from both authorized and unauthorized sources.

Fakes and reproductions abound, but a knowledge of the company's history can help you spot some of the more obvious ones. Advertising slogans changed over the years, for example. Also, the famous 'contour bottle' wasn't introduced until 1915, so anything supposedly earlier but showing such a bottle is a fake.

Merchandise was produced as early as the 1890s, but was only made in large numbers from the 1920s. Early calendars from the 1890s are now very rare and expensive, and early menus are surprisingly valuable. Many later limited-edition items also have a strong following among collectors.

Coca-Cola hired top graphic designers including Hamilton King, Haddon Sundblom and even Norman Rockwell. Sundblom is noted for creating Christmas advertising campaigns in the 1930s using the image of Santa Claus. They were so popular that they gave rise to an urban legend that these campaigns created the modern Santa, who wears red and white because they are Coca-Cola colours. In fact, the image of Santa as we know him already existed.

JONTY'S TIP

Coca-Cola is now sold in over 200 countries and it is therefore easy to find other collectors from around the world. Pre-WWI pieces are rare because expansion only took place outside the US after this time. Such is the interest in Coca-Cola that almost anything connected with the brand is collectable, including this American uniform tag.

Coca-Cola cloth label, 1950s.
£3–5

Other merchandise

Coca-Cola Tiffany-style lamp shade c1920.
£4,900–5,400

Coca-Cola card advertising sign, 1950. £240–260

Pops-Rite Coca-Cola popcorn bag, 1950s.
£3–5

Coca-Cola cup, waxed paper, 1950s. £3–5

The one to look for

This is a point-of-sale sign. Its simple message, 'Drink Coca Cola' was the very first slogan adopted in 1886 and has been used alongside many others over the years.

Coca-Cola enamel advertising sign, 1950. £200–230

The enamel sign has a good, clean image and shows the bottle; it is a classic design. It has suffered some chips, but enamel signs are prized. To achieve the best prices, colours need to be bright, with no fading. Signs from the 1950s are especially popular with collectors.

Coca-Cola trays

Tin trays, from left to right: 1921, £30–35; 1939, £130–155; and 1950s, £65–75
Tin trays were supplied to soda fountains and drug stores as far back as 1897, printed with images from Coca-Cola calendars. There are many fake and reproduction trays around, and genuine ones must be in good condition. A desirable old tray might be worth over £1,000 in good condition, but only £1 if not.

A Coca-Cola advertising sign in a wooden crate, 1950s. £500–550

Coca-Cola Magazine Advertisement, 1964. £3–5

ScoreBoard Coca-Cola phone card, 1995. £60–65

Coca-Cola Disney World Florida coke bottle and case, 2001. £3–5

Guinness

Guinness, the distinctive Irish stout, was first brewed in 1759, and is one of the world's best-known brands today. There are numerous Guinness collectables to choose from, including posters, playing cards, badges, table lamps, mats and trays. For those starting out, it is possible to build an attractive and even valuable collection by concentrating on the smaller, more accessible objects.

There were many memorable Guinness posters, among them John Gilroy's famous 1930s image of a man carrying a girder, which made such an impression on the public that people started referring to the drink as 'girder' in pubs.

Some of the most collectable items are the various Carlton Ware animals made in the 1950s and early 1960s by Wiltshaw & Robinson. They included a sealion, a kangaroo, an ostrich, a tortoise and the famous Guinness toucan. There was also a zookeeper and a drayman. Unfortunately, as they have become very collectable and prices have escalated, numerous fakes have appeared. They can be distinguished by their colours, and it is worth familiarizing yourself with the originals.

How to spot a fake

Right: Wiltshaw & Robinson Guinness Toucan, 1950s. £200–240
Left: Carlton Ware Guinness lamp, 1957. £135–150
The many fake Guinness toucans on the market can be distinguished from the originals by the quality and colour of the painting. Reproductions often display poor techniques and the yellow and orange of the beak are too vibrant. The gradation of colour is also badly executed. On the originals, the orange of the bill fades gradually to yellow. The eye decoration should be neatly painted and the head on the pint of Guinness should be about ¼in (5mm) in depth. It should also be a creamy colour to match the base. Unfortunately, a Carlton Ware backstamp is no proof of authenticity in itself – these backstamps have also been faked.

Guinness merchandise

Guinness advertising plaque, 1930s. £200–240

Carlton Ware ceramic tortoise. £65–75

Guinness advertising card, 1950s. £5–10

Guinness wax paper cup, 1950s. £10–15

The one to look for

This poster was printed by John Waddington, from artwork by Edward Ardizzone. As well as producing artwork for advertising campaigns, Ardizzone (1900–79) is well known as an illustrator of children's books. He also worked as an official war artist during WWII.
Guinness for Strength advertising poster, 1953. £250–300

Humour has always been a strong suit of Guinness advertising and this is a good, well-illustrated example. While humour remains a key component of many Guinness campaigns to this day, the claims that Guinness is 'for strength' or the famous slogan 'Guinness is good for you' would fall foul of modern-day advertising watchdogs, but is typical of the brand at the time.

Carlton Ware cruet set comprising salt, pepper and mustard pots, 1950s. £55–60

Guinness advertising showcard, 1960. £35–40

Carltonware Guinness kangaroo, 1960s. £40–60

Commemorative three-handled porcelain mug, c1983. £70–80

Tins

Tins became popular for packaging during the 19th century as they were durable and inexpensive to produce. The earliest tins, dating from the 1840s, were handmade and were decorated with paper labels glued to the surface. Such tins are now very rare and valuable.

With advances in manufacturing and lithographic technology, it became possible to produce tins more cheaply, in a vast range of colours and, from the late 1880s, different shapes. Mustard, cigarettes, stock cubes, toffees and tea were among the many diverse products packaged, and tins that once contained these products have become very collectable.

One of the big differences between British and American tins is that the former were often designed with a secondary use in mind, whereas American ones were more functional (though there are always exceptions). Biscuit tins are a case in point; produced with middle-class households in mind, who were best able to afford such treats, many were made in the form of toys, such as buses or cars, and could be played with when empty. Other forms included buildings, books and, in the 1920s and 1930s, manufacturers produced tins with moving parts in the form of windmills and aeroplanes.

Although machines would have been used to produce them, the more elaborate designs would have taken many man hours to finish.

The name that springs to mind for any collector above all others is British firm Huntley & Palmer's, who pioneered the use of colourful and attractive tins for their products as far back as 1837. Their biscuits – and therefore their tins – were exported all over the world. Their range of biscuits was extensive and they made many different types of tin in which to keep them. It is possible to form a collection based on the products of this firm alone.

Many tins were produced for special events, such as a Coronation, or for Christmas. Although they do make interesting collectables, they were made in large numbers and many people kept them, so most are relatively common. Of particular interest to collectors, however, are the special tins that were used to send food, such as chocolate, to the troops in the Boer War and WWI. These are worth more if they still have their original contents but most, understandably, do not.

When buying tins, collectors look for good designs and bright colours, and you should always beware of rust and scratches – damage to a lithographed tin is very difficult to restore.

Other tins

Coleman's Mustard tin, c1900. £70–80

Dimitrino & Co Egyptian cigarette tin, 1920s. £80–90

Mazawattee Tea, Old Folks at Home tin, c1920s. £30–35

McVitie & Price's biscuit tin, c1924. £15–20

The one to look for

Huntley & Palmer's began as a small bakery in 1822, and went on to become the largest biscuit manufacturer in the world. Tins such as this one are popular on both sides of the Atlantic, as they are so elaborate and the quality is high.

Huntley & Palmer's Indian biscuit tin, c1894. £270–300

The printed decoration on this tin is intricate, with the Huntley & Palmer's name woven into the complex design. The tin shows some signs of wear and there are areas where the ink has been worn away, but if it is a particularly old and valuable example, like this one, this can be forgiven.

Blue Ribbon Red Label tea tin, 1930s. £35–40

Gray Dunn & Co Wheel of Fortune biscuit tin, c1935. £175–190

National Household Dried Milk tin, 1950s. £5–10

Walter's Palm Toffee tin, c1950s. £25–35

Signs

Rather than being the sole preserve of the collector, advertising signs are often purchased by designers and home furnishers looking for something with a nostalgic appeal to complement the decor. Many signs have become famous, iconic even, and these will attract a premium price. Generally speaking, well-known brands are more desirable than lesser known ones, but if a sign has striking graphics and a strong image, it can still be sought after, especially if it overlaps with another collecting field. When buying enamel signs, watch out for chips and rust where the enamel has worn away. Minor damage may be acceptable if it is an otherwise attractive sign, but not if it affects the image.

Kingov flour *This is a projecting, double-sided sign, and it has an attractive Art Nouveau border. Kingov is not a well-known brand today.*

Enamel advertising sign for Kingov patent self-raising flour, c1900.
£350–400

Fry's chocolate 'Five Boys' *This is one of the most famous advertising images of all time. It showed five boys with various expressions, listed as 'Desperation', 'Pacification', 'Expectation', 'Acclamation' and 'Realization' The boys were introduced in 1886 and used until 1971.*

Enamel advertising sign for Fry's chocolate, 1920s–30s.
£700–800

Melox dog foods *The pet foods firm of Melox produced a range of promotional items for its products, from paperweights to match book holders, bearing their terrier trademark. They also produced trading cards of famous breeds of dogs. This sign, which is in mint condition, dates from the 1920s and is likely to appeal to dog lovers as well as to general advertising collectors.*

Enamel sign advertising Melox Dog Foods, 1920s. £400–450

COINS, MEDALS & EPHEMERA

Black Cat Virginia cigarettes This advertising sign dates from c1920–1930. It is a famous image and has been much reproduced in smaller, cheaper versions and even as fridge magnets. This makes the original version all the more desirable. Like the Melox sign, it will also appeal to animal lovers – some people have themed collections based on animals, and both cats and dogs are popular.

Enamel advertising sign for Black Cat cigarettes, 1920–30. **£200–250**

Sunlight soap Produced by the British firm of Lever Brothers, the soap gave its name to the village of Port Sunlight, built in the northwest of England for the factory's employees. Sunlight is a famous name from the 19th and early 20th century.

Enamel advertising sign for Sunlight Soap, 1920s–30s. **£250–300.**

Técalémit Motoring-related signs have a keen following, and collecting automobilia is a separate field in itself. This sign will appeal to motoring enthusiasts as well as general collectors. It is French and dates from the 1950s. The firm of Técalémit was founded in 1922, specializing in garage equipment and lubricants.

Enamel advertising sign for Técalémit Station Officielle, 1950s. **£250–300**

Packaging

Before the advent of packaging, grocers simply weighed the required amount of goods for each customer. The 19th century saw the development of large food manufacturers, many of which survive to this day. They developed their own pre-packaged goods to standardized weights, which the shopkeeper only had to sell.

This was an important development, and came in the wake of scandals concerning adulterated foodstuffs. Unscrupulous shopkeepers sometimes added cheaper, and other times inedible or even dangerous ingredients to food to make it go further. Hence, many packages of the 19th century openly boast of the 'purity' of their products. The packaging served as a guarantee to a manufacturer's consumers that its products had not been tampered with.

Packaging also allowed firms to achieve 'brand recognition' and to promote themselves to the consumer. Major firms were not slow to take advantage of this opportunity, and competed with each other on the shelves to produce the most eye-catching and attractive packaging for their various products.

Some firms have changed their packaging over the years to reflect changing times, though radical design changes have been rare. Indeed, most manufacturers have kept the same, or very similar, designs for their packaging for many decades or in some cases for well over a century in the interest of brand recognition – among the most familiar examples of this are Oxo, Lyle's Golden Syrup, and Colman's Mustard.

Because packaging was mostly thrown away after use, survivors are collectable. Most old packaging is still quite affordable, however, so there are still plenty of opportunities. Even the humble paper bag is collectable, if it has an attractive design, especially one that relates to a well-known brand. It is also worth considering that many paper bags we use today are likely to become collectable in the future, due in part to a growing public enthusiasm for recycling.

Paper and cardboard packaging are particularly susceptible to mould and rot, as well as insect attack. They can also be subject to 'foxing', which is seen as small brown spots on old paper. This is caused by iron deposits from the manufacturing equipment, causing a chemical reaction in the presence of damp. Bright sunlight is the enemy of any print, including printed packaging, so watch out for badly faded examples.

Other packaging

Taylor's Cough Syrup box wrapper c1885. £15–20

Junket rennet powder box, early 20thC. £5–10

Fry's Shilling Chocolate box, 1920. £10–15

Cardboard ice-cream container, c1930s. £15–20

The one to look for

Collecting ice cream-related items is less popular in Britain than in the United States, where ice-cream parlour and soda-fountain memorabilia find ready buyers. This is because of the strong associations of the ice-cream parlour with American culture.

Verifine Ice Cream container, 1930s–40s. £15–20

Replica food

The self-service supermarket was pioneered by Clarence Saunders, who opened his first Piggly Wiggly store in Memphis Tennessee in 1916, but it wasn't until the middle of the 20th century that self-service became common. Before that customers would be served individually by the shopkeeper, with goods kept behind the counter. Realistic models of foods were used at the front of the counter as a sales aid. The most collectable replica foods are the Victorian and Edwardian wax models, but wrapped dummies of well known brands are also sought after.
Chocoate dummies, late 1950s. £10–15 each

Anco Macaroni bag paper, 1950s. £1–5

ERA moth cartridge, 1950s. £1–5

Packet of Boots Primrose Household Soap, c1960. £1–5

Box of Bronco Toilet Tissue, c1960. £1–5

Entertainment

The ever-increasing interest in popular culture, the influence of Hollywood and the monumental growth in mass communication have all contributed to the cult of the celebrity. Whether your interest lies in the stars of pre-war music halls or silent movies, cult rock bands or the superstars of the latest international blockbuster, you are sure to find memorabilia associated with your idols.

Items to collect include autographs, vinyl records, cult TV-related toys and props from film sets. Whatever you decide, something will tempt you and you will become well and truly hooked. The choice is endless and there are definitely bargains to be had.

We live in an age in which people are fascinated, obsessed even, by celebrity, so it comes as no surprise that the market in entertainment-related collectables is booming. They are constantly promoted, if only indirectly, by radio, television and film and are never out of the public eye.

Starting a collection

Most people already have a basic entertainment collection in their own homes, such as a few items related to a favourite character or film star, and this can be good to build from. Most people have a record collection, so dust off those old vinyl discs and see

Mattel poseable talking Mork action doll, from Mork and Mindy, *1979. £100–110*

Xray Spex, 'Germfree Adolescents', stereo LP record, by EMI, 1978. £25–30

what you have. It is surprising how many gems can emerge from a long-forgotten record collection. If you have disposed of your old records, remember that other people are doing the same, so boot fairs can be a very good place to find them. Although most people are aware that some old records have value, the

majority have only a vague idea of what is of interest to collectors, so bargains can be had. On the other hand, such ignorance is a two-edged sword as it can lead to sellers believing that just because a record is old, it must be valuable. Auction sites such as eBay can be useful for tracking down unusual items, but the usual caveats of buying online apply, so make sure you do your research.

What to buy

Many collectors are genuine fans, so they usually heed the sensible advice to buy something for the sheer love of it. This is just as well, because the movie memorabilia market can be fickle, and interest in music stars can also rise and fall.

There are exceptions, of course, such as science fiction, fantasy and action movies, which remain the most popular genres in film. Series such as *Star Wars*, James Bond and the Indiana Jones films are proving enduringly popular.

Collecting is not just limited to memorabilia as the films and shows themselves are also collected. There is a market for limited-edition DVDs, although it is worth bearing in mind that these are being issued specifically for a collectors' market and are not, therefore, vintage collectables. As a general rule, memorabilia that is of the period is more collectable than later examples.

Kenner Star Wars Return of the Jedi plastic laser rifle carry case, c1984. £40–50

Pull my
Talking Ring!

Special limited-edition video tapes are also collected. In 1998, a VHS single of Madonna's 'Ray of Light' was released, limited to just 40,000 copies. This is collectable today, and is interesting as it came towards the end of the VHS era. As far as films are concerned, some fans like to own every available format of a favourite film, including VHS. Packaging is especially important here; also it is unplayed, sealed items that are of interest – anything else is likely to be worth very little.

In the field of music, there are collectors who specialize in obscure bands and record labels, but this is very much a niche market. If you are looking for collectables that are popular and likely to remain so, go for the big names. Elvis and the Beatles are obvious ones, although the really worthwhile vintage collectables are harder to come by and more expensive. Well-known rock bands with a global following, such as Queen, are certainly worth collecting, and Madonna is also popular. As well as the obvious, such as film props, toys, action figures and records, do not overlook the smaller, simpler things. In 1978, Helix made a Death Star pencil sharpener for the first *Star Wars* film. It cost a matter of pennies in the 1970s, but they can now sell for as much as £40. Such items were popular, but have been used, lost or discarded over the years, making survivors rare and desirable.

The future

Entertainment is a very dynamic area of collecting because the supply to the collector is

Donald Duck celluloid plastic egg cup, 1930s–50s. £55–65

constantly being replenished.

Also, new collecting fields have emerged in recent years. A good example of this is film cels, which became popular in the United States before interest spread across the Atlantic.

Changing technology will continue to create new possibilities for collecting, just as the introduction of phone cards in the 1970s created an entirely new field. It is impossible to say what the future will bring, but whatever comes along will certainly be there to be exploited both by the entertainment industry and the canny collector.

Disneyland postcard, c1999. £1–5

ENTERTAINMENT

Disney

Walt Disney's Mickey Mouse made his debut in the 'talkie' cartoon *Steamboat Willie*, which was premiered in New York on 18 November 1928. Mickey proved such a hit that merchandise soon followed. The first deal was made in 1929 by a businessman who secured the rights to produce Mickey Mouse on a school notebook. After that, various companies competed for the right to produce toys and games based initially on Mickey, and then on other Disney characters as the studios developed new ones.

Markings are important when trying to determine the date of a Disney collectable. Until 1938, 'Walt Disney Enterprises' or 'Walter E. Disney' usually appeared on German and American Disney toys, and 'Walt Disney Mickey Mouse Ltd' on British ones. From 1939, they were marked 'Walt Disney Productions'. If the toy still has its original box it may state that a toy was made with the authorization of the Walt Disney Company.

German firms licensed to produce Disney toys included Distler and Tipp & Co which produced some fine tinplate toys based on Disney's characters. Distler's early designs were often created from memory after seeing the films, so they are not always accurate. The characters changed in form over the years, and this can be a good guide to dating. Mickey was initially slender and almost rat-like in appearance, and the toys reflect this. Similarly, early in his career, Donald Duck had a long bill which evolved into the shorter, curved bill of later years.

Some characters have always been more popular than others, but sometimes it is the less popular ones that are more valuable today. For example, Marx, which in the 1950s was one of the world's largest toy companies, made a tinplate and plastic clockwork model of Pinocchio. The character was not as popular as others in the Disney stable, so relatively few were made. Consequently, they are now hard to find and therefore command higher prices.

Collecting Disney is hugely popular, and the range of items to choose from is vast. Many collectors therefore specialize in one particular character or type of collectable, such as soft toys, or even ephemera, such as napkins and paper cups. In some cases, there is an overlap so that, for example, Disney ceramics might be of interest to a collector specializing in a specific pottery, as well as to Disney enthusiasts.

Disney collectables

Set of Wade Walt Disney's Seven Dwarfs, c1938. **£160–200**

Reprint of 1940 lobby card for Walt Disney's Pinocchio. **£220–240**

Chad Valley Walt Disney's Mickey Mouse game board, c1940. **£25–30**

Walt Disney promotional plaster Donald Duck model, 1950s. **£180–200**

The one to look for

Wade Heath & Co was one of three companies run by the Wade family. In 1933, Wade won the license to produce designs based on Walt Disney characters. This model of Bambi measures 4⅖in (11.5cm) wide and is from the firm's Blow Up series. The eye colour is different from the early Hat Box models, which have brown eyes.

Wade Blow Up model of Walt Disney's Bambi, 1961–65. £35–40

The Blow Up series were larger versions of the Hat Box range, which was introduced in 1956. There were ten Disney Blow Up models, the first of which was Lady from Lady and the Tramp, who first appears in the film in a hat box. This and other models were packaged in a similar box. Pieces are marked with the Wade backstamp and copyright information (shown on the right).

WADE PORCELAIN
COPYRIGHT WALT DISNEY PRODUCTIONS
MADE IN ENGLAND

Walt Disney animation cell, for Peter Pan, 1953. £350–450

Film poster for Walt Disney's Lady and the Tramp, 1955. £500–550

Kohner Walt Disney's Mickey Mouse acrobat, 1960s. £15–20

Pedigree Walt Disney's Mary Poppins vinyl doll, 1964. £550–650

Film memorabilia

Most film fans would love to own a piece of memorabilia connected with a favourite movie, and as the cinema remains a very popular form of entertainment, with the popularity of many films waning and rising, it is not surprising that there is such a demand for related collectables. However, it can be a very fickle market, so the advice to buy whatever appeals to you personally, rather than with an eye to investment, has never been more sound.

In America, props and costumes have been collected since the golden age of Hollywood, roughly the late 1920s to the late 1950s, but it is a more recent hobby in the UK. The most popular collectables today include film props, which were once usually discarded at the end of a production but are now likely to be sold off almost as soon as a film is finished. The most popular film genres as far as collectables are concerned are action films and science fiction/fantasy. This is partly because while other films may use props that are unremarkable and usable many times over, science fiction, fantasy and action films often use props that are tailored to the production and unique. Provenance is most important with film props – be suspicious of items without a letter of authenticity or other proof that they were used in a production. This is especially important if the prop itself is not particularly distinctive and it also helps to distinguish it from replica items that may be on the market.

Film-related collectables also include still photographs, autographs, film cels and press kits, aimed at journalists writing about the movie. One of the biggest areas of film-related collectables, however, remains the poster. Posters and lobby cards were produced in large numbers to promote films, but were often thrown away.

More people are becoming interested in collecting posters and, as a result, the competition is driving up prices. Some films are more popular and well known than others, and some images from posters have achieved iconic status. A popular film, a striking image and good condition, without tears, holes or fading, will always prove to be a winning combination. Be aware that there is a difference between original film posters and reprints, which were made in large quantities for direct sale to the public. Only genuine film posters that were produced for distribution to cinemas and were used for promoting films are of interest to the collector.

Other items

Lobby card for Angels With Dirty Faces, 1938.
£850–950

Gown worn by Elizabeth Taylor in Cleopatra, 1960s.
£1,400–1,800

Prop cat from Superman, 1978.
£900–1,000

Rubber stunt gun and movie stills from Die Hard, 1997.
£1,300–1,500

The one to look for

The Indiana Jones films were hugely successful around the world. These miniature items were used in *Indiana Jones and the Temple of Doom* (1984) in one of the film's finest scenes, in which Indy, Willie and Short Round are pursued underground by the Thugee.

The car is not as detailed as some that were used, as it is a stunt version and was not seen in close-up. The models are made of plastic and have been painted and distressed to match the full-size versions. They were purchased from a former employee of the special effects company Industrial Light and Magic, who was allowed to keep these and other miniatures as mementoes.

Miniature mine car and barrels, by Industrial Light and Magic, 1984.
£1,350–1,500

Film posters

Many collectors concentrate on artists and genres. Stars such as Audrey Hepburn and Marilyn Monroe and the films of Alfred Hitchcock are always popular. Also collected are posters of the same film from different countries, which sometimes used different artwork.

Left: The Dam Busters, 1955.
£400–450
Right: The Seven Year Itch, c1960.
£300–350

Mirror-image plastic lifeboat sign from Titanic, 1997.
£130–145

Backpack from Mission Impossible 2, 2000.
£800–900

Crossbow from Buffy the Vampire Slayer, 2003.
£2,300–2,500

Rubber cavalry officer's helmet from King Arthur, 2004.
£300–350

Star Wars

Star Wars is by far the largest single field of collectables in the science fiction and fantasy genre. Since the first film made its debut over 30 years ago, a staggering range of collectables has been produced, from records and board games to toiletries and telephones, although action figures remain the most popular of all.

Many claims have been made for *Star Wars*, but one that is certainly true is that it revolutionized the action figure market. The figures introduced for *Star Wars* were, at around 3¾in (9.5cm), smaller than the more usual 12in (30.5cm) or 7in (18cm) figures, as they were designed to fit into an accompanying range of spacecraft.

The very first figures were from the so-called 'early bird' package, a special mail-order offer, and these are among the most sought after *Star Wars* figures. It comprised four characters: Luke Skywalker, Princess Leia, Chewbacca and R2D2. The 'early bird' Chewbacca differs from later examples in that his crossbow-like weapon, known as a bowcaster, was made from a greenish plastic. The 'early bird' Luke Skywalker has a double telescoping light sabre, which extends further than later models.

Collectors like to have examples of as many variants as possible. Figures were often released in slightly different versions for different markets, so a figure that is relatively common in the UK may be harder to come by in the US, and vice versa. Be aware, however, that some variants have been faked. A notorious example is that of the Jawa figures, which mostly had cloth capes, although a few early examples had vinyl ones, making them rare. Fake vinyl capes have been made from cut-down Ben Kenobi capes.

Variations are sometimes by accident rather than design. An example is the blue Snaggletooth figure, released exclusively in the US. The toy designers, given only limited information to work from, produced the character with a blue uniform. In the film, the character had a red uniform, so the 'red Snaggletooth' soon replaced him.

The character of Boba Fett, the bounty hunter, also appeared in several variations, so collectors pay close attention to him. An especially desirable version is the 12in (30.5cm) rocket-firing pre-production version. This model failed safety tests and was withdrawn, but a few are on the market and are highly prized.

Also worth looking out for are the 16in (40 cm) versions of Chewbacca; relatively few of these larger versions were made and so are now desirable.

Collectable items

Star Wars Weekly
comic, No. 6, 1978.
£5–10

*Storm Trooper,
Darth Vader and
Snow Trooper, 1977.*
£5–10 each

*Hasbro Mr Potato
Head Darth Tater
figure, 2005.*
£5–10

*Palitoy Escape from
Death Star board
game, 1977.*
£30–35

The one to look for

The *Star Wars* X-Wing Aces game is an electronic target shooting game. Although it is an early example of the use of the emerging microchip technology in home entertainment, it is essentially a rehash of an earlier WWI game called Aerial Aces.

This game is extremely rare if boxed and is something of a Holy Grail to dedicated Star Wars *enthusiasts, hence its high value.*

Kenner Star Wars *X-Wing Aces target game, 1978. £1,500–2,000*

Carded figures

Packaged figures are worth significantly more than loose ones – not only are they protected but the packaging gives information about the contents. Early figures are often known as '12-backs' because the first 12 characters in the range were depicted on the back of the card. In general, the 12-back versions of figures are more valuable than later ones.

Left: Stormtrooper by Kenner, 1978. £270–300
Right: EV-9D9 and Collectors' Coin, 1978. £250–300

Poster for Return of the Jedi, *1983. £40–50*

Star Wars soundtrack, LP record, 1979. £80–90

Palitoy Millennium Falcon Spaceship, boxed, 1980. £70–80

R2D2 telephone, early 1990s. £70–80

Dr Who

The time-travelling Dr Who made his debut on British television on 23 November 1963, the day after the assassination of US President John F. Kennedy. It was promoted as a different kind of science fiction show, with a hard edge and one that would avoid the usual 'bug-eyed monsters' that had become a science fiction cliché. However, the show's second story, written by Terry Nation, featured a race known as the Daleks – and the rest, as another cliché has it, is history.

Dr Who has been shown in many countries around the world, including Australia, New Zealand, Canada, Japan, Hungary and South Korea. It gained a cult following in the United States from showings on PBS television from the 1970s onwards, so there is a market for *Dr Who* collectables on both sides of the Atlantic.

In Britain, the show was a hit from the start, so toys and other merchandise inevitably followed, ranging from toy Daleks to money boxes in the form of the Doctor's vehicle, the Tardis. The programme was cancelled in 1989, although a film was made in 1990. The series was revived in 2005 and is a hit once again, with new lines of toys and collectables to accompany it, some of which are aimed at the adult collectors' market.

Generally speaking, it is the early collectables from the 1960s that are the most sought after, including the early annuals. Well-known toy firms such as Marx, Mego, Tomy, Dinky and Palitoy have all made *Dr Who* products. In the 1980s, Dapol made a line of action figures to complement the series and, although they are not very expensive, they are collectable. As with many action figures, there are variations to look out for. The Dapol figure of Dr Who's assistant Mel (played in the show by Bonnie Langford) was made with both a pink and a blue blouse – the pink version is worth slightly more.

Such was the demand for *Dr Who* toys in the 1960s that some manufacturers seemed almost desperate to cash in. In 1965, Lincoln International made an 'Anti-Dalek jet immobilizer', a plastic water pistol, made in Hong Kong. Cheap and mass-produced in its day, these have become very rare and are now worth £500–600.

Interest in *Dr Who* collectables had been in decline in recent years, with all but the hard core of fans. However, the arrival of new shows on our screens has revived the market once again.

Dr Who collectables

Dinky Toys diecast model of the Tardis, 1960s.
£15–20

Dr Who Annual, No. 1, 1965.
£30–40

Denys Fisher Giant Robot toy, with box, 1976.
£90–100

Plastic Tardis toy with spinning interior, 1976.
£90–100

The one to look for

Although several actors have played the Doctor to date, most people have their favourite and, for many, Tom Baker who played him from 1974–80, is the definitive Doctor. This Denys Fisher figure shows him with his trademark hat and scarf, which should be present and in good condition.

The Doctor's sonic screwdriver, which is usually missing, adds considerably to the value.

Denys Fisher Dr Who action figure, with sonic screwdriver, 1976. £100–120

Daleks

Daleks rank among the most sinister science fiction villains of all time. In 1960s Britain 'Dalekmania' almost seemed to rival 'Beatlemania' and Daleks were everywhere. This toy Dalek has the original box, is an original model rather than a reproduction and was authorized by the BBC. Weapons, or eyepieces on Dalek toys are vulnerable and if missing or damaged will seriously affect the value. This example still has its weapon in the original packaging.

Palitoy plastic talking Dalek, 1975. £180–200

Whitman Dr Who *jigsaw puzzle, 1977. £5–10*

Palitoy plastic talking K-9 toy, 1978. £90–100

Film poster for Dr Who and the Daleks, *1986. £180–200*

Dapol poseable Dr Who figure, 1996. £5–10

James Bond

The first James Bond film, *Dr No*, was released in 1962 and was the start of a series of films that continues to this day. So too do the related collectables. In the 1960s, these were mostly toys and games, but Bond is such a popular and enduring character that there is also a thriving market in limited edition items and collectables aimed at adults. The Bond collector is spoilt for choice, with toys, games, action figures, props, posters and, of course, first editions of the Ian Fleming novels (see page 213).

Because James Bond is associated with high-tech gadgetry, this features strongly in much of the merchandise. Watches are among the most popular and some are rare. They include a James Bond Spy Watch, made in the 1960s by the firm of A. C. Gilbert. This is a name to look out for as they produced many early Bond items, including an action figure of Bond and another of the henchman Oddjob from *Goldfinger*. Both are desirable, but while Bond may have been the hero, Oddjob is more valuable as fewer were sold.

James Bond drove many cars in the films, but the Aston Martin DB5 remains the one that is most often associated with the character. Corgi was licensed to produce toy versions, but even unauthorized

models are sought after. A DB5 was made in Hong Kong in the 1960s by Lincoln International, described as a 'secret agent' car – though there was no doubt which agent they had in mind. It can fetch £200 or more today. Interest in Bond collectables is unlikely to wane for the foreseeable future. There is no end in sight to the series and interest is stimulated further with the release of each new film.

JONTY'S CHOICE

While Corgi's versions of the Aston Martin DB5 are the best known, A. C. Gilbert made this model in 1965. Advertised as James Bond's car from *Goldfinger* and *Thunderball*, this one has some damage to the box. If you are lucky enough to own one with both car and box in perfect condition, it could be worth up to £900.

A. C. Gilbert battery-operated tinplate Aston Martin DB5, with box, 1965. £300–350

Bond collectables

Airfix plastic Toyota 2000 GT construction kit, 1967. £180–200

Ian Fleming, You Asked For It, (Casino Royale), 1954. £180–200

Corgi Toys Citroën 2CV, c1981. £40–45

A. C. Gilbert plastic figure, 1966. £30–35

The one to look for

Several different James Bond action figures were made,
including a very collectable 1965 version by A. C. Gilbert for
the film *Thunderball*. This action figure is also for
Thunderball but was made by Hasbro in 1997. It was part of
the relaunch of the Action Man range, with an emphasis on
action heroes rather than soldiering.

*Hasbro James Bond Action
Man figure, limited edition,
1997.
£65–75*

*Part of a collectors' edition that
also included items from
Tomorrow Never Dies, Goldeneye
and The Spy Who Loved Me, these
were never really intended for play.
The packaging should be in mint
condition and accessories must be
present to achieve maximum value.*

*This James Bond Action Man was made as a limited
edition and comes complete with a film cel. Film cels
have become a collecting field in their own right. This
excellent package also came with a leaflet and poster.*

*Mattel 007
collectors' edition
Barbie and Ken gift
set, 2002. £60–70*

*Milton Bradley
James Bond board
game, 1960s.
£35–40*

*Colgate 007 shaving
kit, 1967.
£60–65*

*Lonestar plastic
Special Agent 007
presentation kit,
1966. £300–350*

Elvis Presley

It is difficult to overstate the impact of Elvis Presley on rock and pop music, or indeed on popular culture in general; John Lennon once remarked that 'before Elvis, there was nothing'. Even more than 30 years after his death, Elvis is still having hits and has a global following. The market for Elvis collectables and memorabilia is huge. In the world of rock and pop collecting, the bigger the name, the better, and they don't come any bigger than Elvis.

Vintage Elvis collectables are highly sought after, with many of those from the 1950s and '60s now beyond the pockets of many collectors. Therefore, more recent collectables, including limited edition pieces that are being produced to this day, find ready buyers. From cookie jars to key rings and from figures to drinking glasses, there is a lot of choice, although there is a difference between the items made specifically for the modern collectors' market and original, period memorabilia. Purists only really consider items to be worthwhile if they were made during his lifetime.

Memorabilia made during Elvis's lifetime includes lunchboxes, badges, dolls, clocks, watches, record players, posters and more. Original packaging will enhance the value, although unboxed items that are original and in good condition will still sell. Signed items will attract a premium, but Elvis's signature did vary somewhat, is not easy to authenticate and there are many fakes, so be warned.

Collectors can even purchase Elvis stamps: issued in 1993, these stamps became the most profitable stamps in the history of the US Postal Service. Many millions were sold, so they are not particularly valuable, although certain postmarks and first day covers, such as the Memphis cover with the Graceland musical gate, are desirable.

Probably the most desirable of all Elvis collectables is clothing worn by the star himself and other personal possessions such as guns. If there is proof that an item has been worn on stage or screen, it will be much more valuable than something for everyday wear. Not surprisingly, such items are highly desirable, as is anything with a direct personal association. Elvis was a generous man and often gave jewellery to his family and friends, some of which has since come onto the market. Provenance is absolutely vital with such items but, if it can be proved that it did indeed come from Elvis, expect to pay a high price.

Elvis collectables

'Love Me Tender', EP record, by HMV, 1956. £100–120

'Don't Be Cruel' and 'Hound Dog', single record, by RCA, c1959. £100–125

Signed photograph, signed on both sides, c1960. £1,000–1,250

A promtional postcard for the film Flaming Star, 1961. £5–10

The one to look for

This Cleveland concert took place on 23rd November 1956,
the year in which Elvis made it big, so the ticket is of
historical interest. There was a strike by newspaper
photographers in Cleveland at the time, so the only
photographs taken at the event itself were by Lew Allen, a
17-year old from a local high school. They became some of
the most famous images of Elvis early on in his career.

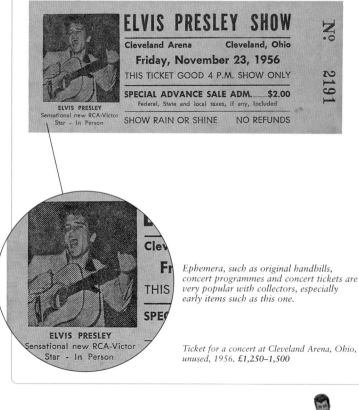

*Ephemera, such as original handbills,
concert programmes and concert tickets are
very popular with collectors, especially
early items such as this one.*

*Ticket for a concert at Cleveland Arena, Ohio,
unused, 1956. £1,250–1,500*

Elvis Express
*magazine, full set of
19 issues, 1962–64.*
£100–120

Film poster for Girl
Happy, *1965.*
£80–100

Film poster for Elvis
on Tour, *on linen,
1972. £450–500*

*Elvis radio,
1977.*
£40–45

The Beatles

The Beatles changed the face of popular music and are undoubtedly icons of the 1960s, but collector interest is by no means confined to those who remember them in their heyday. Their popularity continues as new fans have discover their music.

There is a solid market for Beatles collectables, but there is a difference between recent collectables and original memorabilia and, for the purist, only vintage items will do. Toys and games featuring The Beatles are collectable and range from puppets to colouring books; the latter are usually only worth collecting if they have not been coloured in.

As well as their music, The Beatles are remembered for their films. One of the most popular was *Yellow Submarine* (1968). More than 20 different firms were licensed to produce merchandise; desirable collectables include lunchboxes by Thermos and a model of the submarine, made by Corgi.

Posters advertising Beatles concerts are sought after, partly because they were usually torn down after the show. Few people would have thought them worth saving, so early examples are rare.

Concert programmes also fetch high prices, although magazines from the 1960s that feature the Fab Four are also collectable and are often less expensive. From the fan's point of view, magazines can contain more information than concert programmes, although they lack the kudos of a programme.

The value of a signature

A superb piece, this Beatles LP, 'A Hard Day's Night', is signed on the reverse in blue ballpoint pen by all four Beatles: John Lennon, Paul McCartney, George Harrison and Ringo Starr. There is some general wear and tear to the cover, although this does not affect the signatures. It is very rare to find copies of LP records signed by all four members of the band.

'A Hard Day's Night', signed LP record, by Parlophone, framed with a photogrpah of the band, 1964. £27,000–30,000

Beatles collectables

Beatles badge, 1982, £5–10

Coalport porcelain letter rack, from the Beatles Collections, 2006. £30–35

Pottery mug, promoting the Cavern, 1960s. £75–85

Postcard depicting The Beatles, 1960s. £5–10

The one to look for

This unused ticket is for The Beatles' first stadium concert at the
Shea Stadium, New York on 15 August 1965. It attracted a world
record crowd of 56,000 and is remembered as the first stadium
concert in modern rock music. Ironically, The Beatles played their last
concert just over a year later, opting to concentrate on studio work.
This ticket for the legendary show is for a reserved mezzanine seat
for $5.65. It is in excellent condition as it was never used.

Ticket for a concert at Shea Stadium, unused, 1965.
£2,000–2,200

'Revolver' compared

'Revolver', sealed stereo LP record, by
Capitol, 1966. £200–250

'Revolver', mono LP record, by
Parlophone, 1966. £50–55

The Beatles' 'Revolver' album from 1966 has been voted one of the greatest albums of all
time. Here are two different versions of the same record. On the left is a sealed copy of the
stereo LP with its original price sticker on the front. It has a number '12' near the RIAA logo
on the back cover, suggesting that it may have an Apple label. The record on the right is
less interesting as it has been opened and, presumably, played. It also the mono version.

'Singles Collection',
comprising 26 single
records, 1982.
£145–175

The Beatles Scrap
Book, published by
Whitman, 1964.
£60–70

Linen tea towel
depicting The
Beatles, 1964.
£100–125

Telephone in the
form of a bus with
Beatles advertising,
1990s. £50–60

Other bands

Although Elvis Presley and The Beatles remain the biggest names in rock and pop memorabilia, relics from many other bands are also collectable. They include big names from the 1960s such as The Rolling Stones, Jimi Hendrix and Jim Morrison, as well as more recent artistes. Autographed material remains the most popular but tickets, programmes for exceptional concerts and a diverse range of other material is avidly collected; a lot of memorabilia is still very affordable. In today's commercial world, bands that have long gone can enjoy a resurgence of interest if a hit single is re-issued, or used in the soundtrack of a popular film or advertisement.

Jimi Hendrix *One of the all-time great guitar legends, almost anything connected with him is collectable. This original programme is for the Jimi Hendrix Experience package tour, which opened at the Royal Albert Hall on 14 November 1967. Also on the bill were Pink Floyd, The Move and Amen Corner.* Tour programme, 1967. £200–250

Madonna *After her debut on the pop scene in 1982 Madonna quickly became an icon. She is well-known for using political, sexual and religious themes in her work, especially her songs and music videos. Her continued success stems from her ability to change her image and to reinvent herself. This is a full-length photograph of the star sitting topless on a bed and glancing at the camera over her shoulder. It dates from the 1990s. It is a striking image and has a clear signature in bold blue ink.*

Signed colour photograph, 1996. £450–500

Kylie Minogue *Kylie first came to public attention in the 1980s in the Australian television soap opera* Neighbours *and is now an international singing star with a global fan base. Her popularity declined somewhat during the early part of the 1990s, but she has now returned to form and recent shows have sold out. This half-length colour photograph shows her wearing a jewel-encrusted low-cut black top, and is signed in bold blue ink.*

Signed colour photograph, 2002. £175–200

The Monkees *The 1960s band The Monkees were the forerunners of today's manufactured boy bands. They were hand-picked from over 400 hopefuls for a TV show, modelled on The Beatles' films. While they were never serious rivals to The Beatles, they enjoyed chart success for a time and have a loyal fan base to this day. This concert programme and ticket is for a 1967 show at the London Empire Arena.*

Concert programme and ticket, 1967. £70–80

Queen *This clipped front cover of Queen's 'News of the World' LP, one of their best-selling albums on both sides of the Atlantic, is signed by Freddie Mercury and mounted on hardboard. More than just a lead singer, Mercury, who died in 1991, is remembered as perhaps the greatest showman of rock. It is usually the case that collectables rise in value following the death of a star, and Freddie Mercury is no exception.*

Signed clipped front cover of 'News of the World' LP, 1977. £300–350

The Rolling Stones *One of the greatest bands of all time, The Rolling Stones were formed in the 1960s and are still going strong today. Over the years they have attracted new fans and continue to tour, playing to sell-out audiences worldwide. Although memorabilia from their early days will fetch the highest prices on the whole, this Rolling Stones Oakland Concert poster from November 1989 is still worth a reasonable amount of money. The condition of posters is always important and this one is nearly mint.*

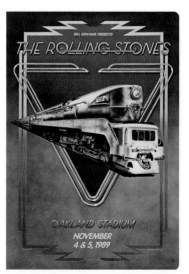

Concert Poster, 1989. £60–70

Records & compact discs

Almost by definition, records are the earliest rock and pop collectables. Vinyl records were becoming collectable in their own right, rather than just for the music, as early as the late 1950s and into the 1960s. Deleted records became sought after and many collectors turned their attention to rare imports.

In the 1970s, record collecting emerged as a serious hobby, which spurred the growth of specialist shops and record fairs. New developments included coloured vinyl, special packaging and 'picture discs', with images on the playing surface of records.

In the 1980s and '90s, Compact Discs emerged and became the preferred format for contemporary releases. However, some CDs are now collectable, with promotional CDs and special limited-edition boxed sets leading the way.

Rarity and condition are the most important factors in record collecting, with some artists being more collectable than others. Some records become rare through special circumstances. An example is the A&M release of the Sex Pistols' 'God Save The Queen'. Copies of this release were destroyed after the cancellation of the band's contract, but a few have survived – this is not to be confused with the reissue on the Virgin label, which is common.

First issues of records are generally more desirable than later ones, and unplayed records, preferably in sealed packaging, are especially prized. Classic tracks, and those by obscure artists, also have a following. However, now could be a good time to buy vinyl records as mint condition copies are fast disappearing and prices should continue to rise.

CDs

Jethro Tull, 25th anniversary four-CD boxed set, limited edition, by Chrysalis, 1993.
£90–100

Madonna, 'The Royal Box', CD, by Time Warner, rare set with video and poster, 1990.
£100–125

Vinyl

Cream, 'Disraeli Gears', LP record, by Reaction, 1967.
£50–60

Marvin Gaye, 'Originals from Marvin Gaye', EP record, by Tamla Motown, 1964.
£35–40

Gerry and the Pacemakers, 'How Do You Like It?', LP record, by Columbia, 1963. £35–40

Manic Street Preachers, 'You Love Us', LP record, 1991.
£20–25

ENTERTAINMENT

What to look for

On the sought-after Vee-Jay label, this LP was the first Beatles record to be released in America. There are many versions of this album, with huge price differences between them. The LP on the right has the tracks 'Please Please Me' and 'Ask Me Why', which were replaced on other versions. It is also unopened and the wrapper shows the orginal selling price.

Right: The Beatles, 'Introducing the Beatles', LP record, by Vee-Jay, 1964.
£4,500–5,500

In this version of the LP, the tracks 'Please Please Me' and 'Ask Me Why' were replaced with 'PS I Love You' and 'Love Me Do'. Although it still has its plastic wrapper, it has been opened.

Left: The Beatles, 'Introducing the Beatles', LP record, by Vee-Jay, 1964.
£575–700

Queen, 'Greatest Hits I & II', two-CD boxed set, by EMI, 1992.
£40–50

The Ramones, 'Mondo Bizarro', autographed CD, signed by Joey, Johnny, C.J. and Marky, 1992.
£125–150

The Dudley Moore Trio, 'Genuine Dud', LP record, by Decca, 1966.
£25–30

Pink Floyd, 'The Best of Pink Floyd', LP record, by Colombia, 1974.
£90–100

Prince, 'Gotta Stop (Messin' About)', single record, by Warner Brothers, 1981. **£180–200**

The Who, 'My Generation', LP record, by Brunswick, 1965.
£50–60

Cult TV

Television has offered plenty of opportunities for merchandising ever since the 1950s. It is a market that is very much led by nostalgia, as people collect items relating to TV shows that were popular in their childhood. This is one reason why children's shows from the *Magic Roundabout* and *The Wombles* to *Bagpuss* and *The Clangers* are so popular to this day.

Through DVD releases and repeats on satellite, cable and terrestrial TV, many shows have found a new audience and a new generation of fans. Brand new versions of some shows have been made, as have films based on popular series, thus further stimulating interest.

Fantasy is a very popular genre, as is science fiction, and even recent and current shows such as *Buffy the Vampire Slayer* and *Xena: Warrior Princess* have a huge following, with many related collectables. Collector interest can fluctuate according to the popularity of the show and whether or not it is still being screened or available on DVD. For example, although it was a classic show, there has been less interest in the Irwin Allen series *Voyage to the Bottom of the Sea*, as it has been rarely shown recently. *Lost in Space*, by the same producer, had a minor revival of interest after the 1998 film release, but interest has since cooled; the fact that relatively little merchandise was released has not helped.

Availability is sometimes a factor, as some programmes had little accompanying merchandise at the time. Producers of more recent shows tend to be much more astute and collectables for popular shows are more readily available. *The Simpsons* has a bewildering array of related licensed merchandise which have been produced since it first appeared in 1989. Adventure shows of the 1960s such as *The Avengers* have a strong cult following, as does *The Prisoner*. Even when shows are not seen regularly on TV interest can be kept alive through DVD releases. The *Prisoner's* 40th anniversary was in 2007 and a special edition DVD was released.

At the moment, TV shows of the 1980s are particularly popular, possibly because people who grew up in that decade are now reaching the age when they are becoming nostalgic for their youth and have a decent disposable income. Shows that are especially popular include action/adventure series such as *The A-Team* and *Knight Rider* and the stylish cop show *Miami Vice*.

TV collectables

Arco A-Team M-24 Assault Rifle target game set, c1983.
£90–100

Mego plastic Buck Rogers action figure, 1979.
£80–90

Mego poseable action figure of Fonzie, c1970.
£15–20

LJN plastic Knight Rider stunt car racing game, c1980s.
£40–50

The one to look for

Spy stories were very popular during the Cold War era. The tongue-in-cheek *Man from U.N.C.L.E.* ran for four series from 1964 to 1968 and collectables include a Corgi model of the show's Oldsmobile car, toy pistols, games, trading cards and action figures, such as the one shown here.

An A. C. Gilbert Illya Kuryakin action figure, from The Man From U.N.C.L.E., *with original box, 1960s.* **£180–200**

This action figure of agent Illya Kuryakin raises his arm and shoots a cap-firing pistol, which should be present along with the U.N.C.L.E. identification card that also accompanied this figure. A. C. Gilbert, the makers, also made figures of agent Napoleon Solo; both are desirable.

Pack of Barrett & Co Magic Roundabout snap cards, 1967. **£60–70**

Muppet Show Miss Piggy bendy toy, 1970–80. **£25–30**

Playmates Toys The Simpsons Convention Comic Book Guy, 2001. **£60–70**

Set of Tintin and Snowy action figures, 1985. **£130–145**

Sporting Memorabilia

The collecting of sporting memorabilia has become firmly established as a worldwide specialist market, enabling youngsters and adults alike to transport their passion from the sports field into the home.

In every sporting discipline, men and women who have achieved excellence in their particular field stand head and shoulders above the rest. One has only to think of iconic figures such as Muhammad Ali, Michael Jordan, Pelé and Bobby Moore to know that their popularity should stand the test of time – and may be as good as money in the bank when it comes to investing for the future.

Sporting memorabilia is a popular and growing field, although it should be pointed out that there is a difference between memorabilia and equipment. Some vintage sporting equipment is of such quality that it is preferred to its modern equivalent for actual use.

American Football League programme, for Dallas Texans v Oakland Raiders, 1960.
£180–220

There is huge international interest in sport and sporting memorabilia, although it probably does depend on location. Baseball memorabilia is highly sought after in the US and can fetch very high prices, but it is not collected much elsewhere.

Brass belt buckle, in the form of two tennis rackets, c1900.
£70–80

Golf is globally popular, as is horse racing and Association Football, or soccer, although the latter has a smaller following in America. Rugby and cricket have many collectables associated with them, although both sports are only played in a limited number of countries, albeit on a large scale. Some collectables, such as bubble gum cards, were originally designed with the young in mind, and sold at pocket money prices. You do not need a high degree of technical or academic knowledge to be able to join in – you just need to love your sport.

What makes it valuable?

Sport is a branch of the entertainment business and, as such, its stars are very important. Any item associated with a famous name will always be sought after, and kit and equipment used by a star in a major game will be the most desirable of all. Provenance is all important and an authentic signature adds value; top brand names with celebrity associations fetch the highest prices.

It is always worth remembering that sport is all about the occasion. For this reason, items associated with popular and successful teams and players or associated with a major event, are desirable. Ticket stubs and programmes relating to a major final will be of far greater interest than those for an average game. If you have collectables relating to a local team and are looking to sell, you should find it much easier to do so in the local area. However, this rule does not always apply, as some teams have a much wider national and even international fan base.

In the case of sporting equipment, technical advances and changes are of particular interest.

Royal Doulton figure of W. G. Grace, HN3640, 1995.
£85–100

Many collectors like to trace the evolution of a sport through its equipment, especially if it is particularly interesting or a landmark piece.

With paper items such as programmes, condition is very important and they should be free of creases and tears. In the

Pair of leather boxing gloves, 1950s.
£25–30

case of books, such as *Wisden Cricketers' Almanack*, date and binding are very important. These volumes have often been rebound and such copies will be less valuable than those with their original bindings. A full set of Wisden will be very valuable, but a long run may also be desirable.

What, where and how to buy
As sporting memorabilia is now such a well-established field, there are many places from which to buy. The major auction houses have specialist departments and smaller ones often include a sporting section in their sales; there are also auction houses devoted specifically to sport.

It is easy enough to focus a collection on a particular team, player or championship, such as Wimbledon in the case of tennis. With cricket, there is such a proliferation of material that collectors tend to concentrate on a particular county or, at

international level, on material relating to the Ashes series.

Would-be collectors should be aware that sporting memorabilia is sometimes faked. A bogus signature can be added, or a replica shirt passed off as a play-worn item. Football programmes for historic matches are also faked and copies of the first FA Cup Final programme at the Empire Stadium in 1923, are known. While fakes are not a huge problem, they do exist, so care should be taken. This is especially true of items that relate to a famous star, since this can turn an otherwise mundane item into something very valuable. Provenance is everything in such cases and the more documentation the better. If in doubt, be prepared to walk away as mistakes can be expensive.

3D Gallery of Football Stars, George Best, from a set of 50 cards issued by the Sun, *1973. £1–5*

American football

Interest in American football is largely confined to the United States, but the game does have a following elsewhere. NFL games are regularly shown in Europe and the NFL's first regular season game outside North America was held in London in 2007. The Super Bowl, as one of America's great sporting spectacles, has a worldwide TV audience.

Collecting American football memorabilia encompasses many items including autographs, trading cards, phone cards, footballs, helmets and jerseys. Cards do not reach the same prices as baseball cards, but they do have a long history, since they have been issued since the 1890s.

There are also collectables such as miniature helmets, posters, plaques, pins, badges, dolls, limited-edition figures and more. Bobbleheads, small figures of players with oversized heads on

springs, have been collected avidly by fans since the 1950s. Anything that is connected with a famous game is collectable, and this includes ticket stubs from classic Superbowl games.

Collectors tend to follow their favourite teams, and vintage items are especially prized. The more famous the player and the more successful the team, the better. Personal items have the same caveat that accompanies any celebrity memorabilia, namely that it should be well documented and come with a sound provenance.

The value of kit such as shirts and helmets will depend on the player, the type of item and whether it was worn during a game; this will also depend on which game. A signed piece of kit will be more desirable than a plain signature. If players are no longer signing, such kit is likely to be more sought after.

Footballs

Leather football used in the University of Chicago v University of Illinois, 3 November 1917.
£500–600

San Francisco 49ers Super Bowl World Championships football, by Wilson, signed by the team, 1989.
£230–280

World League football, by Wilson, 1990.
£25–30

Other memorabilia

Hand-drawn football manoeuvre, by Vince Lombardi, 1958.
£50–60

Signed photograph of Bronko Nagurski, 1960s. £65–75

Signed photograph of the Green Bay Packers, 1962.
£160–200

Super Bowl World Championship game programme, 1967.
£170–200

The one to look for

Kevin Williams played as wide receiver for the Dallas Cowboys before going on to the Arizona Cardinals, Buffalo Bills and San Francisco 49ers. In 1993, he played his 'rookie season' for the Cowboys, and this is one of his jerseys from that season. It is signed clearly on the number.

Created Exclusively for
The DALLAS COWBOYS...
By
APEX ONE.

OFFICIAL LICENSED PRODUCT
44
MADE IN U.S.A.

Dallas Cowboys jersey, worn by Kevin Williams, signed, 1993.
£200–250

The jersey was made by Apex One sportswear and bears a label for the Dallas Cowboys. Designed for cold weather games it has chamois-lined hand-warmer pockets.

Kevin Williams became one of Dallas Cowboys' most popular players. The shirt is 'game worn' and has a few minor tears, which do not detract from the value.

Helmets

Game-used helmet, worn by Bob Lilly of Dallas Cowboys, 1973–74.
£3,000–3,500

San Francisco 49ers helmet, signed by the team, 1987.
£100–130

Riddell NFL 75th anniversary helmet, signed by 32 players, 1994.
£270–350

Super Bowl IV football ticket stub, 1970.
£100–120

Walter Payton Rushing Records 1st cover, signed, 1984.
£60–70

Philadelphia Eagles jersey, worn by Bill Bradley, 1974–75.
£250–300

New York Rangers jersey, worn by Mark Messier, 1995–96.
£1,300–1,600

Baseball

Baseball has a huge following in the US – and an illustrious history which has fuelled a thriving collectors' market. In a sport boasting superstars such as Babe Ruth, Mickey Mantle and Joe Di Maggio, collectors can expect to pay enormous sums for top-of-the-range items.

Big-hitting Babe Ruth, of course, was a remarkable scorer of home runs, and was repeatedly voted the greatest player of all time. Anything connected with George Herman Ruth, who reputedly earned $1 million in salary and prize money between 1914 and 1934, is especially sought after. Other big names include Honus Wagner, Ted Williams, and Ty Cobb.

Such players helped to create the hobby of baseball collecting. For in the late 19th century, cards featuring the most popular players began to appear in packets of cigarettes, sweets, savoury snacks and, most notably, bubble gum. Rare cards can be extremely valuable. In 2007, for example, a 1909 cigarette card depicting the player Honus Wagner sold for $2.35 million. What gave this particular card its lustre was the fact that Wagner had demanded the withdrawal of the card as he did not want his likeness to be used to promote smoking. Only about 50 examples exist.

In recent years, interest in other memorabilia has grown, with programmes, presentation rings, press pins and artefacts connected with the World Series champion-ships being highly prized.

Kit and equipment, especially signed items, are also very collectable. Clothing worn by Lou Gehrig can command high prices. A baseball – signed on the sweet spot by Babe Ruth and in good condition – is especially desirable.

Balls

New York Yankees World Championships ball, with 27 signatures, 1958.
£1,300–1,600

Cincinatti Reds NL Champions team baseball, signed by the team, 1939.
£320–380

Darren Daulton NL All-Star team baseball, signed by 31 players, 1993.
£250–300

Other memorabilia

Photograph of the Crescents baseball team, 1907.
£300–350

Babe Ruth souvenir pin, 1920–1930s.
£1,500–2,000

World Series programme, 1926.
£420–500

Reach baseball trophy, 1930.
£300–350

The one to look for

Mickey Mantle, who played for the
New York Yankees in the 1950s and 1960s,
was one of the all-time greats. He was
inducted into the National Baseball Hall
of Fame in 1974. This figure was made just
four years before his death.

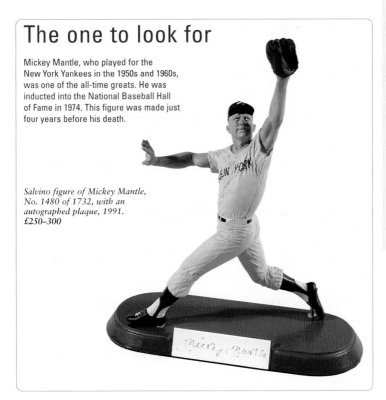

*Salvino figure of Mickey Mantle,
No. 1480 of 1732, with an
autographed plaque, 1991.
£250–300*

Uniforms & jerseys

*Boston Braves silk uniform,
introduced to reflect light
during floodlit games,
1948. £3,500–4,500*

*Houston Astros 'Shooting
Star' game home jersey,
worn by Cesar Cendeno,
1972. £500–600*

*Clearwater Phillies Minor
League jersey, worn by
Ryan Howard, 2003.
£1,600–1,900*

*Goudey Gum Co
card, featuring Lou
Gehrig, No. 92,
1933. £500–600*

*New York Giants v
Brooklyn Dodgers
Opening Day ticket,
1955. £350–450*

*Boston Red Sox cap
worn by Carl
Yastrzemski, c1975.
£1,000–1,250*

*Philadelphia Phillies
baseball bat, signed
by the team, 1980.
£400–500*

Football

Collecting football programmes and other memorabilia such as medals became fashionable in the late 1960s – as the game enjoyed a boom thanks to England's World Cup Final victory over West Germany in 1966. Programmes from that era are among the most sought after today. Pre-1960s programmes have become even more popular in recent years, especially for FA Cup finals and England internationals.

In the 1950s and 1960s, bubble gum or cigarette cards depicting famous footballers were hugely popular. These cards usually came in sets of 25 or 30.

Today, the success of the English Premier League since its formation in 1992 – and its status as the world's most watched sporting league – means the collectables market is as buoyant as ever.

Shirts worn by players are sought after – and the more famous the name, the more you will have to pay. However, shirts of modern footballers have declined in popularity, largely because of the confusion between the many replica shirts available and player-issued shirts. The general rule is the older the better, so shirts and other memorabilia relating to Brazilian legend Pele, Manchester United star George Best and 1966 England captain Bobby Moore are still popular.

England international caps awarded after the Second World War are also prized, especially as they were always embroidered with the year and the opposition. The colour of the cap revealed the oppositions: purple for matches against Scotland, maroon against Wales, and white against Ireland.

Medals can cost anything from £10 to several thousand pounds and their value depends on material, date and winner.

Football caps

England v Hungary international cap, inscribed, 1936–37.
£1,600–2,000

Welsh FA cap awarded to Terry Yorath and inscribed '1976–77'.
£650–780

Caps, awarded to players by the Football Association for participation in international matches, are popular amongst collectors. Post-war English FA caps are embroidered with both the year in which the match took place and the name of the opposing team.

Other memorabilia

The Book of Football, *rebound, 1906.*
£150–180

Photograph of Chelsea v Stockport County match, 1911.
£150–180

Match programme, England v Scotland 31 March, 1928.
£700–850

Enamel Football Association Steward Final Tie pin badge, 1935. £200–220

What to look for

To date, England have won the World Cup just once, in 1966. Even fans who were not born at the time are keen to snap up anything to do with England's finest hour.

Photograph of the England World Cup football team, with 22 signatures, mounted, framed and glazed, 1966. £1,000–1,200.

World Cup Final programme and ticket stub, for England v West Germany, 1966. £250–300.

World Cup Winners shirt, signed by nine England finalists, 1966. £180–220.

Cigarette cards

Cigarette cards, along with bubble gum cards representing famous footballers, were issued in large numbers and were usually offered in sets of 25 or 50. A full set is more desirable than a part one and some cards may be more desirable than others.

Set of 50 W. A. & A. C. Churchman Association Footballers cards, 1938. £35–40

Set of 50 W. D. and H. O. Wills Associated Footballers cigarette cards, 1939. £60–70

Pair of Tom Finney autographed leather football boots, 1950s. £100–120

Leather football signed by Pelé and the Santos team, 1975. £350–420

Signed photo of Manchester United Champions League winning team, 1999. £1,500–1,800

Everton No. 18 jersey, worn by Wayne Rooney, 2003–04. £200–250

Golf

Golf originated in Scotland, where it is recorded as far back as the 15th century – and the evolution of the game since then has contributed to a diverse memorabilia market.

Collectables range from autographs, cigarette cards, golf magazines, postcards, through to ceramics, works of art with a golfing theme such as paintings and sculptures, to golfing trophies.

Balls and clubs are among the best-known golf collectables. Balls can be divided into three eras. The feather-filled ball is the earliest – dating from the early 19th century – and is the most scarce. Today, it can fetch £1,500 to £13,000.

In 1848, the gutta, or 'gutty' ball was developed. It was made of gutta percha, a mouldable, rubbery substance, from which balls could be made at a fraction of the cost of feathers. A hand-hammered example of a gutta percha can fetch around £1,000 at auction. Finally, around the end of the 19th century, the rubber core ball was developed.

Turning to early clubs, most were hand-crafted and made from wood. Until the 1850s, iron-headed clubs, which were usually made by local blacksmiths, were only used as a last resort, because of the relative fragility of the feather balls. The earliest clubs had long, slender wooden heads, but during the 19th century the design changed as the club head became shorter, the face deeper, and the neck thicker.

However, little equipment has survived from before 1800. Even when a collector comes across, say, a club from this period it may command as much as £40,000.

Besides the actual equipment, paintings of the sport are sought after, particularly of four-times British Open champion Tom Morris, a professional player at Scotland's St Andrew's course in the 19th century. Works by British naive painters Francis Powell Hopkins and Thomas Hodge can fetch £1,000 to £10,000.

There is much else to attract the collector. Between 1890 and 1935, pottery, porcelain cups, ashtrays and other mementos decorated with golfing subjects were all produced. Larger trophy pieces, which were sometimes given as prizes, are also worth looking out for.

A word of warning, though. Such is the sport's popularity, particularly in the US, it attracts wealthy collectors, so competition for the best pieces is fierce and, consequently, prices can be very high.

Other memorabilia

Oak model long hazel putter, steel and hickory, c1910. £50–70

Golf iron with a silver head, Birmingham 1914. £500–600

Auchterlonie St Andrews spliced head wood putter, c1920. £150–200

Gibson William Kinghorn Mashie Niblick, c1930. £55–60

What to look for

Early golf balls are among the most prized items of golfing memorabilia. Balls are particularly interesting, but they often look unremarkable to the untrained eye. Even valuable ones can lurk unnoticed in a box of miscellaneous items at a fair or auction.

Feather ball by John Gourlay of Musselburgh, stamped 'J. Gourlay' and inscribed '28', unused. £4,000–6,000 Gourlay, active 1835 to 1855, is one of the most famous makers of feather, or 'feathery' balls.

Gutta percha golf ball, c1870. £55–60 These balls were originally smooth and it was only when golfers discovered that they played better when marked by wear that manufacturers began to add carved markings to their balls to improve the aerodynamics. Gutta percha balls were much cheaper than feather balls and therefore made golf more affordable.

Gutty 'Ocobo' golf ball, by J. B. Halley, with mesh pattern, c1895. £150–200 These preceded dimpled balls and various patterns were used in an attempt to produce the perfectly aerodynamic ball. The more unusual the pattern, the more valuable a ball is likely to be.

Joker mesh pattern rubber cord golf ball, c1920. £10–15 Aerodynamically superior dimpled balls had been introduced in the early 20th century, but the design was patented and Spalding USA bought the rights.

Photograph of the 1902 Open Champion Sandy Herd, signed, 1902. £120–145

Silver golfing trophy, c1928. £300–350

Women's National Open Golf Tournament programme, 1950. £115–135

Ryder Cup flag, signed by the European team, 2006. £2,000–2,500

Fishing

Fishing is one of the world's biggest participation sports, some say it is the biggest, and angling enthusiasts are certainly among the most passionate about their sport. It is a country sport, and angling related items have for many years been a staple of the country saleroom.

Altough there are many fishing collectables and mementoes around, from trophies to collectable ceramics, interest is focused on fishing equipment, such as rods, reels and lures. Fine and early equipment can command high prices. Prices are dependent on age, condition, and maker. Owing to the fact that many fishing enthusiasts like to buy vintage equipment for use, condition is especially important. Reels, for example, should not be dented and should spin freely, without obstruction, to achieve good prices.

The undisputed leader in the field of fishing equipment is the UK maker Hardy. William Hardy started out in business as a gunsmith in Northumberland in 1872, and was joined by his brothers the following year. Hardy fishing equipment soon gained a reputation for quality and reliability, and the firm's clients included royalty. Today, vintage Hardy fishing equipment achieves high prices.

Every angler appreciates a fine specimen, so fish taxidermy is another popular field. The rarest and most interesting examples are those that encase several fish. These are always in demand in the salerooms and often fetch high prices. Stuffed fish are frequently labelled with the species and when and where they were caught – sometimes they are souvenirs of a major competition.

Fish taxidermy is a highly skilled art, and taxidermists often signed their work, just as artists do. One name worth looking out for is that of J. Cooper, who is considered a master and whose cased fish are highly prized.

Books about fishing are always popular with enthusiasts, the best known of all being Izaak Walton's *The Compleat Angler*. First published in 1653, it has been reprinted many times over the centuries; some 19th-century editions can be very valuable. Generally speaking, as with other books, first editions of fishing works are the most sought after.

Fishing equipment

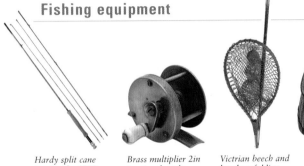

Hardy split cane trout rod, c1975.
£300–350

Brass multiplier 2in trout reel, early 19thC.
£220–250

Victrian beech and bamboo folding trout net.
£80–90

Fishing creel with leather trim, c1900.
£270–300

What to look for

Almost anything by Hardy is sought after, such is the firm's reputation for quality. Individual items such as reels alone can fetch high prices, so a case like this, complete with contents, is highly prized.

Hardy teak fisherman's case, with contents, 1938–52.
£700–800

The fitted teak case contains a scarce Hardy 'Jock Scott' multiplying bait casting reel, line drier, oil bottle and leather pouched reel spanner. It is in excellent condition.

Lures

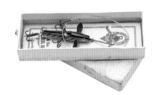

Artificial minnow in original box by R. & Co. **£70–75**

Allcock's patent collapsing spoon lure, c1920. **£20–25**

Collecting lures is a specialist field within the sphere of fishing collectables. Lures come in many different shapes and sizes according to the needs of the angler and some are quite elaborate and decorative. Lures have been made from various materials; early ones were usually made of wood, but rubber and then plastic came later.

Telescopic Salmon gaff, c1900.
£150–165

Hardy wood and brass line winder, c1900.
£450–500

The Science of Dry Fly Fishing, by Fred G. Shaw (The Amateur Champion), 1st ed, 1906.
£200–250

Hardy pigskin fly wallet, 1920s.
£120–135

Tennis

The modern game of lawn tennis was invented by Major Walter Wingfield in 1874, who produced its first ever rules in an eight-page booklet. Winfield took his inspiration from the much earlier game of 'real tennis'. The game proved to be a great success and tournaments began, the most famous being Wimbledon, which started in 1877.

Tennis became a hugely popular pastime in the late 19th and early 20th centuries, as is reflected by the number of novelty items produced, including clocks, teapots, toast racks and even dinner gongs. Jewellery using racket and ball motifs became quite fashionable, and original pieces made from the 1870s to the 1930s – what many collectors consider to be the 'golden age' of tennis – are particularly desirable.

All of these items are collectable today, as are autographs of top players and programmes relating to major tournaments – Wimbledon programmes from the 1930s and earlier are rare. Programmes are bought not only as collectables, but also as valuable reference material. Tennis even has its own equivalent of cricket's Wisden, namely *Ayres' Lawn Tennis Almanack*, which was published between 1908 and 1938, after its founder died. A full set of the Almanack, in fine condition, is valuable today.

Along with trophies, tennis rackets are probably the most collectable of tennis memorabilia. Although it is a relatively young sport, rackets have developed considerably since the early days and good early examples are hard to find. Early rackets are quite different in shape to their modern counterparts. Made of wood and with longer handles than we are used to, they were quite heavy and cumbersome.

A good way to identify and date a racket is to look at the shape of the head, which has evolved over the years. However, do remember that heads can become distorted over time, especially if any of the strings are broken. Another good way of determining the age of a racket is to look at the wedge, the piece of wood between the top of the handle and the frame of the head. On early rackets, the wedge was convex in form. During the 20th century, designs changed in favour of a concave wedge that followed the line of the frame to produce an oval form.

Tennis rackets & other memorabilia

Lawn tennis racket by F. H. Ayres, c1885. £350–400

Wooden tennis racket by Howier & Sons of St Andrews, c1900. £100–120

Slazenger 'Demon' lawn tennis racket, c1905. £150–200

Spalding open throat 'Top Flite' tennis racket, 1930s. £80–120

The one to look for

This tankard, which was made c1947, is the only tennis-themed product produced by the firm of Royal Bradwell for its sporting series; other sports included rugby and golf. The handles reflected the sport; in this case, the handle takes the form of a tennis racket.

The tankard commemorates the Wimbledon winners of 1947, Americans Margaret Osborne and Jack Kramer. Coloured versions of this tankard were made and they are rarer than this brown version.

Royal Bradwell Sporting series tankard, c1947.
£45–50

This tankard is marked with the name of Royal Bradwell, which was a trading name of the notable Arthur Wood pottery, based in Staffordshire.

Box of Dunlop Warwick tennis balls. £45–55

Wooden club tennis racket press, 1920s. £120–160

Bronze Jubilee Lawn Tennis Championships medal, 1926. £90–110

Silver-plated tennis trophy, supported by three rackets, c1930. £200–250

Other sports

Cricket has a wealth of collectable material, including autographed bats, books, magazines, and silver and ceramic objects. Anything associated with legendary player W. G. Grace, such as paintings and biographies, are sought after. Cricket is dominated by books, however, such as the celebrated *Wisden Cricketers' Almanack*, first published in 1864. England and Australia are the key markets, and memorabilia relating to the Ashes series fetches the best prices.

Horse racing is popular around the world and memorabilia ranges from paintings of famous winning horses to cigarette cards. Boxing has a serious following, especially in the United States.

Basketball The value of this Spalding basketball is enhanced by the signatures of two of the game's greats in the US. Bill Russell won the NBA Most Valuable Player Award no fewer than five times, while Wilt Chamberlain is the only NBA player to date to average more than 40 points in a season.

Spalding basketball, signed, 1950s.
£700–850

Boxing As with most sports, vintage boxing kit and equipment, including headguards, is collectable. A link with a famous name would push the price much higher.

Left: Pair of boxing gloves, 1930–40.
£80–90

Muhammad Ali was arguably the greatest heavyweight boxer of all time and anything associated with him will attract interest. Another great boxing image shows Muhammad Ali standing over the prone Sonny Liston during their World Championship bout in 1965. A signed press photograph can fetch up to £200.

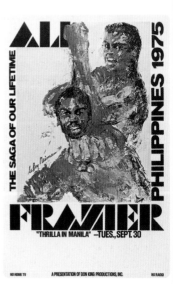

Right: Promotional poster, 1975.
£80–90

Cricket England and Australia contested the first cricket test match in 1877 – and rivalry between the two countries has been intense ever since. As a result, cricket memorabilia relating to matches between the two is highly prized. The cricket bat shown here is signed by both teams and dates from 1934 – the 1930s are considered a 'golden age'. Old photographs are also of interest, especially if they are signed. The one shown here is of the 1924 South African cricket team and is signed by the players.
Left: Signed cricket bat, 1934. £650–780
Above: Signed photograph of the South African team, 1924. £300–360

Equestrian This was a popular theme for cigarette cards which also depicted famous racehorses and celebrated jockeys. The brass and enamel Newbury horse racing badges shown on the left date from 1915. Such badges are appealing collectables.

Left: Silk scarf, commemorating the Derby, depicting the winner 'Trigo', 1929. £120–140

Above: Two brass and enamel Newbury racing badges, 1915. £35–40 each

Buying & Selling

So how do you set about buying, or selling, or both?
What questions should you ask and where can you go to
get all the information you need?

What is it that the dealers know that enables them to
acquire the best bargains? How do auction rooms work
and how do they make their money? What do you need to
know before you go down this particular path? What are
the trade tips that will help you to maximize your profits
at a car boot fair? Finally, there's that mega-market – the
Internet. How do you set about buying or offering goods
for sale and find out what the costs are, and how do you
pay, or get paid?

The following pages will answer all of these questions –
and more.

Car-boot fairs

A day spent selling at a car boot fair can be thoroughly enjoyable if you go well prepared. Passers-by are always attracted by a well laid out display and a friendly approach and are more likely to stop, look and hopefully buy if they feel welcome. So here are my tips to help ensure that your day goes smoothly – and that with a bit of luck you return home with a bulging wallet.

Assembling your equipment

In order to prevent last-minute panics, spend some time assembling everything you are going to need well in advance. Take plenty of newspapers, bubble wrap and plastic bags for protecting and carrying your wares, along with some strong cartons in which to pack delicate items. It is a good idea to take along extra plastic bags for customers to put their purchases in. You will also need one or two bin bags for rubbish. Sticky labels, plain postcards, marker pens and biros for pricing your products are also essential. For display purposes, you will need a small cushion plus safety pins for securing jewellery and other small items, and a hanging rail and wire coat hangers if you are selling clothes. Most importantly, obtain a folding table on which to display your goods. It is also a

Keen buyers will seek out and inspect items of interest.

good idea to have some card-board to stand on in case the ground is muddy or cold. Plan to take some refreshments with you, including hot and cold drinks and some food, as it can be a long day. There are usually lots of people milling about at a boot fair so keep a close watch on your takings – a secure bum-bag is ideal for this purpose, and do not forget to take plenty of small change.

Preparing your stock

Start gathering your sale items together well in advance but be aware of the restrictions concerning the sale of electrical equipment or post-war upholstered furniture. All goods should be clean, so dust wash or

A busy Sunday morning.

polish as appropriate. Wash and iron clothes and fabric – creased or dirty items just will not sell. Make price labels in advance using marker pen or biro that will not run in the rain, and fix to major items. Cheaper items can be priced as you go. When pricing, allow for at least 20 per cent discount and be prepared to reduce prices further later in the day. Finally, wrap breakable items generously in bubble wrap or newspaper and pack in cartons, putting lightweight breakables such as china and glass on top, so that they are ready to transfer to the car. It is also better to be realistic about just how much stock you can handle in one day rather than to overload yourself.

On the day

Dress appropriately in layers so that you will be able to cope with most weather conditions, and arrive at the site early in order to get a good position. Be prepared for the experienced buyers who are likely to crowd round you, hoping for a quick bargain – just keep them at bay until you have unpacked. If your stock is pre-priced you are less likely to be panicked or confused into selling cheaply. Take along a friend or family member to help unwrap, chat to customers and generally keep an eye on the stand. Display tall pieces at the back of the table, shorter ones at the front and group similar items together. Remember anything that cannot be seen will not sell. Secure jewellery, watches and badges etcetera to a cushion with safety pins and remember to rearrange your display throughout the day to make the best of the available space.

As far as money goes, be prepared to offer discounts. Zip your takings into your bum-bag and wait until you get home before counting it. Look friendly and engaged all the time – dealers who read the newspaper don't make sales. Do not cross your arms as it makes you look unapproachable. Chat to people but don't be pushy.

Packing up

At the end of the day carefully wrap any remaining items so that they are ready to take to another boot fair or, if you really don't want them, ask a charity shop if they would like them. Be sure to dispose of rubbish in bin bags, in an environmentally acceptable way. Record the sales and prices achieved and note the best sellers – this is your homework for next time.

Be sure to display your goods so that they can be viewed easily .

Finally...

Please do not be put off if all the above sounds like a lot of hassle. Provided you are well prepared and follow my tips, the chances are you will have a great day out and make some cash into the bargain!

Internet

It is hard today to think of a world without computers or without eBay. The concept was formed in 1995 by Pierre Omidyar as he tried to help his wife, an avid Pez collector, contact other enthusiasts over the Internet. Even though there are countless other auction sites, such as uBid and Bidz.com, it is the American giant eBay whose name has become a byword for the phrase 'internet auction'. I believe it to be one of the main reasons why trading in 20th-century collectables has become so successful recently.

Getting started

One of the main reasons for eBay's success is that it is very easy to become involved. Start

KitKat hand-held game, c1980.
£1–5

by reading the online tutorial, then familiarize yourself with the areas that interest you. Before you buy or sell you must register. For this you will need a working email address, username and password. These will be unique to you, so choose carefully and record them in a safe place. If you want so sell, you need to create a seller's account, which will require credit or debit card details. There is a site map to

Dinky Toys Commer Fire Engine, No. 955,
with box, 1955.
£90–100

help if you get into difficulties. If you choose to sell by auction, you will be asked the length of time you wish to have your lot offered for sale. Consider selling for 10 days, ending on a Sunday evening; this will allow for bidding to take place over two weekends with completion when bidders are likely to be at home.

It is important to display your sale goods clearly, and for this purpose it is worth investing in a high quality digital camera. Photograph items under good lighting and include additional images showing relevant markings, generally on the back or underside, along with any damage or restoration work. Make your descriptions honest, concise and not too flowery. Include measurements, preferably metric and imperial. Never give a false description or withhold information, as there is a strong possibility the buyer will demand a refund later.

Pricing

Quote the cost of postage or shipment that you will charge and indicate your preferred method of payment. Before placing your goods for sale, click on 'completed items'. This will show you similar items and the prices for which they were sold. Finally, ensure you place your sale goods in the appropriate category.

Coca-Cola World Cup football polar bear, c1998.
£1–5

Sales and service

There is a strong possibility that you will be contacted by potential buyers seeking further details. Always deal with enquiries courteously and supply all the information requested, as this may well affect the outcome of the sale. Once the sale has ended, if your item has sold you will receive email notification of the successful bidder's name from eBay. You will then need to contact the purchaser to agree the preferred method of payment for the total sum, including packing and shipping. There are many ways to pay but never send or accept cash through the post and only despatch the goods when your buyer's payment has been cleared through your bank account.

When despatching, ensure your goods are very well packed – small fragile items will be safest packed in polystyrene chips. Make sure your parcels are well taped and clearly addressed, labelled 'fragile' if appropriate. Check out the addresses of local carrier services that can deliver goods that are too large for the post office. There's nothing like the excitement of conducting an auction in your own home! And once you become hooked on eBay as a way of selling your car boot fair bargains, you may well find yourself launched on a part-time business that is both profitable and fun.

It is important to be aware of eBay's fee system and note that all relevant charges will be debited to your eBay account and then your credit or debit card. Costs will include a listing fee proportionate to your starting price, so set this figure as low as you can and be aware that the lower the starting price, the more attractive it will be to prospective buyers. Many buyers are registered with Paypal, a service that enables buyers and sellers to transmit money securely and instantly to or from their credit card or bank account. This is particularly handy when dealing with buyers from overseas. There will be a small charge to the seller for every Paypal transaction.

Four Homer Laughlin Fiesta ware jugs, 1940s–70s.
£40–45

Auctions & Dealers

SELLING AT AUCTION

Selling at auction can be a very effective way of disposing of 20th-century collectables. Auction houses do all the work for you by attracting buyers from far and wide – even from overseas. They will give you a valuation that is without obligation and usually completely free. Before going along the auction path, however, you do need to be aware of the costs involved. Auction rooms charge a percentage of the price realized on the sale of your item (the hammer price). There may also be additional charges for insurance and possibly for photography if your item is illustrated in their catalogue. Alternatively you can supply your own digital photographs; take several shots to include maker's marks and any damage or restoration. A minimum charge may be levied if your item has a relatively low value, and there may be an unsold fee if it fails to reach a high enough price in the sale. Bear in mind also that it is your responsibility to deliver the item to the saleroom and to collect it should it fail to sell. Be patient – you may have to wait a while until a suitable sale comes up and to wait again before you receive payment.

BUYING AT AUCTION

Buying at auction brings its own excitement for there is always the chance of a bargain. There are many auction rooms to choose between – find one in your locality, check dates and viewing times and allow time to view the goods thoroughly the day before the sale. Do buy a catalogue for descriptions and price estimates and do not be afraid to ask the staff for more information on any items you are interested in.

Before you start bidding you should be aware that auction rooms will charge you a buyer's premium (a percentage based on the hammer price) which can be as much as 25 per cent. On the day of the sale you should register with the auctioneer and for this you may need proof of identity. You will then be given a paddle with a number, which you should wave when you make a bid.

Remember that it is easy to get carried away once the bidding

Take time to view the goods before the auction starts.

This is the time to make your bid.

starts, so decide on your ceiling (the maximum amount you are prepared to pay) and do not exceed it. If you are unable to attend the sale, you can leave a commission bid with the auctioneer, but be sure to quote your maximum price.

SELLING TO A DEALER

Selling directly to a dealer can be more time-consuming than selling at auction as you have to take the time to search them out, and you may want to consult more than one. However, the upside is that you should be able to receive your money straight away, without paying third-party commission. It is my experience that specialist dealers will pay more than general ones, so before you make an approach, do your homework. I recently tried to sell a Minton majolica table centrepiece at auction, hoping to make between £400 and £600, but it did not sell. I then found a specialist dealer around the corner and ten minutes later I had a cheque for £650.

The Internet is now a very good source for price comparisons, as are antiques price guides. Alternatively you can visit dealers' shops in your area in order to find a suitable buyer. Dealers are often on the look out for fresh stock to sell.

BUYING FROM A DEALER

One of the great benefits of buying from dealers is that they are usually keen to pass on their knowledge. I myself have learnt a lot from dealers, just by asking questions about their stock. If you do see something you want to buy, make sure you ask the dealer the right questions. These could include: What does he know of its history? Is there any damage to the item or has it been restored? When you purchase always ask for a written receipt to cover your legal statutory rights, just in case you find later that you have been deliberately misled. In fact reputable dealers usually belong to some type of trading association as they have their reputations to maintain.

Two final points: firstly, and most importantly, unless you are planning to sell the piece on for a profit, only buy something you really like. Secondly, always ask for a discount; you may not get one, but if you don't ask, you don't get!

Directory of useful websites

Antiques and collectors' fairs

Adams Antiques Fairs
www.adamsantiquesfairs.com
London's longest-running monthly
Sunday fairs are represented on this
website, which features a calendar
of events.

www.decorativefairs.com
This UK organizer specializes in Art
Deco fairs and there's a full listing of
their events here (mostly in the north
of England). Many are held in
attractive venues and there are
pictures of these online.

Armacost Antiques Shows
www.armacostantiquesshows.com
This fair organizer began in 1985 and
now runs charity antiques fairs in
seven states: Florida, Maryland,
Missouri, Ohio, Oklahoma,
Pennsylvania, and Virginia. The site
lists the dealers represented, giving
website links where available.

www.artizania.co.uk
Browse through a selection of vintage
costume, shoes, lace, and other items
on the site of this specialist costume
and textile fair organizer.

Bowman Antiques Fairs
www.antiquesfairs.com
Bowman's have been organizing
quality antiques fairs in England and
Scotland since 1973. Everything you
need to get you to Bowman's regular
fairs at Bingley Hall, Stafford, UK can
be found on this site. They now
organize six fairs at the Bingley Hall
every year with over 400 exhibitors at
each one.

British Antiques Fairs
www.antiquesforeveryone.co.uk
One of Britain's largest vetted antiques
fairs has regularly updated information
on several prestigious events. This
includes fair previews and exhibitor
information as well as details of the
venues where the fairs are held.

www.cmo-antiques.com
Images abound on the website of this
French organizer, who is responsible
for some major Parisian events.
Exhibitors, organizers, and stock are
pictured, and you can search exhibitor
lists alphabetically or by category.

Cord Shows Ltd
www.cordshows.com
Cord Shows have been organizing fairs
for over 30 years. Their site lists their
annual fairs in New York State and
western Connecticut and gives details
of location, merchandise (rather than
exhibitor list), admission, directions
and special events.

DMG Antiques Fairs
www.dmgantiquefairs.com
The website of one of Britain's major
fairs organizers includes all the dates
of the year's fairs and information on
facilities and opening times. DMG
events include the Newark Fair, which
is Europe's largest antiques fair.

www.nyflamingo.com
This organizer promotes fairs
throughout Long Island, New York and
across the northeastern United States.
The site contains a complete listing of
all the fairs they run, giving directions,
admission fees and opening times.

Gadsden Promotions Limited
www.antiqueshowscanada.com
Experienced Canadian fairs organizers
Gadsden Promotions have events of
various types and sizes on their
calendar. You will find more than just
listings of the events and dates on
their site: there are also full details of
the type of stock, the venues, and
instructions on how to get to each fair.

Galloway Antiques Fairs
www.gallowayfairs.co.uk
Stately home settings are popular with
Galloway Antiques Fairs, who organize
events around Britain. The venues are
pictured on the site, and there is a full
calendar of events. The site is rich in
graphics and animation.

Lomax Antiques Fairs
www.lomaxantiquesfairs.co.uk
A potted history of the fairs of this UK organizer is included on this site as well as a history of the venues, some of which are quite historic. There are detailed directions for those wishing to go to one of the fairs and an email will get you complimentary tickets.

The Maven Co. Inc
www.mavencompany.com
This is the site of fair promoters in New England and Westchester County, New York, who run antiques and collectables fairs, vintage clothing, jewellery and textile fairs, and doll, toy, and teddy bear fairs. There is detailed information about each fair online giving opening hours, directions, dealer lists and bus transportation schedules from New York City.

New England Antique Shows
www.neantiqueshows.com
A slideshow of goods featured at these New England shows is the main feature of this site. The merchandise is mostly country. There is news of forthcoming events, and you can subscribe to an email mailing list for the latest updates.

Professional Show Managers Association Inc.
www.psmashows.org
This is a group of American fair managers/organizers who are dedicated to advancing the professional standards of the antiques fair business. A Code of Ethics encourages honest representation with dealers and the public, and high ethical and business standards.
A Calendar lists all associated fairs by month or state and there is a separate listing of weekly markets

Renningers Antique & Farmers' Markets
www.renningers.com
This manager owns three large antiques and farmer's markets, which are open at weekends. Two are in Pennsylvania (Kutztown and Adamstown) and one is in Florida (Mt Dora). In addition, each of these markets hosts two or three 'extravaganzas' each year, which are large fairs (with over 1,000 dealers). They also run two major fairs, one outside Boston and the other outside Philadelphia, each with over 500 dealers.

SRP Toy Fairs
www.srptoyfairs.com
Toy cars, trains, and ephemera are all found at SRP's specialist events, which are mainly held in the south of England. Their website includes prices charged for space at these events and, if you are a dealer, you can actually book space at the fairs directly online. The site also has a calendar, listing all the year's events.

Stella Show Management Company
www.stellashows.com
This US organizer runs 22 fairs, mostly in New York City and New Jersey, as well as the Chicago Botanic Garden Antiques and Garden Fair in Glencoe, Illinois. This company has put the term 'triple pier' into the antiques vocabulary, taking over three passenger piers in New York to fill them with antiques, folk art, and collectables

20/21 British Art Fair
www.britishartfair.co.uk
British art of the last and new century is included at this fair and on its Internet site. There is a floor plan online and list of exhibitors with links to websites where they are available. Also included are details of the fair's informative lecture programme.

World Wide Antiques Shows
www.wwantiqueshows.com
This organization has been running more than 50 years and holds three large fairs each year in Denver, USA, with over 190 exhibitors in each fair. Pictures of some of the booths are on their website. It also provides directions on how to get to each one and there is an online application form for would-be exhibitors.

www.antiquesireland.com
Irish dealers' site, which includes information on fairs.

www.caskeylees.com
Leading American organizer offers information on its shows that are held in various states.

Resource and Gateway sites

Goantiques
www.goantiques.com
GoAntiques has over 1,450 dealers from 29 countries who have filled their Virtual Warehouse with antiques, collectables, estate merchandise, and antique reproductions.

Antiqnet.com
www.antiqnet.com
This site will put you in touch with, and link you to, the websites of insurance firms, restorers, shippers, educational resources, publications, and various other services. However, that is not all – you will also find fair organizers, online auctions and a shopping mall, which has various items for sale by dealers at fixed prices that you can buy directly online. There is an online demonstration of the buying and selling process to help you get started.

Antique Alley
www.antiquealley.com
This site has a large classified section, which lists objects for sale from both dealers and non-dealers. There are no pictures, except for a small selection of highlights, but the relevant dealer's email is given so that you can contact them directly for further details.

Antique Hot Spots
www.antiquehotspots.com
This site lists many Internet antiques and collectables sites and has international links as well as American ones.

Antiques and Art Australia
www.antique-art.com.au
As its name suggests, this website offers a gateway to antiques and art Down Under. You can choose from more than 1,500 items that are for sale in the virtual gallery, and also follow the links to the top dealers' associations of Australia and New Zealand, as well as to the Australian Antique Collector magazine.

The Antiques and Collectibles Guide
www.antiquecollectorsguide.co.uk
Here you will find the Antique Dealer & Collectors' Guide website. Where you can obtain comprehensive and up to date information on fairs and auctions taking place in the UK.

Antiques Atlas
www.antiques-atlas.com
This site gives a geographical guide to antiques in the United Kingdom and Ireland. Click on an area of the map to find a breakdown of shops, auction houses, centres, fairs, museums, and other places to see and/or buy antiques and art. Full listings of places are given, including their opening hours. You can also search a database of items for sale from around the world and get in touch with a vendor. No transactions take place through the site – any deals are directly between you and the seller.

Antiques Trade Gazette
www.antiquestradegazette.com
This site compliment the popular weekly trade paper that comments and lists auction sales and all the major antique and collectable Fairs within the UK. Although subscription only, there is an ever increasing auction price comparison site with over a million items to look at.

The Internet Antiques Guide
www.iantiquesguide.com
This site claims to be the largest Directory of Antiques Resources on the Internet with links to over 5,000 dealers. It is a comprehensive guide to dealers, conveniently categorised into their specialist areas, a calendar of flea markets with their home page highlighting the latest headlines from the world of antiques and collectables

Belgium Antiques
www.belgiumantiques.com
A vast and comprehensive introduction to the antiques world in Belgium and the Netherlands, this site (available in English) offers a guide to dealers, auctioneers, trade associations, fairs, and markets – and there's even shipping information. You will also find details of educational courses and stolen items, as well as an online guide to styles and periods. An interactive map of the two countries helps you to find the location of specific dealers, and there is travel information, should you decide to visit.

Clougherty Jeans
www.cjeans.com
This New England site does not have any items for sale, but has links to many dealers, as well as to the MADA (Maine Antique Dealers Association) and NHADA (New Hampshire Antique Dealers Association). It is also an extensive listing of New England auctions and fairs as well as links to publications, including *Maine Antique Digest and Antiques* and the *Arts Weekly*.

Collector Cafe
www.collectorcafe.com
This is a non-commercial web portal that caters for the needs of the collector, providing information, articles, a bulletin board, and collecting resources. Ninety different collecting fields are catered for here, and there is also a listing of various specialist dealers as well as classified ads. Go to your area of interest, read an article, then see a list of relevant dealers and other websites, with instant links to them.

Collector Network
www.collectornetwork.com
This site is dominated by coins, banknotes, and stamps, but it is also expanding into other collecting fields. It features an online shopping mall, a news stand with links to the sites of collecting publications, and bulletin boards for you to contact and have debates with other users. Perhaps its most useful feature is, however, its web directory, which features links to almost 10,000 sites, from general antique sites to specialist sites devoted to topics ranging from advertising to sporting collectables.

Collector Online
www.collectoronline.com
This US site is essentially an online antique mall but it offers much more than just that. It provides the Inventory Management System free of charge, which helps dealers manage all aspects of their online selling. It also allows dealers to sell items on multiple auction sites as well as in a 'booth' within its own online mall. You can search this mall using a category system and there is also a request form that you can use to get them to do a thorough search for a particular item for you.

Collectors Universe
www.collectors.com
This site is aimed at collectors of autographs, coins, currency, records, sports memorabilia, records and music memorabilia, and stamps, and each of these subjects has a separate area within the site. There are online price guides for each, and an extensive library of articles on collecting these items. Useful definitions of collecting terminology are also included.

Curioscape
www.curioscape.com
On this American site, you can search approximately 13,000 independently owned shops for that coveted item, be it a Chinese snuff bottle or a lunchbox. Browse through a feast of items illustrated in colour, and click on the picture of your choice to make your purchase online (prices are given in US dollars).

The Great British Antiques Web
www.antiques-web.co.uk/fairs.html
As its title suggests, this is a thorough and extensive listing of antiques fairs taking place in the United Kingdom, including specialist fairs such as Art Deco events. Contact details are given, as well as links to the pages of individual organizers and their websites where applicable.

Goantiques.com
www.goantiques.com
One of the largest sites to exist GoAntiques has over 1,450 dealers from 29 countries who have filled its Virtual Warehouse with antiques, collectables, estate merchandise and antique reproductions

LiveAuctioneers
www.liveauctioneers.com
LiveAuctioneers offers a gateway linking bidders to traditional auction events broadcast in real-time via the Internet. It connects auction houses and bidders worldwide through eBayLiveAuctions.com. It lists sales at more than 500 auction houses and claims to be the second-most frequently visited auction-related Web site for fine art, antiques and collectibles, following only eBay. LiveAuctioneers also offers a leading online database, with an archive of nearly 4 million auction results, illustrated by more than 28 million images.

LAPDA
The association of Art and Antique Dealers. As this is the largest trade association in the UK you will find links to many of the countries top dealers with lists of fairs and stock search

New England Antiquing
www.antiquing.com
This site covers the world of antiques in all five New England states. Antiques shops and centres are listed by state, or you can search for what is available in a particular town or city. Some antiques are for sale online and there is also a list of dealers who have online inventories, as well as a list of auctioneers.

Ruby Lane
www.rubylane.com
This American site is a great place for finding, buying, and selling antiques, collectables, and fine art. A global search produces items from many online auctions and private sellers and most of these are accompanied by pictures. Online shops are divided into categories such as antiques, collectables and fine art shops. Items offered in the antiques section must be pre-WWII, and those offered as collectables must be at least 20 years old. There are links to Ruby Lane's own shops, which allow you to go into each one and see their catalogue.

SalvoWEB
www.salvo.co.uk
A gateway to information on anything to do with architectural antiques, garden statuary, and salvage, this site provides links to a multitude of dealers in this field. It also provides a listing of forthcoming UK auctions featuring these objects, warnings of stolen items in circulation, and information on publications. There's also a list of buildings that are due for demolition, and a link to an American site that offers similar useful information in the United States.

World Collectors Net

www.worldcollectorsnet.com
Run 'by collectors, for collectors', this site offers an online magazine, message boards, and a shopping arcade. There's also a news section, which gives the latest on limited-edition products, location filming for antiques TV programmes, and much more.

Dedicated car boot web sites

The Car Boot Sales and Boot Fair Directory
www.boot-fair.co.uk
This web site has a free listing of many of the major sites of car boot fairs in the UK conveniantly split into regions with opening times, entrance fees and winter closing dates were applicable.

UK Fayres
www.ukfayres.co.uk
This is a subscription-based site with listings for UK car boot sales, computer fairs, antiques fairs, toy fairs, craft fairs, jumble sales, book fairs and others. The site claims to hold over 84,000 different listings.

Car Boot Calendar
www.carbootcalendar.com
Established for over 10 years the car boot calendar is published five times a year. Each issue lists thousands of events in date order within the UK.

Yourbooty
www.yourbooty.co.uk
This is a non subscription-based site listing sites and other information but is less comprehensive.

Index

Acknowledgments

We would like to acknowledge the great assistance given by our consultants. We would also like to extend our thanks to all those who have assisted us in the production of this book.

Phil Ellis

Wood, Moulds, Bakelite & Plastics, Tools, Telephones, Cameras, Radios, Computers & Technology, Clocks, Toys, Ephemera, Entertainment and Sporting Memorabilia.

Phil Ellis is a freelance writer and editor, specializing in antiques and collectables. He has a long standing fascination for the past writes for and has written for numerous publications, including the weekly *Antiques Magazine*, where he was Assistant Editor for 11 years. He has contributed to several Miller's publications and is the author of *Miller's Sci Fi & Fantasy Collectibles* (2003).

Will Farmer, Fielding's Auctioneers

Glass, Silver, Stainless steel, Copper & brass and Other metals.

Will is a Director and valuer with Fieldings Auctioneers, Stourbridge, which he established with his business partner Nick Davies. Will has a keen passion for Art Deco ceramics and 20th-century glass. He has just completed filming the 30th season of *Antiques Roadshow* for BBC Television.

Nick Goodman

Fashion

Nick Goodman is a freelance writer and editor.

Steven Moore

Ceramics

Steven is a freelance arts and antiques consultant, writer and broadcaster. He is a member of BBC TV's *Antiques Roadshow* experts team and has just completed filming the 30th season of the programme.

Fieldings Auctioneers

for providing images of glass. Fieldings Auctioneers, Mill Race Lane, Stourbridge, West Midlands DY8 1JN

Pepe Tozo for suppling images of computers and technology. www.tozzo.co.uk

John Mole, Curator, Digital Museum of Cornish Ceramics for supplying images of Troika. www.cornishceramics.com

Mark Winwood for the jacket design and photographs. www.markwinwood.com

Jonty Hearnden would like to thank **Sue Adams**